SCHOPPEN

MODERSCHEID

FRONT 16 DEC

I SS PZ
16 DEC

99
106

394
14 CAV

SIXTH
SS PZ
ARMY

HEPPENBACH

AMBLEVE

DIEDENBERG

V
XXX
VIII

LOSHEIM

LANZERATH

TD

HOLZHEIM

16

TD

TD

GERMAN MILITARY ROAD

ERIC WOOD OPERATED IN
THIS AREA 19 DEC - 22 JAN

MANDERFELD

16

18
VG

FE

BORN

17

MEYERODE

GERMAN MILITARY ROAD

6 WAY CROSS-
ROADS

HERRESBACH

KOBSCHEID

ROTH

150
PZ
16 DEC

17   MEDELL

ERIC WOOD'S
BODY

AUW

14 CAV

19   HERVERT

17

LAUDESFELD

16

422

16

18

WALLERODE

SCHONBERG   17

HEUEM

17-21

422
END

H

G   17

19

E

SCHLAUSENBACH

16

16

17

16

SAINT-
VITH

81 ENG
17-21

21-22

81 ENG

19/20

17-21

423
END

A

B   C

D

F

17

SIEGFRIED LINE

16

21-22

22

3/423
18

19

RADSCHEID

OBERLASCHEID

17

17

16

20

MUTZENICH

17

16

18

18

LOMMERSWEILER
PART OF 1/424
EARLY 17

BLEIALF

BUCHET

17

16

17

422
423

19

17 DRIVEN BACK
BY CCB 9

WINTERSCHEID

16

16

16

SELLERICH

MASPELT
20

18

GROSS-
LANGENFELD

16

16

HERSCHEID

16

NIEDERMEHLEN

19/20

18

WINTERSPELT

17

BRANDSCHEID

SIEGFRIED   LINE

A=3D 423
B=1st 423
C=2D 423
D=3D 422
E=2D 422
F=1st 422
G=MOTOR POOL
  STAND 19/21
H=2/423 AM 17

18

18
1
3

17

EIGELSCHEID

STEINMEHLEN

48

BURG-REULAND
3
2

18

1/424
17

HABSCHEID

16

423
424

WEINSFELD

18

106
XX
28

16

WATZERATH

62 VG

16

GROSS-
KAMPENBERG

16

ASSEMBLY
AREA

MASTHORN

PRONSFELD

116
(ELTS) 16 DEC

FIFTH PZ ARMY

MATZERATH

18

17

LEIDENBORN

424
112

LUNEBACH

ADVANCE 18 DEC. 1944 ON
SCHONBERG
GERMAN PENETRATIONS

0   1   2 MILES
SCALE

ST. VITH

LION IN THE WAY

★

NORTHERN FRANCE

★

RHINELAND

★

ARDENNES–ALSACE

★

CENTRAL EUROPE

St. Vith
LION IN THE WAY

The 106th Infantry Division
In World War II

By COLONEL R. ERNEST DUPUY

WASHINGTON
INFANTRY JOURNAL PRESS

FIRST EDITION

TO THE GOLDEN LIONS

AMERICAN SOLDIERS WHOSE RAW COURAGE
AND STOUT HEARTS CONQUERED ECLIPSE

Contents

✦✦✦

FOREWORD ix

Chapter 1: THE BULGE 1

Chapter 2: BIRTH OF A DIVISION 5

Chapter 3: INTO THE LINE 9

Chapter 4: THE STORM BREAKS 21

Chapter 5: THE SECOND RED DAY 63

Chapter 6: THE THIRD DAY 103

Chapter 7: THE FOURTH DAY 133

Chapter 8: THE FIFTH DAY 158

Chapter 9: THE SIXTH DAY 165

Chapter 10: A FORTIFIED GOOSE EGG 172

Chapter 11: THE END OF THE SALIENT 177

Chapter 12: TOTTING UP THE SCORE 191

Chapter 13: THE SECOND ROUND 195

Chapter 14: TURN OF THE TIDE 202

Chapter 15: INTO THE LOSHEIM GAP 213

Chapter 16: LAST LAP OF BATTLE 219

Chapter 17: PRISONERS BY THE MILLION 224

Chapter 18: TALLYHO AND FINIS 233

Appendix I: OPERATION GREIF 235

Appendix II: ORDER OF BATTLE 236

Appendix III: ORGANIZATION AND TRAINING 239

Appendix IV: DISTINGUISHED UNIT CITATIONS 249

Appendix V: AWARD OF CROIX DE GUERRE WITH SILVER-GILT STAR 252

PHOTOGRAPHS 253

Maps

1: The Golden Lions Committed. (Area Occupied by the 106th Infantry Division, 11 December 1944) 10

2: The Northern Flank 20

3: The Losheim Gap. (Positions of the 14th Cavalry Group and 422d Infantry, 16 December 1944) 24

4: The Southern Gateway. (Positions of the 423d and 424th Infantry Regiments, 16 December 1944) 36

5: The Tragedy of the Schnee Eifel 138

6: Parker's Crossroads. (The Big Picture) 184

7: Last Stand of the 589th Field Artillery Battalion 185

8: The First Fight at Manhay. (25 December 1944) 196

9: The Second Fight at Manhay. (26 December 1944) 198

10: First Offensive. (Attack Across the Amblève, 13 January 1945) 204

11: The Fight for the Ridge. (15 January 1945) 208

12: Into the Losheim Gap. (25 January 1945) 216

13: Journey's End. (7 March 1945) 220

14: The POW Area of the 106th Infantry Division 228

Foreword

The task of writing the history of the 106th Infantry Division was undertaken at request of the 106th Infantry Division Association. In agreeing, the author made the one basic proviso that he should write the story in accord with all available evidence, without bias, and as an impartial critical analysis.

Except as otherwise specifically noted herein, the narrative is based upon official after-action reports, interviews by historical research teams, and such other official records as are available in plenitude in the files of the Historical Division, Department of the Army. Thanks are due to Major General Edwin F. Harding, Chief of the Historical Division, at the time of this writing, for his cordial invitation to make use of all records, and to all members of his staff for their courteous assistance.

The 106th Infantry Division Association laid open all its files. Major General Alan W. Jones, former Division Commander, Brigadier General Leo McMahon, former Division Artillery Commander and Lieutenant Colonel H. B. Livesey, Jr., former Division Chemical Warfare Officer and later Secretary of the Association, have assisted in the collation of data.

To Colonel Malin Craig, Jr., Field Artillery, former Executive Officer of Division Artillery, special thanks are due. Colonel Craig's personal diary, his collection of data unavailable elsewhere, in addition to his own continuous and painstaking research into knotty points brought up by the writer, combined to make a major contribution to the work.

The comments and personal recollections of Major Generals Robert W. Hasbrouck and William M. Hoge, respectively commanding the 7th Armored Division and CCB of the 9th Armored Division during the action in and around St. Vith, have been of great value in reconstruction of the operations.

Major General Donald A. Stroh, commanding the 106th during the later period of its life in ETO, has been most helpful in furnishing a very complete report on the Division's colossal task of guarding German POWs.

The interesting photographs contributed by George R. Hayslip and Francis Aspinwall have lent graphic illustration.

The author is also indebted to a number of officers and men of the Division who have taken time and trouble to contribute eyewitness accounts of various portions of the operations. Credit for their respective contributions is given in notes at the end of each chapter.

Thanks are herewith extended also to all others assisting, whether or not noted herein by name.

To sum up, unless specifically otherwise listed in footnotes, the facts contained herein come from official Department of the Army records. The conclusions drawn and opinions expressed are those of the author.

This is the story of an American division that found itself the hard way—on the field of battle; a division whose first taste of combat came with the tidal wave rush of an enemy's major counterblow. It is the story of American men battling against fate, rising superior to themselves in that first thirty minutes of combat which makes or breaks the soldier.

Here and there in the narrative names crop up—names of individuals whose acts of heroic self-abnegation happened to have been noticed and made of record. These must be taken as examples, not exceptions. For each individual mentioned there were scores of others whose equally meritorious and gallant deeds remain masked by the fog of war.

In the gathering of these data the author has been struck by the fierce pride of organization demonstrated by all members of the Division with whom he has been in contact, and by the existing spirit of loyalty and mutual respect—up and down—between officers and men of the Golden Lion.

R. ERNEST DUPUY
Colonel, USA, Retired

Washington, D. C.

ST. VITH

LION IN THE WAY

Chapter 1: The Bulge

On 16 December 1944, the German enemy launched a counter-offensive against the Allied Expeditionary Force, then knocking at his Siegfried Line. Dreamed up by Hitler, executed by Field Marshal Walter von Model who was commanding German Army Group B, its objective was to split the British and American armies by a shrewd stroke duplicating the drive of 1940 against the French. Antwerp, just become a vital port of debarkation for Allied supply, was the ultimate goal.

Time was vital to the enemy. An American assault was already in motion just north of St. Vith, in Belgium, striking for the dams controlling the raging Roer River. Once these dams were in our hands, he knew, the big Allied offensive for the Cologne Plain would start. With St. Vith, focal point of five main highways and three rail lines, in German hands, the way would be open for a northward swing to roll up the U.S. First Army's blow at the dams, suspend indefinitely the coming invasion of the Rhineland, and open the road into Belgium. Hence Von Model's timetable called for the capture of St. Vith in the first twenty-four hours of the attack.

The enemy effected complete tactical surprise. Strategically, his capability to make a counterattack somewhere had been for some time weighed and admitted by Supreme Headquarters, though the SHAEF G-2 summary for 10 December 1944, somewhat flippantly dismissed the capabilities of the enemy armored reserve, admittedly building up and refitting. Where it was and for what purpose it might be used were question marks. The probability was that it was in the Cologne–Trier area and that its most efficient use would be for a flanking stroke against our armies when they should later burst out across the Roer into the Cologne Plain. The probability of the counterblow coming through the Ardennes was discounted by the High Command to a certain extent.

The offensive was launched over a 75-mile front in the forested volcanic hill masses of the Eifel, and into the equally jumbled hill country of the Belgian Ardennes at the northern tip of the little Grand Duchy of Luxembourg. This was a region of evergreen-crested hills, drained by many narrow rivers running between steep banks through the thick woods.

The roadnet was poor. Rapid advance westward, once the Belgian–Luxembourg borders of Germany were crossed, depended on possession of two vital road junctions: St. Vith on the north and Bastogne on the

1

south. In the northern zone, cross-country deployment of armored vehicles off the road was almost impossible until the high ground immediately north, south and west of St. Vith was gained. The winter season, with a snow coverage of from three to five inches, still further impeded vehicular movement.

On the other hand, from the enemy standpoint, the terrain selected was the best for his purpose at the time, since he knew our army groups were lining up for offensive action through the Aachen gateway to the Cologne Plain on the north, and were threatening the Moselle corridor to the Rhine on the south, both pathways of conquest leading into Germany. Hence the American forces in the Ardennes–Eifel area would be weakest. This was verified by good preliminary enemy intelligence work.

Aided by fog and bad weather, which had impeded for many days any Allied aerial observation and nullified to a great extent the superiority of our air forces, the Nazi coup was launched, sliding down both sides of the Schnee Eifel hogback which points southwest at the tip of Luxembourg.

On the north was the Sixth SS Panzer Army, *Obergruppenführer* (Colonel General) Joseph "Sepp" Dietrich commanding. On the south was the Fifth Panzer Army, Lt.Gen. Kurt von Manteuffel commanding. The German Fifteenth Army on the right at the same time threw a corps against the northern shoulder of the invasion area in the vicinity of Monschau, while on the left the German Seventh Army struck toward Echternach, the southern shoulder. In all, some twenty-two enemy divisions were involved, ten of them panzers. Of these, nine divisions, three of them panzers, were in the initial jumpoff.

One entire panzer brigade, the 150th—English-speaking Germans— was dressed in U.S. Army uniforms and used captured American tanks and vehicles, supplemented by German matériel camouflaged as American, to confuse and terrorize in the first mad rush. Small detachments of similarly disguised English-speaking German soldiers were rushed in jeeps and also dropped by parachute into our rear areas, to add further confusion and sabotage to the attack.[1]*

From north to south in the affected area our own situation was as follows: the right flank of V Corps, around Monschau, was held by the 99th Infantry Division, through which the 2d Infantry Division was attacking in the Roer dam operation. Maj.Gen. Troy H. Middleton's VIII Corps, the right flank of U.S. First Army, filled the remainder of

---

* Notes are at the end of each chapter.

the Ardennes line. Its left flank unit was the 106th Infantry Division with the 14th Cavalry Group attached and maintaining contact with the 99th Infantry Division. South of the 106th were, in succession, the 28th Infantry Division, the 9th Armored Division (less one combat command) and the 4th Infantry Division.

The mission of VIII Corps was one of aggressive defense, prepared to advance on Cologne upon First Army order.

The German blow was the first and only real counteroffensive the enemy had been able to mount since we landed on the Normandy beaches. Into it he threw all his available reserves in the west. Its success depended on his ability to accomplish three things: first, to bludgeon a gap in our lines; second, to exploit the breakthrough by widening the shoulders of this gap; and third, to go far enough and fast enough in the initial rush to capture sufficient Allied supplies, particularly gasoline, to make the operation self-sustaining.

Accomplishing the first task, the enemy failed to gain the other two goals.

On the northern shoulder the 99th and 2d Infantry Divisions, later reinforced by the 1st Infantry Division, held stubbornly and Sixth SS Panzer Army failed to break through into the Monschau Forest and up on the Elsenborn Ridge. Nor could it, although assisted by the right-flank elements of Fifth Panzer Army, attain St. Vith in time. In the south the 4th Infantry Division could not be budged.

The assault, initially canalized by the stand of the 106th Infantry Division—in the Schnee Eifel and in front of St. Vith—developed into four prongs. The two center ones actually pushed to within sight of the Meuse; the two flanking ones were checked by the stubborn resistance of the divisions on the shoulders. The 106th Infantry Division's defense, bolstered by the 7th Armored Division and other units, developed into a salient threatening the whole of Fifth Panzer Army's northern flank, while it continued to delay the advance of Sixth SS Panzer Army's westward movement. At Bastogne the 101st Airborne Division's island of resistance split Fifth Panzer Army, which was forced to flow north and south of that vital road junction.

Lacking a real communications network, the German reinforcing and supply columns were practically immobilized, to become easy prey to our air forces when at long last the weather cleared. By that time U.S. First Army had moved sufficient reinforcements to a new defensive line which would later become a springboard for offense, while from the south Patton's amazing U.S. Third Army was driving offensively into the enemy's left flank.

After many days of violent battle the German counteroffensive failed.

In the gamble the enemy squandered his entire strategic reserve. The "Battle of the Bulge" ended as an American victory.

The story of Bastogne has been told. In front of St. Vith the fortune of war placed the 106th Infantry Division, newly arrived from the United States and only four days in the line, squarely in the path of the enemy blow.

The expression "fortune of war" is used advisedly. Let us dismiss here and now any theory that the arrival of the untried 106th Infantry Division in the sector influenced the enemy decision to attack. Had the German plan been executed on schedule, the 2d Infantry Division would have received the blow as delivered.

The dream of a counteroffensive through the Ardennes was first conceived by Hitler in September 1944. Discussions began at his headquarters early in October. D-day was initially set for 26 or 28 November, but it had to be deferred because of the difficulty of concentrating troops in the area, conditions of secrecy, and the delays incident to movement over lines of communication being shattered continuously by our air forces.[2]

Notes To Chapter 1

[1] *Operation Greif* was the German code name for this maneuver, which included a small band of English-speaking desperadoes disguised as American soldiers, trained and led by a scar-faced Nazi named Otto Skorzeny. These men were to infiltrate all the way to Paris, with the mission of assassinating General Eisenhower. This entire operation was, of course, in violation of the laws of war.

[2] Consensus of answers by *Reichsmarschall* Hermann Goering, Field Marshal Wilhelm Keitel, Col.Gen. Alfred Jodl, Field Marshal Karl Gerd von Rundstedt, Lt.Gen. Kurt von Manteuffel, Col.Gen. Sepp Dietrich, and other high-ranking staff officers of OKW to Allied interrogators.

Chapter 2: Birth of a Division

The 106th Infantry Division came into existence by War Department authorization 29 November 1942. It was to be one of the then newly authorized one hundred divisions, later cut down to ninety, which were to go overseas following a training more rigorous and more thorough than had ever before been given American troops before they went into action.

The theory was that each of these new divisions would begin and end as homogeneous groups—recruits brought in around a hard core, called a cadre, gathered from already trained units. The training, laid down by Army Ground Forces, would be progressive from the beginning, balanced and coordinated, to the end that when each division moved to the battle front it would be a team. Its officers and men would know one another, would know their business. The only thing lacking would be that first thirty minutes of combat, the vital kill-or-be-killed moment which comes only with battle.

It was a sound theory. Unfortunately its preceptors did not take into account the abnormally large casualty lists which would call for replacements, nor did they realize that Army Service Forces would mount to an empire within and without the United States; an empire of sound, able-bodied men fit for combat but placed in noncombatant positions and hence unavailable for conflict. Nor did they foresee the unwarranted but prevalent impression which rose during the early summer of 1944 that the war would soon be over.

The 106th Quartermaster Company was activated at Camp Forrest, Tennessee, on 15 December, and the 806th Ordnance Company at Camp Perry, Ohio, on 23 December 1942. The 106th Division Artillery Band and the 423d Infantry Band were activated 15 February 1943, at Fort Jackson, South Carolina. The former was originally the 222d Field Artillery Band, 40th Infantry Division (Utah National Guard) and the latter the 123d Field Artillery Band, 33d Infantry Division (Illinois National Guard).

On 15 March 1943 the Division as a whole was formally activated. Cadres for all the other units except the Ordnance Company came from the 80th Infantry Division.

Brigadier General William C. McMahon was first designated to command, but was later transferred to command of the 8th Infantry Division. Brig.Gen. Alan W. Jones, then Assistant Division Commander of the 90th Motorized Division, was named to command the

106th on 20 January 1943 and on 18 March of that year was promoted to major general.

Colonel Herbert T. Perrin, of the 1st Division in World War I, was appointed Assistant Division Commander 2 February 1943, and became brigadier general on 18 March. Col. William C. Baker, Jr., was appointed Chief of Staff.

The original Artillery Commander was Brig.Gen. Ronald C. Brock (who in World War I had commanded the 106th Field Artillery Regiment of the 27th Division). He was relieved by Brig.Gen. Leo T. McMahon in December 1943. The Artillery Executive was Col. Malin Craig, Jr.

Since the day the Division was activated it followed the normal routine of training, through basic and unit programs, running the gamut from recruit drill and orientation to combat infiltration courses.

On 12 August the outfit was shaken up by the new tables of organization providing cannon companies, division special troops and a division band; this last absorbed the two existing bands.

Regimental and division exercises and field problems of all sorts began on 3 October, and continued to 8 January 1944.

Originally, the Division was one in which the stress in the enlisted personnel was on youth. In September 1943, two-thirds of the entire enlisted personnel were twenty-two years of age or under; more than three-quarters of the men were twenty-five years old, or under.

From 20 January to 27 March 1944, the Division participated in the Second Army maneuvers in Tennessee, a period of gruelling tests and sham battles under field conditions. During this time the organization received a draft of 1,157 men from Army Specialized Training Program schools, while seven hundred enlisted men were ordered away to the Fort Meade Replacement Depot, the first of many such drafts.

All in all, it may be considered that at the end of the Tennessee maneuvers the 106th was an average infantry division in which officers and men had been together long enough and had gone through sufficient combined battle training to make it that. Insofar as training is concerned—and one must always take into account that battle and battle only is the pay-off on the discipline and training of an organization—the 106th Infantry Division was ready to take the field. It was at the height of its training efficiency, a height which unfortunately it would never again attain until reforged in the fires of war.

It was in this state of development that the Division moved from the maneuver area to Camp Atterbury, Indiana, where the War Department axe began to fall on its then existing strength of 708 officers, 42 warrant officers, and 12,523 enlisted men.

In April, 3,145 men were drafted out; during May, 877; in June, 195; in July, 136; and in August, 2,894; a total of 7,247, or sixty per cent of its enlisted strength. More than 6,000 went to Fort Meade as replacements for overseas service. These figures do not take into consideration the normal and healthy attrition of 159 men sent to officer candidate schools.

The worst of this drainage was the fact that key men were being seized. These drafts of strength were accomplished under rigorous screening which insisted on taking the best, and only the best.

It would be a grave injustice to the men of the 106th who did remain and go into battle to say that they were but the culls. The point is that many men who had developed early, who first had shown aptitude, who already were of the grade of private first class, or higher, were the men chosen to be removed from the Division before it ever left the United States.

In their place came groups from Army Specialized Training Program, from the Army Air Forces, the Army Ground Forces replacement depots, and volunteers for infantry. These volunteers came from antiaircraft and coast artillery units for the most part, with a sizable complement from military police and Army Service Forces units.

Let's look at this situation for a moment. One cannot say that these men were of inferior quality. One can say—and this writer here says it—that one cannot take more than fifty per cent of a trained unit's complement away, fill it up with other men and expect the unit to be fit to enter battle as a combat team. It just can't be done, no matter how good the replacements, or the cadre, are. The spark of team play gained by rigorous training, the patina of *esprit de corps,* the pride of organization, are missing.

On the other hand, one can infilter small increments of replacements into a combat-tried unit and, after a short period of training and shake-down, expect results. Even this has to be done carefully. It was one of the weaknesses of our system during the war, decried by all commanders, that we had to send our replacements into front line units without sufficient shake-down time.

The men who came to the 106th were from all branches except the infantry. Some came willingly, some not so willingly. That didn't help, either. Given time, and a complete reshuffle of training, it would not have been bad, of course. Making a combat team takes time. But it was later than someone in the War Department thought.

For on 20 October 1944, the 106th Infantry Division was moving on the high seas, on the way to England.

No one questions the necessity for replacements. One questions the policy that robs Peter to pay Paul.

Advance parties steamed for England on 8 October 1944. The Division as a whole moved to Camp Myles Standish on 10-11 October. From this embarkation center they moved by increment.

The 2d Battalion, 424th Infantry, left New York on 18 October, on board the *Queen Mary*. The rest of the regiment and the entire 422d Infantry went 20 October on board the *Aquitania*. They landed at Greenock, Scotland, on the Firth of Clyde, eight days later and went to the Midlands—to Adderbury, Banbury and Chipping Norton.

Division Artillery and Special Troops streamed on board the *Wakefield* on 10 November, arriving at Liverpool on the 17th. They then moved to the same general area as the rest of the Division.

Training of a sort, but more particularly the drawing of matériel and equipment, took up the time until 1 December.

Chapter 3: Into the Line

The Division moved from England 1-2 December. The artillery, embarking at Weymouth in LSTs on 1 December, anchored that night off Le Havre where they tossed drearily for three days, then progressed up the Seine to Rouen, moving thence to Yerville to bivouac for three more interminable days. The infantry elements embarked 2 December at Liverpool, on board SS *Monowai,* their vehicles being carried in LSTs, to hang also in Le Havre estuary in bad weather until 6 December when they landed at Le Havre itself in snow and mud.

All elements moved by motor to Yerville, then started a dreary, chilly ride across country to Limesey, from which they hopped to St. Vith to another bivouac in the snow. No one who participated in that comfortless trek will ever forget it.

Days of rain, snow and mud; days of misery for the men packed in trucks as they rumbled through France and into Belgium, were prelude for the 106th's entry into battle. Inability to change clothing or foot-gear sopping and soggy with icy water is not conducive to the joy of living. When such things precede the vital test, when the discomfort and misery are added to the uncertainty of battle, the men undergoing them must be of tempered caliber, men so inured to the rigors of discipline they subordinate personal matters for teamwork. And the combat teams of the 106th, unfortunately, were not yet of that caliber; the Division was paying for the frequent drain on it for replacements, with constant influx of new personnel.

This was the last, long mile. When the Division finally ground to a halt again, it was in the midst of the 2d Infantry Division. The sector would be taken over gun for gun, man for man; thus read VIII Corps orders.

The long columns rolled into St. Vith, halted, then rolled again. As they progressed into the dreary, forest-bordered roads of the Ardennes, getting colder and colder, spirits went down. The excitement of going into battle thrives on sun; here there was no sun. Chill winds, gloomy little settlements set in the folds of the hills, mud and ice when they dismounted, and always the grey black vista of evergreens. An eerie region, the Ardennes.

They took over an area which had been won by the 4th Infantry Division 13 September, astride the fortifications of the Siegfried Line which here runs along the crest of the Schnee Eifel, a hogback ridge nosing down southwesterly from the Eifel area and pointing to the

9

Map 1: *The Golden Lions Committed. (Area occupied by the 106th Infantry Division, 11 December 1944)*

junction of the Belgium–Luxembourg–Germany boundaries. The depression to the north, a succession of winding valleys in which rise the headwaters of the Our River in the vicinity of Losheim, is called the Losheim Gap. South of the Schnee Eifel ridge the Prüm River drains. Both these streams run at first generally southwesterly, then turn south after they leave the higher ground of the Eifel to parallel one another until they empty into the Sauer River in the vicinity of Echternach, more than twenty-five miles to the south.

Two smaller streams, the Ihren and the Alf, rising from the northern slope of the Schnee Eifel above Bleialf, drain, respectively, into the Our to the west and the Prüm to the south. From Losheim the railway line to Malmedy pokes through the Gap on the north, while on the south another railway follows the devious valleys of the Prüm, Alf, and Ihren to cross the Our on the way to St. Vith.

There are other innumerable watercourses in this network of jumbled hills but the terrain features mentioned above definitely bound the Schnee Eifel battleground. North of the Our and east of St. Vith is the forest of Büllingen, and west of it the partly open mound of the Langert Berg.

The forest of St. Vith comes up to within a mile of the town. Directly to its east and to the south the Reiners Berg, Our Berg and Stein-Kopf are three partly wooded hills accidenting the terrain. St. Vith, Division headquarters, lies approximately ten miles west of the original front lines, but much farther by the winding roadnet.

Once west of the Our River the plateau opens out with opportunity for maneuver of armored units across country until the woods of Grand Bois and Bois d'Emmels spread their belts in front of the Salm River, next terrain barrier, on which lie Salmchâteau and Vielsalm, roughly ten miles from St. Vith.

In compliance with VIII Corps Letter of Instructions dated 7 December, the Division was to take over from the 2d Infantry Division "man for man and gun for gun," on or about 11 December. The Corps mission was one of aggressive defense, prepared to advance on Cologne on First Army orders.

Since every action and reaction in war depends upon four elements—mission, means, enemy and terrain—let's examine them now in this particular situation. We said that Gen. Jones' mission was one of aggressive defense. Just what does that phrase mean? To different persons, different things, perhaps; but the interpretation given by two great captains—Stonewall Jackson and George S. Patton—is probably the best: Keep the enemy in front in constant turmoil by a succession of attacks which, while perhaps minor in themselves, retain for one the initiative.

The means: one infantry division and one reinforced cavalry group, totaling nine battalions of infantry, two squadrons of cavalry, five battalions of field artillery, and one battalion each of tank destroyers and antiaircraft artillery. As reinforcement, the fires of nine battalions of VIII Corps Artillery were available on call.

The enemy as known to Jones: elements of two partly trained *Volksgrenadier* divisions with their supporting artillery, two panzer divisions supposedly lurking somewhere in the rear in reserve; in front of the enemy a liberal crop of minefields.

The terrain: as described in detail above, and implemented by a roadnet which must be considered carefully, since modern armies must move on roads to accomplish their missions. Into the 106th Division area came the following main roads, stemming from an adequate network in enemy-held terrain paralleling the front, and coming to a single focal point, St. Vith:

From the northeast (and entering through the sector held by the neighboring 99th Infantry Division) the Schleiden–Büllingen–Amblève–St. Vith highway. From the east the Kronenburg–Hallschlag–Manderfeld–Andler–Schönberg–St. Vith highway through the upper Our Valley. From the southeast the Prüm–Sellerich–Bleialf–Schönberg road to St. Vith, and below it the Pronsfeld–Winterspelt–St. Vith road.

Out of St. Vith, to continue around the clock, sprouted roads of vital importance to our own general success: the Oudler–Troisvierges–Bastogne road, branching a third of the way down south to a road paralleling the west bank of the Our—and our own front lines in that sector—all the way to Diekirch; the Poteau–Vielsalm highway, key to every road west to the Meuse; and the Ligneuville–Malmedy highway going north.

In addition, there was the railroad from Pronsfeld in enemy terrain to St. Vith, linking there with main lines to south, west and north.

Thus, one sees, the one absolutely vital spot in the entire divisional sector, from both defensive and offensive viewpoint not only of the Division but also of the U.S. First Army, was St. Vith, a spot to be held at all costs.

To get to St. Vith the enemy from the east had but two routes (always excepting roads through sectors held by neighbors of the 106th): down the Our Valley north of the Schnee Eifel, up the Pronsfeld–Winterspelt road to the south of it. Schönberg was the cork to one, the Heckhalenfeld hill mass to the other.

In the Schnee Eifel itself, within the American lines, one other main road runs from Roth on the northeast over the hill crests through Auw, Radscheid and Bleialf to Heckhuscheid and Grosskampenberg. We will hear more of this road, nicknamed by our people "Skyline Drive," and of its branch running north from above Bleialf to Schönberg. For the moment, however, we may dismiss them, since they are not themselves access roads to St. Vith.

From this somewhat sketchy estimate of the situation the reader may draw his own conclusions as to the solution of the problem of "aggressive defense" in this sector, remembering always that Gen. Jones, for his part, was also ordered to take over in place the exact dispositions of the 2d Infantry Division.

These dispositions consisted of a line of fortified villages across the Losheim Gap to the north, linked to a segment of the old Siegfried Line in the Schnee Eifel, thence to another succession of village strongpoints on the southern flank. A rigid, cordon defense, this, the puncture of which at any given point would endanger all the rest of the line.

In a nutshell, the sector which the 106th took over from the 2d consisted of a salient jutting into the enemy lines some eight miles at its deepest point, and twenty-two miles long in air line, from Lanzerath on the north to Grosskampenberg on the south.

To the 106th were attached the 14th Cavalry Group, the 275th Armored Field Artillery Battalion (105mm), the 820th Tank Destroyer Battalion and the 634th AAA Battalion. The first-named two units were to replace the 2d Division's Task Force X, guarding the headwaters of the Our River and the Losheim Gap.

The 422d Infantry and its supporting 589th Field Artillery Battalion (105mm) would relieve the 9th Infantry and its 15th Field Artillery Battalion; the 423d Infantry and 590th Field Artillery Battalion (105mm) the 38th Infantry and 38th Field Artillery Battalion; the 424th Infantry and 591st Field Artillery Battalion (105mm) the 23d Infantry and 37th Field Artillery Battalion.

Up in the north the 14th Cavalry Group, with the 275th Field Artillery in support, took over on 11 December. The 422d Infantry, on its right, had gotten in on 10 December; the 589th Field Artillery Battalion, supporting it, was the first unit of the Division to accomplish the relief, by the way, at 11:30 A.M., 10 December, having gotten in the previous afternoon and started its registration by 4:00 P.M. Pfc. Earl Copenhaver pulled the lanyard of the A Battery howitzer which barked the first round away.

The 423d Infantry also got in on 11 December, but the 424th Infantry on its right did not complete the relief until the next day.

It should be noted that both the 422d and 423d Regiments actually occupied old German positions, the exact coordinates and dispositions of which were, of course, known to the enemy down to the nearest yard. These positions were not chosen by the 106th Division; they were inherited. Why the 2d Division or VIII Corps, for that matter, had allowed this always potentially dangerous gamble, is not known. One suspects that the winter cold and the "quiet" aspect of the area had engendered carelessness.

On the other hand, the positions held by the 23d Infantry of the 2d Division, and now taken over by the 424th Infantry on 12 December, had been deliberately selected for defensive purposes, withdrawn nearly five thousand yards from the German Siegfried Line.

The position of the 424th Combat Team can be considered as well adapted for an elastic defense. Its principal fault was that it had the Our River in its rear. Again, it was an inherited position, for which neither blame nor praise belongs to the 106th Division but to its predecessors. It is understood that this position, refused somewhat from the old line, was taken up by the 23d Infantry Combat Team at the direction of the VIII Corps commander some time previous.

The 81st Engineer Battalion at Heuem, two miles west of Schönberg on the main road to St. Vith, was divided in support of the combat teams, with Company A at Auw attending to the 14th Cavalry Group and 422d Infantry. Company B was at Schönberg with the 423d Infantry, and Company C was at Heckhalenfeld with the 424th Infantry. Its mission was combat zone road maintenance. The 168th Engineer Combat Battalion, a Corps unit, was in close support and attending the rear areas.

General Jones held out the 2d Battalion, 423d Infantry, as Division reserve, at Born, north of St. Vith and generally nine miles behind the lines. Incidentally, the 1st Battalion, 424th Infantry, although Col. Reid, commanding the regiment, states that he did not know it, was considered by Division to have been also earmarked for Division reserve. This was later to occasion some friction and delay at a most crucial time. The 592d Field Artillery Battalion (155mm howitzers), in general support, was in the vicinity of Landesfeld, having taken over from the 12th Field Artillery Battalion.

To sum up the dispositions of the 106th Division at 7:00 P.M., 11 December, when Maj.Gen. Jones assumed responsibility for the sector, the outfit was much overextended, with its southern combat team, the 424th, the only element capable of conducting any sort of mobile defense.

Seven infantry battalions and one reinforced cavalry squadron, which was the total on the line, cannot do much along a 22-mile front. We will take up the detailed disposition of the combat teams later.

For supporting artillery, in addition to units mentioned above, Corps had earmarked, as available on call from the 106th, fire from the 174th, 333d and 402d Field Artillery Groups (nine battalions)—sizable fire power which was later to be sorely needed.

Ammunition for the organic Division artillery was a problem which, starting with the arrival of the Division in England, was not settled until after it had gone into the line. In Britain it was only after great difficulty that sufficient 105mm shells were obtained to calibrate nine of the new howitzers issued, and this just forty-eight hours before loading.[1]

Supply people were filled with assurances that there was plenty on the "far shore." Nevertheless, despite efforts to draw it, not a single round could be obtained, and the four field artillery battalions trundled into their positions without it. In fact, Gen. McMahon was forced to decline to relieve one of the 2d Division's light artillery battalions on 9 December because of this fact.

The 2d Division artillerymen had ammunition in fairly plentiful supply at their positions, and before leaving provided some for their relief gunners.[2]

Once in position, however, the artillerymen's reiterated pleas were soon heard. The ammunition trains began hauling from dumps as far away as Liège, and actually, by 14 December, had their basic loads, as McMahon on his inspections of all batteries, found. The only gripe of the gunners now was that the ammunition lots were so many and so mixed as to add to the difficulty of accurate fire.[3]

The medics of the 331st Medical Battalion were well scattered, with headquarters and clearing station at St. Vith. Collecting companies were disposed: A at Andler, B at Buchet, and C at Steinebrück. Company A had the additional task of handling two collecting stations, with one ambulance each, at Manderfeld for the 14th Cavalry Group, and at Winterscheid for Troop B, 18th Cavalry Reconnaissance Squadron. Good dispositions were made for further evacuation.

Division headquarters was at St. Vith, as had been said. Here also was headquarters of Division Artillery, and of the 634th AAA Battalion, whose elements were scattered over the area. The rear echelon was at Vielsalm.

Numb, soaked, frozen—no change of warm clothing available, for their barracks bags had not caught up with them—the 106th tumbled from their trucks and took over "man for man and gun for gun," as the Corps directive read. And the 2d Division, old-timers who had been enjoying a brief rest in this area, were in a hurry to get off. Some outfits were actually on the move as the newcomers came in.

Wisecracks flew as the men of the 2d touted the "rest camp" the 106th was coming into. The officers, too, assured the newcomers of their good fortune as they hurriedly turned over schedules of fire, schedules of patrols.

"It has been very quiet up here and your men will learn the easy way," remarked Col. Francis H. Boos, commanding the 38th (Rock of the Marne) Infantry Regiment, to Col. Cavender, commanding the 423d Infantry.

In some cases the turning over of data was slurred. Company C, 422d Infantry, for instance, didn't even get information of the elements to right and left when it took over.

The Johnny-come-latelies could pick up where the old-timers left off. The 2d was on the way to a fight. *Let's go, soldier!* Some of the infantry weapons were imbedded in mud. *Never mind, give us yours. Hurry, hurry! You don't know how lucky you are to be here.*

So the 106th's men went fumbling out into the snow and muck, stumbling in water-soaked foot-gear. The forests were eerie; over there somewhere was the enemy. He made himself known by occasional small-arms fire, occasional bursts of "Screaming Meemies," the mortar shells that sound as if they are right on top of you even if they're a quarter-mile away.

The hutments and pillboxes looked inviting and safe, even if the 2d Division had taken the stoves away with them. Old-timers always do. The billets in the villages, too, were warm, as far as they went, and that was something to be thankful for. But where old-timers would at once have gone about the business of drying out socks, the newcomers were perhaps a bit timid. It might seem as if they were only play-soldiers. Or perhaps they didn't know. Anyway, they didn't—or couldn't—take care of themselves, and the trench-foot rate soared almost immediately.

Those villages—houses huddled about crossroads in depressions—"sugar bowls" the 106th called them. Sugar bowls they were to be, too—for the enemy—for from the surrounding high ground all these so-called "strongpoints" could be brought under fire. But the 106th didn't know that—yet.

General Jones did not like the dispositions of the Division when he made an inspection. Neither did Perrin, the Assistant Division Commander, nor McMahon, the Artillery commander. And Mark Devine, the tough cavalryman commanding the 14th Group, was outspoken about it. Devine said he wanted to get a counterattack plan. So did everyone, and the Division was working on one, almost immediately. However, until VIII Corps gave them a directive there wasn't much that could be done about it. The VIII Corps directive was received 14 December. And in the meantime each regimental commander was asked to turn in a plan of his own. The 422d's came into Division headquarters just before noon on 15 December. There was a G-2 conference at Division headquarters on 14 December. One gathers that the repeated assurances of the 2d Division that this was a quiet sector, and the general impression that the 106th had been put here for training, a sort of warming-up for the real thing, permeated the atmosphere.

Lieutenant Colonel Stout, 106th's G-2, opened the conference by noting that there were two panzer divisions about fifteen miles back of the enemy line, as available reserve in case we attacked. He described the enemy in front of the Division, the 18th and 26th *Volksgrenadiers,* as inexperienced and placed in the area for training and indoctrination. Stout quoted liberally from a Corps G-2 estimate of about a week previous.

"This must be old stuff to you," Stout remarked to Lt.Col. W. M. Slayden, Assistant G-2 of Corps, who had been detailed temporarily to the Division to help it get on its feet. "Old stuff, for you wrote it."

Stout stressed the poor roadnet in front of them, with few available routes for armor except north-south. He inferred that the woods were generally too dense for armor to operate across country, which was quite true.

All elements reported on enemy activities. Out of these emerged a picture of greater activity on the north, diminishing on the 424th's sector to the south. Devine's S-2, speaking for his cavalry group, said there had been slight patrolling activities, and a great deal of mortar and artillery fire. He felt that his sector was more vulnerable to attack because it was flatter, with a collection of towns, and was less densely wooded than the rest of the Division's area. Devine was not intrigued by his thin-spread condition. To man some of his "strongpoints" he had had to dismount automatic weapons from his vehicles, a grave loss of mobility.

The 422d Infantry reported some patrol activity and a lot of enemy fire. The 423d Infantry had sent several patrols out as far as eight hundred yards, but had contacted no enemy, though sporadic artillery fire was being received. In the 424th sector no artillery fire had fallen, nor mortar fire, and there was no evidence of enemy activity at all.

As a matter of fact, out in the front lines, and particularly in the sectors of the 422d and 423d, there was some evidence of enemy activity. From time to time the noise of motors swelled through the trees.

Throughout the Division, one senses from the evidence, existed an odd mixture of complacency, false sense of security and jittery nerves. The last, quite naturally, was to be expected from men just prior to and during their first contact with the enemy. The natural inclination, the nearer one gets to the front, is to magnify in importance the slightest rumor, incident or evidence of hostile activity.

Military intelligence consists of skillful interpretation of such information; the screening and correct totting up of evidence depends both on the experience of the operator and on the particular situation concerned; one does not learn from books alone. Regiment screens battalions and lower units, division screens regiments, and corps screens divisions. The result is passed down again.

So, when we come to the complacency and sense of false security existing in the higher echelons of the 106th Division during this preliminary period, much of it reflects from the attitude of Corps. For instance, when a battalion S-2 in the 422d Infantry was criticized by regimental headquarters for reporting movement of "convoys," and told that the correct word was "motors," since all that had been heard was the noise of automotive engines,[4] that attitude was engendered by corps G-2 opinion. Corps had informed Division that the Germans might be playing transcriptions over loudspeaker amplification systems to simulate a massing of forces. And it was fact that the Germans from time to time during the war had used just such a ruse.

Naturally again, commanders and staffs of troops just arrived in the sector would lean heavily on the opinions of the higher command, which could be expected to have reliable knowledge of the situation. In this case one suspects that the perhaps rose-tinted glasses of VIII Corps intelligence personnel had much influence on Division intelligence evaluations.

However, at this 14 December meeting Stout did urge on all elements the necessity for groping deeper to find the enemy, plot his minefields, and capture prisoners. Slayden concurred; no new identifications had been obtained for two weeks.[5]

Out along the front enemy artillery fire ranged from 88s to mortars. Occasionally a snow-weighted trip wire would explode a mine or booby trap to put edge on new and straining nerves. Occasionally our outposts would glimpse the enemy—the artillery OPs were on the *qui vive* for this, and dropped concentrations practically down the Krauts' throats at the slightest provocation. In the infantry lines B Company, 423d Infantry, occupying Siegfried Line positions overlooking the little town of Brandscheid, scored a number of kills with small-arms fire after it got in. The engineers began rebuilding trails; drivers began to learn the bad places in the roads like Purple Heart Corner, on the Bleialf–Schönberg road. And so they drifted for a few days while it snowed, and rained, and life in general was miserable. There happened the usual plethora of reports demanded by higher headquarters, the usual gripes between front-line units and the service people. The 106th was short in a number of vital items, and it was like pulling teeth, it seemed, to get them.

Not that the Division's own service personnel were not battling with Corps and Army. They were, and they accomplished a lot. Overshoes were gotten up—needed most by the 422d Infantry, where trench foot rates had jumped. The poor 422d, landing 6 December, at Havre, had stood almost all night in cold and rain before moving out, and incidentally had been the last regiment to draw overshoes, with the usual results that happen to the people on the end of the line. Typical of the existing red tape was the 423d Infantry's request for barbed wire on 15 December, and the dump's retort that "at least forty-eight hours advance notice must be given."

Anyhow, it was a "quiet" sector. The sun must shine some day soon and hearts were high at the opportunity to get some battle indoctrination before the big push to the Rhine broke.

NOTES TO CHAPTER 3

[1] Brig.Gen. Leo T. McMahon to the writer, 10 September 1946.

[2] *Ibid.* Also Col. Malin Craig, Jr., to the writer, 4 September 1946.

[3] *Ibid.* This is a technical point which only an artilleryman will appreciate. Since each lot of powder produced by the manufacturer varies slightly in muzzle velocity, necessitating adjustment of fire control and changes in data at the battery, your artilleryman naturally prefers to have sufficient of any particular lot to do his work with the least number of minute changes.

[4] Lt.Col. Joseph C. Matthews, Executive Officer, 422d Infantry, as quoted by an interviewer of the Historical Section, ETO.

[5] The 106th, it must be remembered, had assumed responsibility for the sector only three days before the meeting.

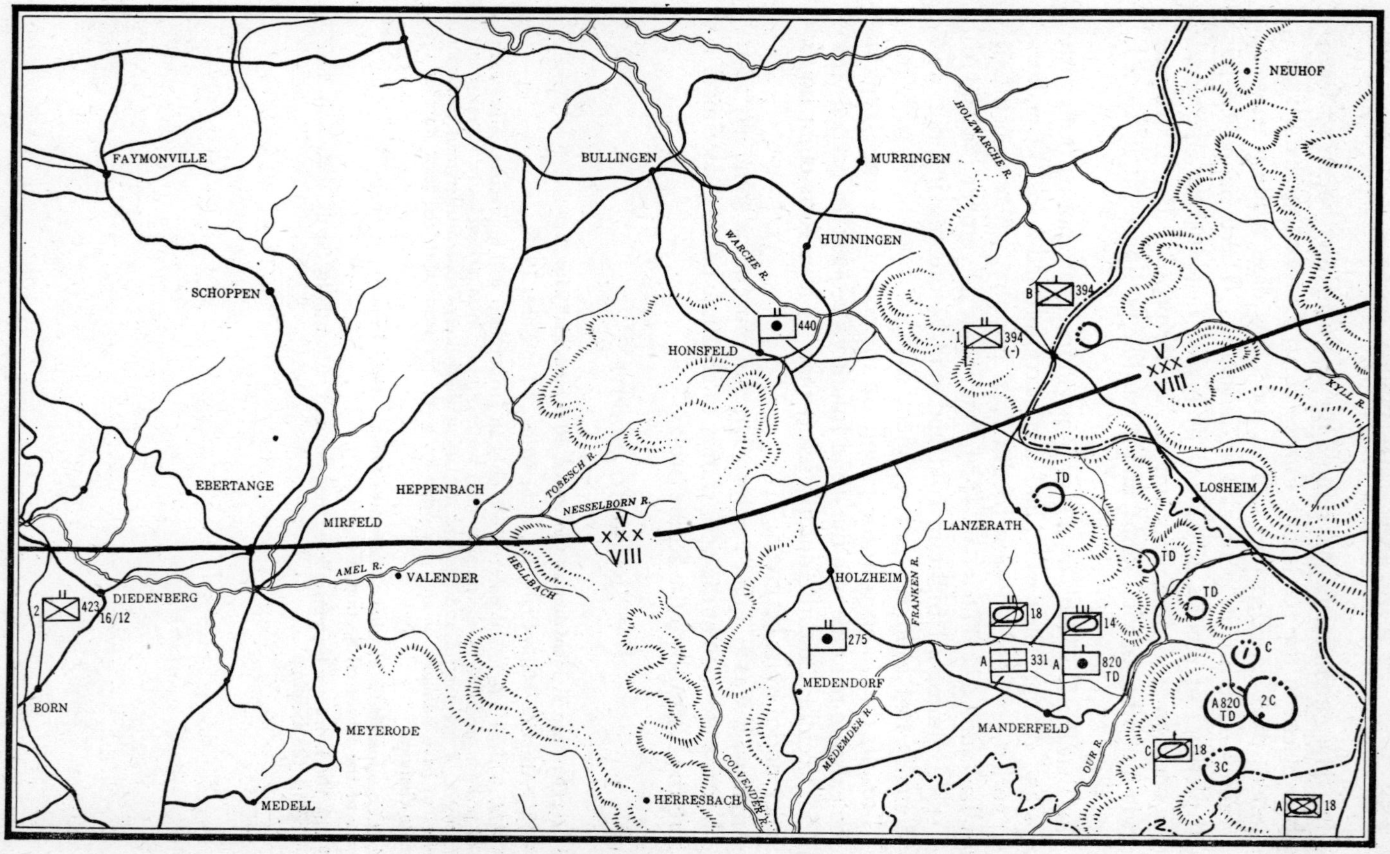

Map 2: The Northern Flank

Chapter 4: The Storm Breaks

Dawn had not yet come at 5:30 A.M., 16 December when an enemy barrage of all calibers up to and including 14-inch shells from railway guns came crashing all along the line and deep into the 106th Division's sector. The 14-inch shells were dropping into St. Vith, rocking Division headquarters. The intense fire came down on crossroads, strongpoints, critical places whose coordinates were as well known to the enemy as his finger tips. Flares—red, green, amber, and white—flickered over the treetops. Here and there searchlights bounced off the low-hung clouds to reflect an unearthly light on roads and other open spots. Wire communications were ripped apart. Although little damage was done to personnel, the sudden impact of shelling was a thing to fill the heart with terror. In the forests, tree bursts showered branches and splinters, sent tree trunks crashing into the snow. Screaming Meemie *(Nebelwerfer)* shells rasped nerves already raw and tense.

In rapid succession three messages came to Division headquarters, giving a quickly sketched picture of the situation. From the 423d Infantry, at 5:50 A.M., relayed over an artillery line: "423 Inf AT Co shelled by arty since 5:30. 2nd Bn 423 Inf alerted. Lines out with AT Co, 2nd Bn and Tr B, 14 Cav Gr." From the 28th Division on the south at 6:20 A.M.: "28 Inf Div received heavy shelling by arty. Reserve alerted." And from the 99th Division on the north, at 6:32 A.M.: "99 Inf Div taking a hv shelling all along S part of sector. No atk by foot troops reported." Thus reads the story in the G-3 journal.

Hell was breaking all along the line. As Gen. Jones says of his reactions early that morning: "When they begin to drop 14-inch shells it's the real thing." But other people, it seemed, in Division and in Corps, were still Doubting Thomases. VIII Corps, at 9:00 A.M. queried: "Please advise us when any reserve strength is committed—even regimental reserve." And back at Vielsalm the Division bandsmen broke up their first rehearsal, put away their instruments and moved out to St. Vith under arms, as Headquarters Security Guard.

By 6:15 the shelling had stopped. Vague figures in white snow suits, figures who screamed and whooped as they danced through the trees, flittered along the front. The clatter of tank treads reverberated on the roads. At last this was something tangible. American artillery, mortar, machine-gun and small-arms fire came down on the enemy spearheads.

North of the Schnee Eifel the Nazi advance, at first estimated as an infantry regiment reinforced by fifteen tanks, barged into the Our Valley

21

generally toward Schönberg. South of the ridge they pushed from
Pronsfeld through Habscheid on Winterspelt and the Alf–Ihren River
valleys. The prongs would converge at St. Vith—must converge there
within the first twenty-four hours if Sepp Dietrich and his Sixth SS
Panzer Army were to keep their timetable. His I SS Panzer Corps
must make room for II SS Panzer Corps on its heels. And on Dietrich's
left, Manteuffel's Fifth Panzer Army was attacking, spearheaded more
cannily by *Volksgrenadier* infantry to make the holes through which
the armor would come. And so from Honsfeld on the north to Grosskampenberg on the south Dietrich's 1st SS Panzer and the 18th and
62d *Volksgrenadier* and 116th Panzer Divisions of Manteuffel were
assaulting the 106th's front, the roads behind them jam-packed for
miles with the weight of the great counteroffensive.

Up in the Our River valley the rush went through the 14th Cavalry
Group strongpoints like a welder's flame through soft iron. Its reserve,
the 32d Reconnaissance Squadron, early committed, was of no avail
against that weight. Lanzerath, Krewinkel and Roth were overrun.
Enemy tanks were clattering and banging through Auw before noon.

The 422d Infantry's left flank, threatened by this advance, was refused to the north, its regimental reserve committed; our artillery was
putting point-blank fire on tanks poking up from Auw—was actually
engaging in a close defense fight. By late afternoon Division had committed the 2d Battalion, 423d Infantry, from reserve to protect this
left flank, northeast of Schönberg, and to assist the threatened artillery
battalions to withdraw. North of the Our the cavalry was now scattered
like chaff, contact with the 99th Division lost.

On the south the enemy advance lashed north from Habscheid to
Grosslangenfeld, wedging between the right of the 423d and left of
the 424th Infantry regiments and threatening Bleialf. At the same time
the *Volksgrenadiers* were also pounding up the Habscheid–Winterspelt
axis, and during the morning the 1st Battalion, 424th Infantry, had
been released to its regiment to maintain its hold on the southern key
to St. Vith.

There was no doubt now that the 106th Division was fighting—
fighting for its life in its first engagement. The engineers were being
committed as infantry in their respective sectors, service companies and
batteries were engaged, and the division was learning the hard way that
"sugar-bowl" strongpoints commanded by surrounding high ground are
no strongpoints at all.

Organically, Gen. Jones now had no further forces with which to
influence the action. But at 11:20 that morning Corps had telephoned
that Combat Command B, 9th Armored Division, then at Faymonville,

had been placed at the 106th's disposition. It could reach St. Vith shortly after daylight the next day. And the 168th Engineer Combat Battalion, at St. Vith, had also been turned over to the 106th Division.

By that evening the threat from the north appeared to Jones to be the more dangerous. He knew that the 14th Cavalry Group was unravelling and contact had been lost with the 99th Division. So he decided to throw the armored troops, who had been in the area and knew the country, up into the Our Valley to restore the situation. He was still worried, however, about that nasty fishhook now threatening Winterspelt and Bleialf to the south.

If anything went wrong, the 422d and 423d Infantry had no maneuver ground, no terrain to give, whereas the 424th Infantry on the south could, if necessary, give ground to cushion the blow. On the other hand, if it did so, the other two regiments would be in a bad way. They must either be pulled out now—this was between 8:00 and 10:00 o'clock at night—if they could disengage themselves, or remain and stick it out, threatened by encirclement.

Jones, who had with him Lt.Col. Slayden, the VIII Corps assistant G-2 who had been loaned him, called Maj.Gen. Troy H. Middleton, the Corps commander. They discussed the situation in guarded terms, for the enemy might be tapping the line. The upshot was that, the conversation finished, Jones turned to Slayden and told him that Middleton had given him Combat Command B, 7th Armored Division, and had assured him that it would be in St. Vith at 7:00 A.M. next day.

One gathers that Jones did not feel he should urge too much the withdrawal of the 422d and 423d, since to give up that ground and uncover the direct route to Bastogne and the Stenay gap—gateway to Verdun—except in vital necessity, would not redound to the credit of the Division. Conversely, unless the high command had good reason, little would be gained by sacrificing two infantry regiments. Middleton had left the decision to him.

Now, packing in each hand, so to speak, the punch of an armored combat command with which to retrieve the situation, things looked better to Jones. He made his decision. He would send CCB, 9th Armored Division, down south toward Winterspelt, and CCB, 7th Armored Division, coming from the north, directly east to clean out the situation on the northern flank. The 422d and 423d Infantry Regiments would hold in place.

"No one," says Slayden, "could question the soundness of this decision with the facts as known to Gen. Jones at the time. It was probably my fault. When it was announced to Gen. Jones over the phone that CCB, 7th Armored Division, would arrive at St. Vith at

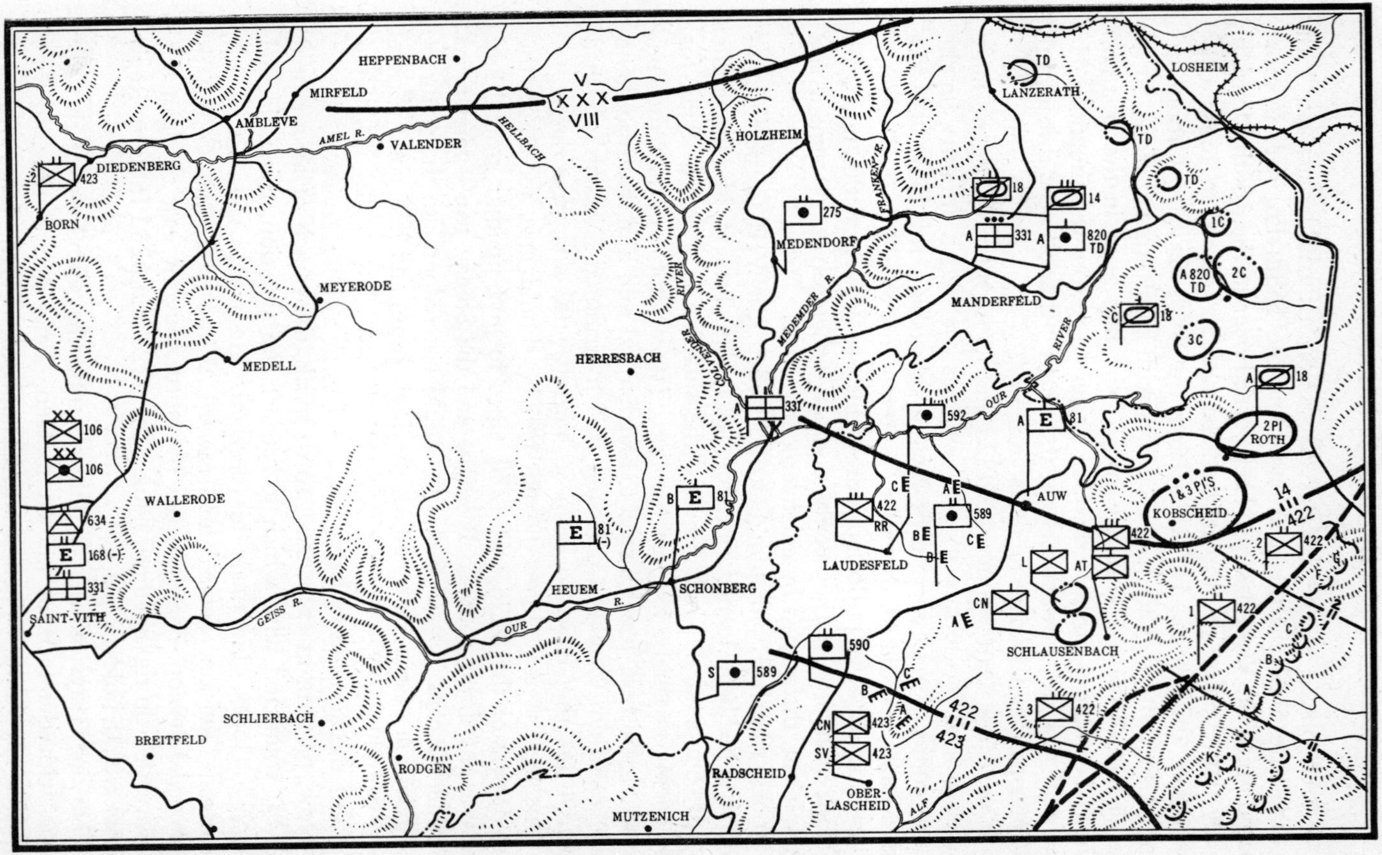

Map 3: The Losheim Gap. (Positions of the 14th Cavalry Group and 422d Infantry, 16 December 1944)

7:00 A.M., 17 December, I knew this was overoptimistic [the 7th Armored Division was at Scherpenseel, Germany, up in the Ninth Army zone to the north]. It was impossible, and I should have said so, but that would have put me in the position of calling the Corps commander a liar."

So there the matter lay that night, with the enemy pressure squeezing in, and the two armored combat commands due in the morning. Looking on the lighter side of life VIII Corps formally announced postponement of a "Posit" (proximity) fuze demonstration scheduled for the next day. Up in the Schnee Eifel, as well as on the flanks, the chill of death settled down in the evergreens as half-frozen fighting men hugged their weapons and cheered themselves as best they might that tomorrow would be another day. To get the real picture of what had happened to the 106th Division on that first day one must examine in detail what occurred on the ground.

THE LOSHEIM GAP

Mark Devine's 14th Cavalry Group, with one squadron, the 18th Reconnaissance (reinforced), on the line, and the other, the 32d, in reserve back at Vielsalm over twenty miles away by road, was supposed to be the stopper in the Losheim Gap. Thin-spread over a seven-mile front, partly immobilized by the nature of their positions, the cavalrymen made as effective a stopper as would a handful of buckshot in an open sluice gate.

Group headquarters was at Manderfeld, key to the Gap insofar as movement southwestward into the Our Valley is concerned. Through it runs the main Hallschlag–Losheim–Manderfeld–Andler–Schönberg road to St. Vith. The route from Schleiden up to the northeast passing through Lanzerath, joins the former road at the Hasenvenn crossroads on the western edge of the village. Lesser roads and wood-trails form a somewhat tenuous network of communication in the tumbled, forested hills. Here Col. Devine had the assault-gun and light-tank outfits, Troop E and Company F (the tank element in a cavalry squadron is a company) of the 18th Reconnaissance Squadron.

Manderfeld itself sits on the edge of a shelf, spreading into a draw coming down eastward from the heights by the crossroads into the Our Valley. Commanded by high ground to the north, the west and, across the river bed to the east, it is one of the "sugar bowl" positions.

The remainder of the 18th Squadron and Company A, 820th Tank Destroyer Battalion (reinforced), which was attached to the group, were scattered from hell to breakfast.

Troop C, its command post at Weckerath, had its 1st Platoon in the hamlet of Afst, nestling in the valley of the Schnitz, a tiny tributary of the Our. The 2d Platoon, with a platoon of Company A, 820th TD Battalion, was a thousand yards to the southeast in the top of the same valley at Krewinkel, and the 3d Platoon was on Hill 570 about another thousand yards southwest of Krewinkel, in a triangle of wood-trails.

Troop A, less 1st and 3d Platoons, was at Roth, a mile and a half directly south of Krewinkel, with only a devious trail connecting it with a two-gun detachment of the TDs. Roth, astride the main road tapping the lateral Prüm–Losheim road, which runs across the highest point of the Schnee Eifel and which provided a jump-off line for the enemy, corks the southern entrance to the Our Valley via Auw. Troop A's 1st and 3d Platoons were at Kobscheid, one mile southwest of Roth on a smaller lateral road, affording further protection to the Auw gateway; they were in close contact with the left flank of the 422d Infantry in the Schnee Eifel fortifications.

Company A, 820th Tank Destroyer Battalion, was further scattered toward the north. One detachment held a roadblock at Berterath, two miles directly northeast of Manderfeld (twice that distance by road) controlling the northern entrance to the Our toward Schönberg. Another detachment was posted at Merlscheid, a woods-trail road junction a mile and a quarter north of Manderfeld, leading to the north-south road into the Our Valley. A third was posted in the vicinity of Lanzerath, three miles north of Manderfeld on this same road.

Periodic patrols northward kept contact between these tiny TD posts, with cavalry headquarters at Manderfeld, and with B Company, 394th Infantry, the right-flank unit of the 99th Division. The latter unit was near Losheimergraben, a huddle of dwellings at the junction of the Losheim–Büllingen and Schleiden–Schönberg–St. Vith main roads.

As far as can be ascertained, there were no minefields protecting this far-flung sector, many of the cavalry automatic weapons had been dismounted to arm the strongpoints, and, by order, most patrolling was done on foot. It would appear to have been far from a good cavalry mobile disposition. Again, one had an inherited situation. That, it seems, was the way Task Force X of the 2d Division had operated; therefore, the newcomers carried on, but grudgingly; Devine didn't like it.

The 275th Armored Field Artillery Battalion (105mm) commanded by Lt.Col. Clay, in direct support of the cavalry sector, was emplaced in the vicinity of Medendorf, two and a half miles by direct air line west of Manderfeld, whence it could put fire wherever desired. One cannot quarrel with this position, which was linked with observation posts well forward. A smart outfit, the 275th, as it was to prove in the days of travail.

Troop C's 1st Platoon, sending a patrol out of Afst the night of 15-16 December found unusual activity—prelude to the deluge. Lt. Ajax L. Crawford, commanding, took eight men up the hill trail into Allmuthen, three-quarters of a mile northeast of his position. Finding a buzz of movement in the hamlet, the patrol circled it, noted it filled with enemy, had an unexpected brush with an equally surprised force of Krauts, and got back with loss of one man.

That was shortly before the enemy barrage started. As the artillery fire came down, the 2d Platoon, under Lt. Kenneth C. Ferrens, at Krewinkel, found itself caught by infiltrating infantry from three sides. When the barrage lifted, the enemy, many of them in snow suits, came in on all the outposts. The 1st and 2d Platoons were both driven back on Weckerath. The 3d Platoon, surrounded on its crossroads position, was ordered by Capt. John T. Walker to "plough through the bastards to Weckerath."

Lieutenant Ledru L. King gathered his men, succeeded in starting his vehicles despite the cold motors, and they hit the road. Germans in snow suits on both sides of the trail, opened fire, which the cavalrymen returned as they ran the gantlet. Just as they neared Weckerath an enemy group beside a barn opened fire, but Sgt. Webster wiped them out with a burst of canister from his 37mm cannon. They got in to find Weckerath itself surrounded. Lt. Schnee, liaison officer for squadron headquarters, got the remnants out through another hail of fire and the now much-battered C Troop made it into Manderfeld. The 275th Field Artillery then turned its attention to Weckerath, and the hamlet and all the Germans in it went up in flames as the artillery concentration pulverized it, about noon.

Troop A at Roth to the south was smacked at once by infantry and tanks. It held out until 11:00 A.M., when Capt. Stanley E. Porche phoned Lt. Lorenz Herdrick, commanding the Kobsheid garrison: "We're moving back. Your friends to the south are moving back [he evidently meant the 422d Infantry; if so it was an erroneous conclusion]. It's up to you whether you withdraw on foot or in vehicles. I advise you to go on foot." One of the TD 3-inch guns in Roth knocked out an enemy armored car, but was then outflanked. The other gun, it seems, was badly sited, and could not bring fire to bear. Porche and his men did not get out. Of the ninety cavalrymen and TD men in Roth, three were killed, the rest made prisoner.

With the loss of Roth the road to Auw was opened, and enemy armor began to roll west.

Lieutenant Herdrick's Kobsheid garrison, Troop A's 1st and 3d Platoons, found itself engaged hammer and tongs as soon as the enemy preliminary artillery fire died about 6:15 A.M. Screaming Nazis—someone said it sounded like the Rebel yell—came dashing in following a green flare in the pallid fore-dawn. From the command post, the troopers started hurling hand grenades, some of which were picked up and thrown back by the attackers.

Private Edward J. Sklepkowski of the mortar squad grabbed some fast-fuzed booby-trap grenades, began throwing them through a slit in the wall of the CP. They exploded in the air with excellent results. A group of snow-suited Krauts huddled into a pigpen beside the house and thirty of them were bagged. In all, the Kobscheid men believe, they killed 150 Jerries in that first assault. The enemy small-arms fire and artillery hampered the gathering of prisoners. German wounded kept up shrill calls of *"Kamerad!"* and *"Wasser!"*

Lieutenant Clark, forward observer of the 275th Field Artillery, kept his head, directed fire. For some God-granted reason both wire and radio communications stayed in until 8:00 A.M. and the 275th's howitzers encircled the town with precision fire. As the assault got hotter, Clark tried to get his battalion to place fire directly on him, but they wouldn't do it. Then communications went out and the garrison was on its own the rest of the day.

By dusk the main battle had swept to the west and south, behind them, with heavy firing. A battered contact patrol from the 422d Infantry on the south staggered in to tell of confused and bitter fighting between Auw and Schlausenbach. Herdrick decided it was time to get out. Destroying their vehicles, the garrison, in three detachments, led repectively by Herdrick, Clark and Mess Sgt. Fred H. Humphreys, set out into the snow-packed forest, single file. They tried first for Auw, but the enemy was there. Moving generally northwest they managed in some fashion—their stories are vague—to link the next day with the 27th Armored Infantry of the 9th Armored Division. They had spent a few hours in some infantry regimental supply bivouac, they had picked up a lone Negro artilleryman of the 333d Field Artillery Battalion (Corps Artillery), the only man left of his particular outfit.

So much for the original front-line elements of the 18th Squadron.

From group headquarters in Manderfeld Col. Devine had called Division at 6:40 A.M., asking permission to move his 32d Cavalry Reconnaissance Squadron, which he had already alerted, from reserve billets at Vielsalm to a position halfway between St. Vith and Manderfeld. At 7:00 A.M. he reported: "Front lines still intact; things well in hand."

Division released the 32d to him at that time, and by 9:32 A.M. the squadron, less its tank company, was bound for Manderfeld, via the St. Vith–Setz–Schönberg–Andler road.

The 32d Squadron, formerly Chicago's "Black Horse" Troop of the Illinois National Guard, was a perky outfit. It had been in Panama and had seen action on Attu. Company F, the tankers, had stripped their vehicles for much needed overhaul, and were caught with their pants down, through no fault of theirs, by the alert. Capt. Horace N. Blair stirred things up and by noon the company was ready for action—less its intercommunication radios. It was smart work. Blair decided to go without the radio and hit the road an hour and a half behind the rest of the squadron.

By 11:00 A.M., when the 32d Squadron's advance party came rolling into Manderfeld, the situation was pretty bad. In fact, while Col. Devine was at an OP his staff had started packing. The 820th TD's detachments to the north had been mostly overrun—seven of their ten guns were lost and five were already being used against the Americans. Contact had been broken with Roth and Kobscheid, and the enemy was apparently getting into Auw. But Devine, coming back at 11:00 A.M., was enraged. He ordered the records unpacked. "We'll stay here," said he, ordering a patrol to Auw to investigate.

We have said that Devine was not satisfied with his original dispositions and was worried about counterattack. One of his plans was to move E Troop, 32d Squadron (in a cavalry reconnaissance squadron, E is the assault-gun troop, armed with six 75mm howitzers, each mounted on a light tank chassis) into a supporting position near Manderfeld. The troop had already reconnoitered such a position at Hasenvenn crossroads a thousand yards west of Manderfeld. This morning, therefore, leading the squadron, E Troop under Lt. Earle A. Lawton at once pushed north from Andler up the Medemder Valley on the Manderfeld road, and went into position at 10:45 A.M. with four of its six guns. They had a field of direct fire covering the road leading north to the village of Hasenvenn itself. While some enemy harassing fire was dropping, it did not inconvenience them too much. Here the troop tied in with the fire direction center of the 275th Field Artillery. Here, too, came drifting back the remnants of the 820th TD detachments from the far northern positions.

Troop C, following, was now rolling into Manderfeld. Behind it on the road were A and B Troops, the former now just at Andler, five miles southeast.

Devine ordered C Troop to cover his north flank, under the support of E Troop's guns. He sent two platoons of A to the high ground south-

west of Manderfeld, and the rest of the troop north up the Andler–
Holzheim–Honsfeld road to Holzheim, three miles northwest of
Manderfeld, covering the now open gap between the 106th and 99th
Divisions. He radioed B Troop to stand at Andler in reserve. This
disposition, leaving him one troop in hand for reserve, and the tankers
still to come, was not bad provided the right flank was secure. And as
yet no word had come from the patrol reconnoitering towards Auw.

Devine had already asked for additional infantry support, suggesting
that the 99th Division drive down on Auw, while he attacked from
Verschneid. Division repeated this suggestion to the 99th, but of course
without result. The northern neighbor was by this time well embroiled
itself.

It was some time during this period that Lt.Col. Paul A. Ridge, commanding the 32d Squadron, went back to get ammunition, turning his
command over to Major John L. Kracke, squadron executive. Ridge,
according to observers, was in a highly nervous state. He was later
relieved.

Captain Charles Martin, commanding C Troop, pushed two platoons
up the road to Hasenvenn, where they promptly got into a fire fight with
enemy elements pushing in from the overrun TD positions. E Troop's
four guns did some snap-shooting, breaking up at least two hostile concentrations. Direct fire on a reverse slope swept a snow-covered hedge-
row to complete the enemy discomfiture. But he was persistent, continuing to slide in on both sides of the road, from five hundred to eight
hundred yards from the gun positions. And now he began to plaster
mortar fire on this troublesome delaying force, together with shells
from some of the captured American 3-inch TD guns. By 2:30 P.M.
the crossroads position was hot, and two of E Troop's guns had to be
withdrawn to defiladed positions slightly northwest.

While waiting for his patrol to come from Auw with the true picture,
Devine had decided to take the offensive himself and ordered Major
James L. Mayes, S-3 of the 32d Squadron, with C and E Troops and
two remaining platoons of the 820th TD Battalion, to take Losheim and
retake Krewinkel.

At 2:30 P.M. Task Force Mayes attacked up the road past Hasenvenn
village, got to the road junction just west of Merlscheid, and there was
pinned down by stiff opposition. About this time the patrol from Auw
came back to Manderfeld, badly cut up. Auw was definitely in enemy
hands and the Our River valley behind the cavalry was open to him.
Devine, who had much earlier informed Division of his intention, if
not reinforced, to withdraw to the line Holzheim–Andler, was ready to
leave. Both his flanks were in the air, one of his two squadrons was
smashed.

Task Force Mayes would cover the withdrawal. Troop A at Holzheim and Troop B at Andler would establish the new line. Company F, the light tanks, which had arrived at Andler at 3:30 P.M., had already been told to wait for further orders and Blair had pulled his tanks out of road traffic into a draw near Setz.

Amazingly enough, this daylight withdrawal was successful. Group and both squadron headquarters, with what was left of the 18th Squad-. ron and the TDs, hightailed out of Manderfeld for the west. Then Mayes, using 1st and 2d Platoons of C Troop as his own screen, together with the original two guns of E Troop, pulled the rest of his little force through his own particular knothole into the gathering dusk. By 4:00 P.M. this crust was ready to break and did, safely. The 275th Field Artillery, leapfrogging, got its batteries back to positions near Nieder Emmels, two miles northwest of St. Vith.

Group headquarters and the 18th Squadron were in Holzheim by dark, 32d Squadron in Herresbach, with C Troop on the delaying line. But what was left of the 18th was moved on, swinging north through Honsfeld and thence in a wide arc down to Medell, four miles northeast of St. Vith. Group installed itself at Hepscheid, just east of the St. Vith–Büllingen road, one mile north of Heppenbach.

Troop A had already swept this ridge-line delaying position for infiltrated enemy, as well as two dismounted platoons could sweep a three-mile zone. Capt. Franklin B. Lindsey's B Troop, all this time in reserve, had established a defensive position on the southern flank above Andler. Now Troop A at Holzheim came in for more grief. Lt. Reppa was anxious about that still blank north flank. He knew that there were American troops in Honsfeld, four miles away. He asked and received permission to move his troop to Honsfeld, where he arrived at 9:00 P.M., to find an unidentified captain of the 99th Division who had organized by sheer will power a rag-tag-and-bobtail fighting force from stragglers and from a 99th Division rest camp nearby.

Reppa joined forces with this unsung hero. He sent a patrol up north again to try to contact the 99th Division and in the meantime stood by. Through the town toward the rear crawled an incessant stream of traffic in the dark. Vehicles were using only their cat's eyes, sometimes were guided by a man walking in advance. Sgt. George Creel, armored-car commander of the 2d Platoon of Troop A, was sitting in his car in the middle of town when a particularly heavy vehicle, preceded by a man on foot with a flashlight, rumbled by. It was a tank; a big one. The flashlight swung carelessly and Creel's eyes bugged out as the beam for a second fell on a swastika mark! Right behind it were several other heavy vehicles and halftracks crammed with men.

The big tank nosed up to a house, swung its gun and fired, point-blank. Creel and his crew couldn't get their own gun working. The village flared with shots and cries, scattered tommy-gun and burp-gun bursts. That was the end of both Troop A and of the unidentified captain's extemporized force. They melted into the night in one of those unpredictable panics, abandoning vehicles. Some worked themselves back to Hepscheid where the 14th Group headquarters troop was billeted, many hiked as far back as Born and Medell by the next day.

To sum up the cavalry situation by nightfall of 16 December, the Losheim Gap was wide, the left flank of the 422d Infantry bare as the paunch of Kipling's "Purser's Sow." And through the northern gap an increasingly heavy enemy infiltration was coming between the 99th and 106th Divisions.

What Happened at Auw

The cavalry screen once penetrated, Auw, three miles behind the 422d Infantry's left flank and back door to the Schnee Eifel positions, became a keypoint. Through Auw, two and a half miles west of Roth, runs the winding, hilltop road to Bleialf—the "Skyline Drive" tapping all the rear regimental echelons of the 106th Infantry Division. From Auw a side road also branches northwestward into the Our Valley and the Schönberg–St. Vith highway.

The saga of Auw belongs to the engineers. More particularly it is the story of T/5 Edward S. Withee, Company A, 81st Engineers, hailing originally from Maine. Company A, attached to the 422d Infantry, was billeted in the village, which, although in something of a "sugarbowl" like all the settlements in the area, sits in the high ground dominating Kobscheid in the Taufen ravine, one mile east through the woods trails, and Schlausenbach, little more than a mile southeast, where the 422d Infantry command post was situated.

Company A apparently had done pretty well for itself in its billets. Company headquarters was in one house, and each platoon had separate establishments among the sullen inhabitants. When the storm of the enemy barrage pulled the engineers out of their sleep on the morning of 16 December, they found, to their surprise, that the villagers were already awake, dressed, and huddled in their cellars. They attribute this to a young woman who during the previous evening had been observed going from house to house.

In any event, some fifteen rounds of enemy shell fell in the village, the command post receiving four hits. No casualties resulted, but the company's 20-ton trailer was demolished. The fire died away. Capt. Harold M. Harmon had work to do, shelling or no shelling, so he turned out his three platoons as usual at 8:00 A.M. The 1st Platoon, under Lt. William J. Coughlin, went to the 422d's headquarters at Schlausenbach, the 3d Platoon, Lt. David M. Woerner, to the area of the 3d Battalion, 422d Infantry. This last unit, as it turned out, would share the fortunes of the doughboys. The remainder of the company went to work in the vicinity of the village, repairing shell holes. Harmon left for Heuem, five miles to the west, where headquarters of the 81st Engineer Battalion was situated, for the usual morning conference of company commanders.

At about 9:30 A.M. the crackle of nearby small-arms fire opened. Wearing white snow suits, the enemy infantry had infiltrated from Roth onto the ridge to the east, to within a few hundred yards of the party. Lt. William E. Purtell's 2d Platoon dove from their work to previously prepared positions for close defense, while company headquarters personnel began returning fire from their own command post building. With the poor visibility of that foggy morning, the enemy were hard to pick up at first.

Coughlin's 1st Platoon, hearing the firing from Auw, dashed back in their vehicles, running through a spray of small-arms fire, and into their own quarters, whence they too opened small-arms fire. This brought the situation to the point where there were three small groups, in three different buildings, without intercommunication, potting away at the Nazi infantrymen milling about the edge of the village.

Captain Harmon, coming back from his conference at Heuem, ran into the 422d Infantry area. There he passed two artillerymen of the 589th Field Artillery lying in a ditch, firing their carbines. There were Germans only two hundred yards away, they said. Harmon hauled them into his jeep and they dashed for the artillery command post under a hail of rifle bullets. Harmon then continued toward Auw, and just outside the village popped into the head of an enemy infantry column, the leading man of which opened on him with a burp gun. Though the vehicle was riddled they made it through to the edge of town.

It was now nearly noon. Roth, it will be remembered, had just fallen, opening the road. The 1st Platoon had rooted out one enemy concentration in a barn across from their position by setting it on fire with machine-gun tracer ammunition. Ten Krauts running for safety were picked off by the cooks, firing from the company headquarters building. But things were really warming up as Harmon looked into the village. One after another, Tiger tanks came clattering in. Harmon, on the nose southwest of the village, saw four of them, and two self-propelled guns.

The beleaguered engineers in the strongpoints saw them, too, and began to pot at them as the big tanks, with open turrets and infantrymen riding them, started up the main street. The engineers nailed several Germans before the enemy realized the situation. The reinforcements dropped off, returned the fire; tank lids clattered shut and the vehicles, with swinging guns, began snouting into the fight. The 2d Platoon's position was being encircled. Purtell got his men out in the nick of time; in what vehicles they could grab they raced for the Andler road, taking Harmon with them.

The tanks opened on company headquarters and Rutledge and his men were pried out. They, too, made for Andler, on foot. All four tanks now turned on the building in which Coughlin and his 1st Platoon were fighting. Eight rounds of 88s came smacking through the building. It was time to go. Behind the house was an open field over which they had to pass. Unless the enemy's attention were distracted, the platoon would be mincemeat before it made the woods.

Withee solved that problem. "I'll stay," said Withee. "Get going." He could not be budged. So Coughlin and his men raced for the trees in safety, while Corporal Withee, submachine gun blazing at four Tiger tanks not thirty yards away, drew the enemy's attention for the moment.

The platoon—what was left of it—got back into the 592d Field Artillery positions. The Krauts closed in on the building. Withee, by the grace of God, was captured, not killed. Not until months later when he returned from a prison camp did his comrades know that he was alive. In his honor the Edward S. Withee Recreation Center at Eupen, Belgium, had been named. So Withee can boast that he is the only soldier in the U.S. Army—officer or man—after whom an army post has been named while he was still living. Better than that, Withee wears today the Distinguished Service Cross for one of the most gallant actions that any man can accomplish. "Greater love hath no man . . ."

Captain Harmon and the remnants of Company A got back to Heuem to make another try for Auw later on, but that belongs with the story of the 422d Infantry. Auw was in enemy hands, the way was opening into the Our Valley's southern bank, and into the back areas of the infantry and their supporting artillery.

But wickedly accurate American artillery fire was now dropping into Auw, was interdicting the road from Roth, and generally still interrupting the German advance. Something had to be done about it. The tanks at Auw began nosing westward up the hill bound for the left and rear of the 422d Infantry and its supporting artillery now uncovered.

The 422d was ensconced in a four-mile strip of pillboxes of the old Siegfried defenses running along the northwest slopes of the hogback, just beneath the crest. With its 2d, 1st and 3d Battalions ranged in that order from north to south, the regimental main line of resistance began directly east of and adjacent to Kobscheid where the cavalry had a garrison and ended on the right a thousand yards north of Hontheim, joining the 423d Infantry.

Its left flank, therefore, was entirely bare to any eruption into the Our Valley, once that thin cavalry screen to the north was removed, uncovering the Roth–Auw–Schönberg–St. Vith road which juts westward from the enemy line of departure—the lateral Prüm–Losheim highway. Worse yet, from the local viewpoint, should an enemy attack gain as far as Auw, the entire rear communications net of the Schnee Eifel positions was threatened, southwest, all the way to Bleialf.

Attainment of such objectives was, of course, the goal of the Nazi spearheads reaching for St. Vith from Losheim.

Colonel George L. Descheneaux's command post was at Schlausenbach, through which runs a secondary road connecting Auw, a mile and three-quarters north by east, with Wascheid and Gondenbrett in enemy terrain to the southeast. The village was the usual "sugarbowl," with the Mertesberg knob jutting over it across a steep-banked ravine to the east, and high ground to the south and west, on which were situated the positions of L and Cannon Companies. Antitank Company platoons were stretched to the north, east and west of Schlausenbach.

The 2d Battalion had two of its rifle companies in line from north to south—G and F, with H (heavy weapons) Company sandwiched in between them in the pillboxes. E Company was in battalion reserve.

In the 1st Battalion the order ran C, B and A Companies from north to south with D (heavy weapons) Company in general support. The 3d Battalion had I and K Companies in line, while its third rifle company, L, was in regimental reserve. One heavy machine-gun platoon of M Company was on the left with I, the other with K. The mortar platoon was in rear in general support.

The 589th Field Artillery Battalion (105s) supported the regiment from positions in the slopes south of Laudesfeld, two miles northwest of Schlausenbach. It was situated astride Skyline Drive from Bleialf to Auw, its command post, motor park, mess and billets on the south side of the road stretching some three hundred yards toward Auw from the junction with the side road to Laudesfeld on the north. Battery A was in a wooded patch southeast of the road junction. Battery B was on the north of the road, at the edge of the woods; and Battery C still farther to the north on the same wooded fringe.

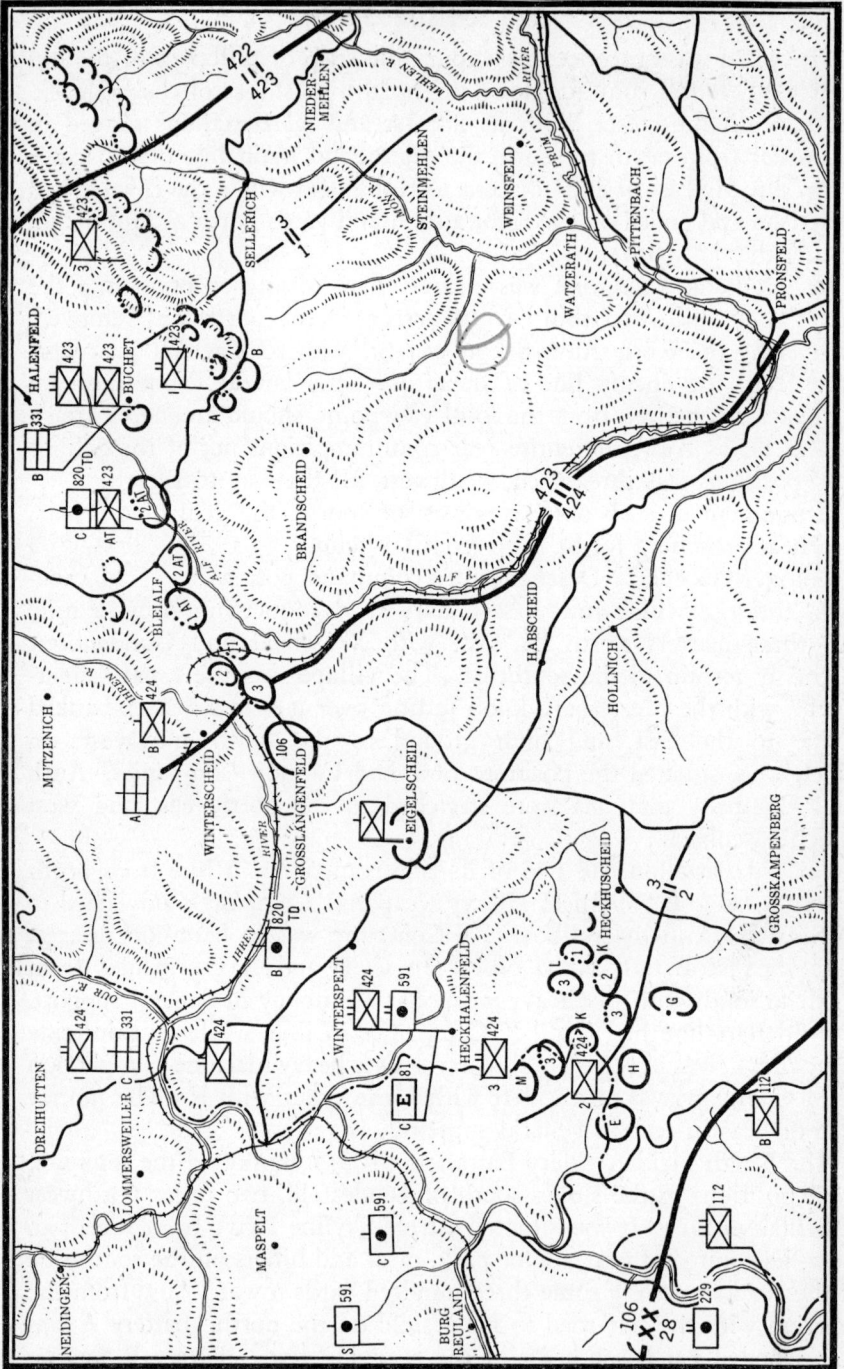

Map 4: The Southern Gateway. (Positions of the 423d and 424th Infantry Regiments, 16 December 1944)

Access to the Battery A and B positions was by corduroyed trails leading directly to the highway, but Battery C was reached only from the front, through Laudesfeld or by a foot trail running southeast into the main road some five hundred yards before it turns sharply north to slide down to Auw.

The general support battalion of the Division, the 592d Field Artillery Battalion (155s), was emplaced nearby, its firing batteries studded around Laudesfeld. Its longer-ranged, heavier weapons could reach to Prüm.

The 422d's regimental sector bestrode no main highway, but a network of woods roads, trails and slashing ran up from the Losheim–Prüm highway through the position. The outpost line of mutually supporting strongpoints and roadblocks lay on the southeasterly slopes of the forested hills above the Mehlin rivulet, which drains into the Prüm River two miles below, two miles northeast of Watzerath, in front of the 423d Infantry sector. Across the ravine, in which nestle the villages of Wascheid and Gondenbrett, the hills rise again, the highway to Prüm running along their crests.

The 422d, then, sat looking—where observation could be had—at the enemy outposts in the ravine and on the hills southeast. It could see him, occasionally, and it could hear him. On 14 December a German patrol, headed by an officer, was bagged in front of the 1st Battalion. On the leader was found a copy of the Rundstedt attack order, which much excited all concerned when it was translated. According to Capt. E. C. Roberts, executive of D Company, it was rushed to regiment. "We never heard any more of it," states Roberts.[1] It heard quite a lot of the enemy on the night of 15 December, rumblings of motors and tractors, and reported the facts. And a prisoner, a Polish deserter, captured the night of 15 December by a 2d Battalion patrol, told of a coming offensive, to be staged some time between the following night and Christmas. The offensive, he said, would be assisted by searchlights which would be thrown against the clouds to simulate moonlight. The information probably reached Division about the time the attack actually started.

The 422d had prepared counterattack plans, three of them, all built about the use of L Company in regimental reserve; and of the Antitank, Cannon, Service Companies, and of Company A, 81st Engineers. The plans envisaged possible enemy penetration from three directions—the cavalry area to the north, a smash between the 422d and the 423d, and finally an attack directly through the position.[2]

The regiment was set for a defense in place, however, a defense which lacked any elasticity—again an inherited situation. Major Douglass E.

Post, assistant executive officer of the regiment, states that when the counterattack plans were discussed at a battalion commanders' meeting, Col. Descheneaux, queried as to possible routes of withdrawal, responded: "There will not be any withdrawal. You will hold in place at all costs."

The 422d covered the ground between its left and Kobscheid by patrols every four hours, backed up by machine-gun fire. A good crisscross system of defensive fires all along the sector was tied in with the supporting artillery, covering all possible routes of approach. Since the regiment had received no mortar ammunition until 14 December, the supporting 589th Field Artillery had had to reconstruct its gun pits, sinking the trails to permit close-in high-angle fire. Most uncomfortable factor of the entire situation was that the regiment, since it left England, had never had time to dry out.

What happened in the 422d Infantry sector that first day of battle is as jumbled as the terrain itself. It can be told only as the doughboys and artillerymen fought it, piecemeal. To put it briefly, the 422d was engulfed by the German advance sweeping wide around its northern flank. Its center and southern flank were irritated only by sporadic diversionary prickings.

The Nazi opening barrage stormed down, cutting telephone lines, paralyzing communications. Little damage was done to personnel, however, for the positions were pretty well protected. While infantry and artillery signal details moved to patch the lines, the infiltrating enemy came drifting up the draws and through the woods on the Mertesberg heights to the left and rear of the 2d Battalion, on the north. They came up, too, from the direction of Auw, even while that place was being fought for.

Infantry and artillery felt the pressure at once. Worse still, they were getting it from the rear. Sporadic small-arms fire began falling into the artillery area as the barrage died down, probably coming from snipers already infiltrated. At the same time the 2d Battalion, 422d Infantry, began to get into the fight, and calls came in for artillery support, which kept the gunners busy.

An enemy combat patrol hit G Company's outpost squad. Staff Sgt. Arnold W. Almond, H Company's mortar observer at the outpost, immediately called for fire directly upon his own OP. His unselfish act, plus arrival of reinforcements, repulsed the attack, Almond coming out unscathed from his log shelter.[3]

Company F's outpost received the next tentative thrust, about 7:30 A.M., which was beaten off. A combat patrol was pushed toward Auw (Staff Sgt. Richard A. Thomas of this patrol led back to safety some of the scattered engineers from the village of Auw during the morning).

The 589th Field Artillery sent out patrols for local protection. One, under Lt. Leach, moving toward Auw, got but three hundred yards into the woods when it was pinned down by fire. It reported infantry coming up from Auw.

Captain Beans, the 589th's communications officer, and his assistant, Lt. Hockstad, going to the forward switching central near the infantry regimental command post, arrived as the 2d Battalion was being hard pressed. Company G was running short of ammunition. Tanks and infantry, they were told, had been reported on the left flank. Beans and Hockstad, returning to their own command post, were ambushed by an enemy five-man patrol in snow suits; Beans was hit three times, Hockstad nicked.

The 422d Infantry now became engaged on both flanks, its 1st Battalion in the center quiescent. On the north, by 9:35 A.M., it knew of the approach of four tanks. A company of infantry in snow suits, supported by more tanks, was moving toward Roth—this was part of the more serious attack engulfing the cavalry garrisons; and, closer in, infiltrating infantry poking up from the Schneifelforsthaus over Hill 672 in the Olzheimer Wald were hotly attacking G Company, beginning to embroil the rest of the 2d Battalion. The 3d Battalion, on the right flank, was by this time meeting an enemy force estimated at one battalion of infantry, which kept I and K Companies busy in a fire fight.

While the infantry was occupied, with most of the sound and fury coming from the north and rear, the 589th Field Artillery Battalion continued to serve its pieces in support, although considerably hampered by intermittent counterbattery and interdiction fire from the enemy side, apparently put down from map data and without observation.

Descheneaux, at his regimental command post, taking stock, could see that his center was not affected, though there had been a brisk enemy concentration of about one infantry company in front of B Company. That had been quickly disposed of by infantry and artillery fire, as had two infiltrating raids on observation posts.

Eighty-one rounds of enemy shell had fallen near the regimental command post by 8:30 A.M. Company M reported an estimated 125 enemy infantry moving southeast from the ravine between Auw and Kobscheid at 10:45. But, more serious, some fifty enemy in snow suits were now seen on the open ground between Auw and Schlausenbach, while burp-gun bursts were heard from the woods. Col. Descheneaux pulled his reserve company, L, into position generally along the slopes of the Frons ravine north of his command post and alerted all concerned for possible counterattack. In the 1st Battalion, two direct hits on his command post mortally wounded Lt. Col. Kent, commanding.

The enemy appeared to be digging in. A prisoner was bagged, carrying on him a copy of his battalion combat order. Descheneaux by this time, about 11:30 A.M. (the message was received at 12:25) queried Division to find out if they wanted "to hold or get group out of Auw."

Enemy cross fire from the rear now complicated the situation in the artillery area. Lt. Thomas J. Wright, Jr., Executive Officer of C Battery, 589th Field Artillery, pushed forward to an observation post of the 634th AAA Battalion where he could see Auw and the gathering tanks, and began adjusting fire. Lt. Leo J. Fromenko, the forward observer with the 422d, was also able to see the activity about Auw and began to harry the enemy there, using radio communication to the guns. Unfortunately, C Battery could not clear the mask to fire effectively, but both other batteries did.

Two bazooka teams from the 592d Field Artillery having reported to the 589th, Major Elliott Goldstein, Battalion Executive, took them up to reinforce the outpost near the crossroad where the Wascheid–Schlausenbach road cut the highway, where there was also a section of D Battery, 634th AAA Battalion.

There was no doubt in the artillerymen's minds now as to the seriousness of the situation. A tank thrust one mile and a half behind the infantry regimental command post and its installations, two and a half miles behind the front line units, would threaten the entire sector. If those Krauts could smash down the road towards Radscheid with any weight behind them the entire Schnee Eifel position was gone.

About 2:00 P.M. the enemy tanks—remember we last noted them pushing up the hill out of Auw—nosed into sight. Capt. George F. Huxel, assistant S-3, who had set up an observation post in the attic of the artillery communications building, first spotted them, but could not adjust on the lead vehicle, which now began to blaze at the outpost, the tank commander leaning out of his open turret.

The outpost took him on with small-arms and 40mm fire; the bazooka smacked the tank to immobility, then Battery A threw two direct hits on it. Scratch one tank. Huxel managed to put fire down from a C Battery howitzer on the second tank, and it, with its remaining companion, scuttled to cover. Once hull-down, one of the tanks now began to return the fire. B Battery, its fire directed by its CO, Capt. Arthur C. Brown, and by Goldstein, adjusted on the flashes in the twilight and apparently hit it, for it ceased firing.

How the lead tank was caught bears telling. Lt. Eric Fisher Wood, Jr., Battery A's executive, when he heard the tanks approaching rushed to a hillock on the battery left flank where he could see them, and shouted his commands to No. 4 piece in direct fire. The gunners could plainly see the tank when they opened fire, and yelped with glee as they saw the shell strike.

Wood then swept the vicinity with short-cut time fuze to clear out any enemy infantry, while he also pounded away at the turrets of the two other tanks, visible for a few moments over the crest. His prompt handling of the situation broke up the attack. We shall hear more about Lt. Wood.

Despite the defeat of the tanks it was evident that the enemy was building up his infiltration on the north flank. He had also gotten astride of the one exit road from C Battery's position. The 589th should get out. Unless assisted, however, daylight withdrawal was unthinkable. And contact with the infantry had been lost.

The 592d Field Artillery, though hammered like all other elements by the initial barrage, was nevertheless able to handle all its missions in the morning, in support of the 589th's fire. Battery C's forward observer, Lt. Rex C. Matson, and his party, had been ambushed on the way to Roth, early in the morning. When word was received from the 589th of the situation about Auw, bazooka teams were sent to reinforce it and patrols were organized and pushed northward to protect the battery positions. The news from the north was confirmed shortly after noon, when Capt. Barnard Richman, commanding Headquarters Battery, got into the fire direction center, on foot, with a dozen of Coughlin's 1st Platoon of Company A, 81st Engineers. Richman reported he had been ambushed in Auw, his driver killed. Running into the engineers, he had brought them across country with him.

Captain Samuel N. Richbourg, battalion S-2, attempted to adjust C Battery's 155mm howitzers on the tanks coming up from Auw, but could not get observation. Then Lt. A. V. Siekierski, forward observer, standing, incidentally, on a pile of live ammunition, managed to place several volleys from the left platoon on Auw, adjusting on the church steeple, and messing up the enemy columns now pressing forward on the much needed road.

Enemy response was vigorous. Tanks or self-propelled guns opened up. One over landed on the Service Battery mess shack, killing several men. Then, about 4:30 P.M., artillery and mortar fire came down in earnest into Battery A, so hotly that the personnel were withdrawn temporarily to defiladed positions. Battery A lost here and later that night thirty-six officers and men. They went back to the pieces at 6:30 P.M.

But the 592d Field Artillery was beginning to run short of ammunition; the ammunition train had gotten no farther than Schönberg when it was blocked by enemy fire. Like its brother, the 589th, the 592d was in a hot spot, though its commander, Lt.Col. Weber, was not worried about the situation.

The infantry position, meanwhile, was in a critical situation. Descheneaux had, of course, sent patrols out toward Auw at the first flurry. Sgt. Thomas actually penetrated to the village with a four-man patrol, sized up the situation and got back with word that the Krauts had the place. Incidentally, Thomas brought back some more of the engineers.

In midafternoon Descheneaux committed Company L and Cannon Company in a counterattack toward Auw. This would be shortly after 2:00 o'clock, just as the artillerymen met the first tank rush. The 422d commander now knew he faced a crisis; he had received word, through Division, that tanks and infantry—"quite a bit," the message said— were penetrating from the direction of Weckerath toward Auw before noon. He knew from his patrols that Auw was taken, and he knew the spearhead of the attack had already hit to his left and rear.

The two companies, L and Cannon, moved generally northwest over the brow of Hill 570, running into a snow flurry which impeded visibility. They tangled with both enemy tanks and infantry. In the advance Cannon Company, under Lt. Irvin Juster, leaving its gun crews at their weapons, fought as riflemen, using their carbines, directing the fire of their cannon by walkie-talkie radio. They did not get to Auw, but their attack certainly stabilized the situation momentarily, halting the enemy up the Radscheid road.

As Cannon Company pressed its attack toward Auw it sent a patrol on a wide encircling movement in an attempt to crush machine-gun fire coming from a clump of woods to the northeast. When orders came to fall back and organize a perimeter defense about its original company area, Pfc. Eldon E. Marks volunteered to take the word to the patrol, now hidden amongst the trees.

Creeping, crawling, and finally making a dash for the timber, while his comrades watched enemy small-arms fire kicking snow spray at his heels, Marks made it safely, and the patrol got back.

Descheneaux had proposed to Harmon, commanding Company A, 81st Engineers, that he join this attack from Heuem, where he had the remnants of his outfit, and a detachment of some thirty engineers pushed up to the vicinity of Wischeid, where they ran into heavy enemy mortar fire and were forced back. It was a good attempt by the infantry commander to take the Auw Nazis between two fires.

Division had taken what steps it could to retrieve the situation on the north. The 2d Battalion, 423d Infantry, alerted at its billets in

Born at 7:07 A.M., was ordered at 9:30 to move to the vicinity of St. Vith. Lt.Col. Joseph P. Puett got his battalion rolling as soon as he could, assisted by trucks which Division sent to facilitate the move. At St. Vith at 12:15 P.M. Puett was ordered to Schönberg, with a platoon of the 820th TD Battalion attached, to secure the roads leading north and south from the town. These orders are recorded in the S-3 journal at 5:00 P.M. as "VOCG."

Puett's force began detrucking at Schönberg at 1:15 P.M., and at once started to dig in, completing the defensive setup by 5:30. Reconnaissance patrols, foot and motorized—two of them had skirmishes with the enemy to the north—brought in data which enabled Puett to report a sound résumé to Division by 7:10 P.M.: "Enemy shelling Schönberg heavily. Cavalry have withdrawn and are mining the road five hundred yards north of Andler. Enemy have completely taken Auw. The 275th Armored Field Artillery have also withdrawn. Am patrolling in three directions and will have more information at 2000 [8:00 P.M.]"

According to Puett the cavalry at Andler—this would be Troop B, 18th Squadron—began to beat a retreat about 8:00 P.M., despite his warning to the commander that if he let Schönberg fall two regiments would be cut off. He says the cavalryman—unidentified—told him he could hold till late next morning, but instead himself proceeded on the way back to St. Vith.

By this time Division was convinced that the 589th and 592d Field Artillery must be withdrawn and that the 422d Infantry alone could not cover the move. Gen. McMahon, artillery commander, had already sent instructions to both battalions to displace as soon as they could break away.

General Jones at 8:30 P.M. telephoned Puett at Schönberg, ordering him to move up the Schönberg–Andler–Auw road, attacking southeast to relieve the left flank of the 422d Infantry and at the same time enable the artillery to displace. He was to send back the trucks when he arrived.

To Division at 8:45 P.M. came a message from the 422d Infantry, sent at 7:23 P.M.: "Battalions still in original positions. Company L plus odds and ends plus TD platoon around regimental command post. Shall I withdraw left battalion through Schlausenbach?"

Division didn't reply till 11:11 P.M., by which time Gen. Jones had made his decision with reference to the action he proposed to take with the two promised armored combat teams next day. By radio and by liaison officer came the message to Descheneaux: "Withdraw your left battalion to line Schlausenbach–east to left of your center battalion.

2d Battalion, 423d Infantry, moving to line high ground south of Auw–
to Wischeid. Acknowledge receipt."

Up at Schönberg Puett withdrew his battalion from its dug-in positions, entrucked in the midst of the flow of retreating traffic, and took
the Schönberg–Bleialf road south, down to the engineer cut-off, thence
up Skyline Drive northeast again. It was a difficult drive, blacked out,
in sleety drizzle, and the doughboys floundered. It was not until guides
from the 589th Field Artillery made contact with them that they were
able to get in, arriving in the artillery area about midnight. In the
meantime, Descheneaux in the 422d Infantry was hauling his own 2d
Battalion around to face north.

There is room for speculation on this move of Puett, who seems to
have no doubt in his mind that he was following orders. The intent of
the Division Commander[4] was that Puett would take his battalion instead up the Schönberg–Andler–Auw road, in order to attack southeast
in front of the artillery positions, relieving the left of the 422d Infantry,
and freeing the artillery at the same time.

Whether or not Puett could have accomplished this is a moot question. The cavalry were mining the road at Andler. If he got by that
point up to Wischeid there is not much doubt that he would have run
headlong into the German advance. In that case, without artillery support, which he did not have, his goose might have been cooked in short
order. The expression as recorded in the division G-3 journal in the
informative message to Descheneaux: "High ground south of Auw to
Wischeid" would indicate merely a deployment of the 2d Battalion,
423d Infantry, from northwest to southeast, with the northern flank
still wide open.

What does matter is that this battalion's displacement from Schönberg left the road wide open to the enemy when the cavalry was knocked
back next morning. The author, however, is of the opinion that unless
the 7th Armored Division had arrived when Gen. Jones expected it
to, whether or not Puett's battalion should have stayed at Schönberg is
merely academic argument. If it were there it could not later have
formed the rear of the 423d's perimeter next day, as will be related.

The artillerymen meantime were buzzing around their howitzers like
angry bees all that night, to get them on the road. New positions had
been selected for the 589th in the vicinity of its Service Battery position
three miles south of Schönberg, for the 592d back near St. Vith. In the
latter outfit Weber, who had told Gen. McMahon he could stick it out
when the first displacement order came at 7:00 P.M., received a more
peremptory order two hours later and by 11:00 P.M. all batteries were
ready to take the rough trek back.

It was rocky going over that woods road linking with the Auw–Radscheid road at a sharp forty-degree angle, around which each big howitzer had to be jockeyed by backing and filling while machine-gun fire from enemy positions less than eight hundred yards away buzzed overhead—too high, fortunately. But the battalion got away, lurching and scraping into the night, less one gun section and several other vehicles—including the mess truck—of Battery A, which, turning the wrong way, ran through Bleialf into an enemy artillery concentration. First Sgt. John C. Beck worked his way to the 590th Field Artillery positions to get help and reported in from there.

Captain Genero M. Mondragon, commanding Battery A, who had nursed his outfit through the terrific shelling, and, with Staff Sgt. Joseph L. Fielder, had braved hostile fire to drag several wounded men to safety, was the last man out of the position. Refusing to abandon the wounded of the gun section caught on the road, Mondragon was made prisoner some time that night. He was later killed by our own aircraft while a prisoner of war.

It was different in the 589th, where Lt.Col. Thomas P. Kelly, Jr., was working against fate to get C Battery out of its impossible position, from which the one exit road ran right into a Kraut nest of dug-in armor. Batteries A and B got into march order with some difficulty. In the former, where enemy small-arms fire continued to fall, wheels sank into mud to the axles.

Eric Wood, Battery A executive, now acting battery commander, Capt. Aloysius J. Mencke having been captured at an OP, tore into things. Two trucks he hitched to each howitzer and swayed the floundering pieces one by one into the road. Each prime mover carried eighty-three rounds of ammunition.

Snow blew patchily into sweating faces in the night. The wind howled; enemy flares flickered now and then over the trees, each one of which might shelter a foe infiltrating through Puett's infantry screen. Midnight passed with the 589th still working to get free.

To sum up the local situation in the 422d Infantry sector at the end of that night, its left battalion was being refused to the north against a very dangerous threat to its left and rear areas; but the 2d Battalion, 423d Infantry, was also up there, prolonging the line to the west. The supporting artillery was falling back to new positions. Its 1st and 3d Battalions were practically untouched in their fortified positions.

The regiment had not done too badly in its baptismal day of battle. As for the future—the 7th Armored Division would be in position next morning to counterattack. The 422d knew that; their Division Commander had told them so.

As for the artillery now displacing, both battalions had accomplished more than they suspected. They had repulsed in gallant and efficient fashion the first tank thrust. But, even more important, the only reason why the enemy moving up along the Roth–Auw axis was not already flooding the Schnee Eifel back areas was the smashing concentrations of 105s and 155s which all that afternoon and evening had denied the German free movement through Auw.

BLEIALF AND THE ALF VALLEY

Below the Schnee Eifel the enemy eruption came southeasterly down the Prüm Valley, swung around Pronsfeld and struck northwest, licking viciously to the north around the tip of the hogback the while it hit toward St. Vith. This was the junction of the 423d and 424th Infantry sectors, divided by the line of the Alf Valley, in the upper reaches of which is Bleialf, sheltered by the Muhlenberg and Alferberg ridges in the 423d's territory, by the Winterscheid plateau within the 424th area.

Bleialf itself, five and a half miles by air line over the ridge from Prüm to the southeast, lies on fairly open ground on the north slopes of the Alf and astride the Roth–Auw–Radscheid road running through Bleialf over the nose separating the Alf and Ihren valleys, southwest through Grosslangenfeld to join the Pronsfeld–St. Vith road at the Weissenhof crossroads. So, as Auw to the north was one door to the rear areas of the Schnee Eifel defenders, thus Bleialf was the southern opening. In addition, one thousand yards north of the village at the Justenschlag road junction, there branches off a short cut to Schönberg. This last road is important, for along it came the normal flow of traffic between St. Vith and Division headquarters and rear installations and the main lines of resistance of the three infantry regiments.

The engineers had put a lot of effort into maintaining this road, and at a hairpin turn north of Justenschlag had corduroyed a steep short cut toward Radscheid. This by-pass, known as Engineer Cut-off, played a prominent part in the action after the enemy had blocked off Auw. Up it came the 2d Battalion, 423d Infantry, to the Laudesfeld plateau, down it came the 592d Field Artillery, on the night of 16 December; down it would come the 589th Field Artillery next morning.

The 423d Infantry, on a five-mile-wide front, like the 422d occupied a part of the old Siegfried defenses on the Schnee Eifel. But at the crossroad in the mountains where a woods trail along the crest cuts a northwest-southeast secondary road between Bleialf and Prüm, and a mile northeast of Brandscheid, the main line of resistance left the defensive works. The 423d, it will be remembered, had but two battalions under regimental control; its 2d Battalion was in Division reserve.

In the Siegfried Line, from north to south, linking with the 422d, came in turn the 3d and 1st Battalions of the 423d. In the former L, K and I Companies were on the main line of resistance, the last with two platoons echeloned to the right rear, one platoon refused to the southeast at Buchet. The 1st Battalion had C and B Companies in line, with A refused to the southwest behind B, whose outpost line looked down into enemy activities in Brandscheid on the right and the hamlets of Sellerich and Herscheid on the left.

Between the right of the 1st Battalion and the left of the 424th Infantry at Heckhuscheid was a three-mile gap across the widening Alf Valley.

The 423d Infantry's portion of this gap, with the railway line from Pronsfeld to Winterscheid as boundary between regiments, was filled by Antitank Company and part of Cannon Company emplaced in and about Bleialf on the northern slopes of the Alf, a complete rifle platoon from the 3d Battalion, and C Company, 820th TD Battalion, attached. Prolonging the line to the west of Bleialf was B Troop, 18th Cavalry Reconnaissance Squadron, also attached to the 423d. These elements thus formed a defensive zone echeloned a mile and a half behind its line infantry battalions. This conglomerate group was constituted as a provisional battalion commanded by Capt. Charles B. Reid. The cavalry troop on the far right linked with the 106th Reconnaissance Troop at Grosslangenfeld, attached to the 424th Infantry. The last-named regiment was responsible for the western portion of this big bow in the lines.

Theoretically, and always provided the front-line troops were backed up by a heavy reserve capable of counterattacking an enemy thrust from Pronsfeld, the disposition was not bad. As part of a stone-wall defense of a salient, unsupported by adequate reserves, the 423d was being dangled enticingly in front of the enemy, just as was its brother regiment, the 422d, with only that thin cavalry screen on its left in front of the Losheim Gap. Once again it must be reiterated that this was an inherited situation, and that the Division Commander did not like it.

Service Company was at Halenfeld, and the regimental command post at Buchet, all this a short distance behind the main line of resistance of the line battalions. The battalion command posts were right in the main line of resistance. The 590th Field Artillery Battalion (105) was in direct support of the regiment, from positions east of Hill 575, north of Radscheid. A regimental security platoon had been organized, by detail from various units, to man the observation posts in the outpost line. The lower units didn't like this drain on their manpower. Incidentally, nobody likes special-duty details.

The ammunition and automatic-weapons situation was not satisfactory. Antitank Company needed more weapons, six light machine guns and eighteen BARs or M3s. The 1st and 3d Battalions, too, were calling for more, and particularly for .50-caliber machine guns, and ground mounts for them. There was a shortage of ammunition, particularly mortar stuff. Col. Cavender took it up with Division.[5] Division went to work on Corps.

The enemy was more active in this sector than the G-2 conference at Division on 14 December indicated. Krauts were milling in and around Brandscheid, not two thousand yards from B Company's outposts, like hornets in barn eaves. Twice self-propelled 88s were seen there, and they occasionally took pot shots in the 423d area. The 590th Field Artillery put several concentrations into the place, sending the SPs scuttling for cover. The artillery put down a concentration on Sellerich, too, early on the morning of 14 December, when the noise of a truck concentration was heard. Screams followed the arrival of the 105s.

A twelve-man enemy patrol was driven back in front of Antitank Company, not far from the mine at Muhlenberg. The doughboys in the lines were on a constant alert. Shadows, echoes, practically every waving blade of grass—where grass showed—was magnified into an enemy. Calls for artillery fire were frequent, too frequent, as a matter of fact. But troops coming up the front for the first time are like that, always. On the other hand, one gathers that perhaps the regiment was not sufficiently security-minded in the use of the telephone, which was being tapped from time to time. Some infiltrating enemy cut telephone lines in the 3d Battalion area 13 December, and, not far from B Company a voice in English called "Help!" several times—suspectedly a Kraut ruse.

Machine-gun fire from the old Siegfried pillboxes around Brandscheid was sporadic; the Nazis occupied some of these a short distance from the 1st Battalion. And flares, principally amber, were noted every night. A number of them were in the Alf Valley. The 422d Infantry called in early on the morning of 14 December to pass on word of an enemy motorcade heard in the vicinity of Hontheim in front of the 3d Battalion. An artillery concentration was put down on it. An enemy road-block on the Muhlenberg–Brandscheid road was discovered by the 820th TD Battalion, 14 December. The infantry put their mortars on it.

All in all, the 423d Infantry should have realized that the enemy in front of it was busy at something. The ammunition situation would be relieved some time during 16 December, it seemed. Service Company would distribute it, but its use would be strictly regulated. Half might be expended by battalions, the remainder held for regimental disposition. Snow suits arrived 14 December and were distributed the next day for use by patrols; twenty-five each to the two battalions and to Antitank Company.

The night of 14 December, Company A's kitchen burned up, by accident, and fire was discovered in an abandoned building in M Company's area. During the night of 15-16 December the normal patrols outside the outpost line found things quiet. However, C Company reported the noise of a railway[6] train behind Brandscheid. An unidentified two-engined plane circled over the area. Burp guns and mortar fire sounded spasmodically. A bright light in front of I Company was considered to be an enemy ammunition dump fired by our artillery, and an enemy patrol was fumbling in the Halenfelder Wald, deep in the 3d Battalion area.

The 1st Battalion reported its wire to the artillery cut, at 8:45 P.M. An unidentified voice cut in on the regimental line before the cutting, but when switchboard checked, the intruder hung up.

Flares were going up from time to time. Antitank Company outposts loosed off several rounds at an unidentified noise. But the consensus at regiment around midnight was—"nothing stirring."

At 5:30 A.M., 16 December, the enemy barrage came down, cutting wire communications with Antitank Company, 3d Battalion and Troop B, as well as the 590th Field Artillery.

Searchlights stabbed the fading darkness up the Alf Valley, reflected down from the low-hung clouds over Bleialf. *Volksgrenadiers* swept over Antitank Company's positions. They poured through the railway cut southeast of the village, blocking off B Troop, 18th Cavalry Squadron, on the right of the regimental sector; they boiled out of the woods on the Alferberg nose directly into the village. They also hit at B Company from the Sellerich road, cutting communication between Bleialf and the rest of the command.

The only available reserve was Service Company, at Halenfeld. Cavender ordered it out as infantry to retake Bleialf. At the same time, 9:05 A.M., he reported to Division that B Troop was hit and was calling for help and that he was committing his reserve, and asked for B Company, 81st Engineers. He had, he said, some seventy men of D Company also available and was rounding up the rest.

The regimental S-3 journal, noting this conversation, adds to it the cryptic remark: "Detroit [code name for 9th Armored Division] one thousand yards west of Purple Heart Corner [on the Bleialf–Auw road behind the 422d Infantry]." The 9th Armored, of course, was still miles away. One wonders what led to this remark—what false hopes were raised, and by whom?

Division turned the engineers over to Cavender, who sent a liaison officer to meet them as they moved from their billets at Schönberg, in trucks, prepared to fight as infantry. Cannon Company, less its platoons already driven in, was also pushed down to Bleialf. They fought as riflemen. Capt. James L. Manning, commanding, was killed leading his men in. Capt. Feas of Service Company took this conglomerate unit into the fight, where it came under command of Capt. Charles B. Reid, commander of Antitank Company and the composite battalion.

As the morning waxed, and the 423d reports 16 December as "clear and cold," it was evident that the enemy had taken Grosslangenfeld in the 424th Infantry sector—"The colonel's classmate is being hit," remarked 1st Battalion—and had driven his wedge up into Bleialf, forcing B Troop, 18th Cavalry Squadron westward, out of touch with the 423d. It never regained physical contact.

The engineers, detrucking a halfmile west of Bleialf, went into action. Capt. Hynes sent Lt. Gordon's platoon into town for a reconnaissance in force, while the rest of the company covered the advance from a position on the Winterscheider knob to the southwest.

Chief Warrant Officer John A. Carmichael, arriving from battalion headquarters with a truckload of ammunition, accompanied Gordon's platoon as a volunteer. Heavy fire was met from the cluster of houses. Two five-man patrols worked their way inside the village. Carmichael, commanding the left patrol, forced the enemy on that side to take refuge in two houses. Leaving his men to keep them pinned down, Carmichael, under heavy fire, worked his way out of town to one of the platoons of C Company, 820th TD Battalion, on the hills above. From there he directed fire on the strongpoint, blasting the Krauts out. Lt. Gordon's platoon then mopped up that section.

But the engineers could not do it all. There were too many Germans in the village.

Cavender had raked up all available men for the drive to regain Bleialf—Antitank Company, 3d Platoon and headquarters group of Cannon Company, all available officers and men of Headquarters and Service Companies. Reid got them into the village, and in a house-to-house battle with the Nazi bagged some seventy-five enemy prisoners and regained all but the fringe of houses down the road toward the railway line. Lt.Col. Frederick W. Nagle, regimental executive, was sent down to take command of the Bleialf force at noon. The 590th Field Artillery turned loose its fire in support very effectively. In the 1st Battalion, Companies A and B maintained their positions.

During all this heavy fighting on the right, the 3d Battalion was untouched. It assisted in the fight by bringing fire to bear on the Sellerich–Brandscheid road.

By afternoon the situation had been temporarily stabilized. B Company, 81st Engineers, took up a defensive position on the ridge just east of Bleialf, with Service Company on its left. No contact could be made with the cavalry troop on the right, except by radio.

Troop B, 18th Cavalry Reconnaissance Squadron, had had a tough morning. Its three reconnaissance platoons were grouped in order from left to right—1st, 2d and 3d—just south of the railway tunnel, one thousand yards east of Winterscheid, where troop headquarters was situated.

The first rush of enemy following the barrage fell on the 3d Platoon, then against the other two. The 1st Platoon was cut off from the Antitank Company strongpoint on its left. A fire fight surged about all three positions. By noon Capt. Robert G. Fossland, troop commander, found himself out of touch with both the infantry on his left and the 106th Reconnaissance Troop on his right in the 424th Infantry sector. His advance positions were running out of ammunition. He reported his situation to Col. Cavender, who, over the radio told him, "If you can't hold, you may withdraw."

The platoons, severely mauled, hauled back into Winterscheid about 2:00 P.M., under cover of a group of three armored cars commanded by Lt. Richard V. Winkler, and Fossland by nightfall had organized a perimeter defense in the village, into which intermittent mortar and shell fire dropped all through the night.

The 590th Field Artillery was kept active, supporting the hard-hit right flank, and served its howitzers throughout the day, despite heavy counterbattery. Capt. John Pitts, commanding Battery A, was killed by one of these bursts. The approach road between Radscheid, Oberlascheid and Halenfeld was under interdiction fire most of the time. That night the battalion kept putting down fire along the Bleialf–Sellerich road, on Brandscheid and other spots where troop movement and concentrations were reported. Wire communication with regiment and battalion was out, radio failed or was jammed time and time again.

As that first day drew to a close, the 423d Infantry was in a tight situation. Cavender, of course, had tried to get his 2d Battalion all day long, but it was being committed by Division up on the north. He was still holding his original positions, but had no reserves left. His right flank was in the air to all intents and purposes, the cavalry troop being buttoned up in Winterscheid, and contact lost with the 424th Infantry which semed to be having troubles of its own. What was going on on the right? At midnight Cavender, who had informed Division during the evening, "Will hold present position until ordered differently," asked St. Vith for word as to immediate status of the division on the right of the 106th and was told that the 28th was still holding its defensive position.

All day long buzz bombs droned over the 423d sector, bound for Liège and London.

And that night, in the 3d Battalion command post, about 8:00 o'clock, a radio program from the United States, relayed either by the BBC or by Algiers, announced to the little group hunting the ether for information that a German offensive had reached the Belgian border in three places.

"Well," remarked somebody, "the people back home seem to know more about it than we do."[7]

What nobody but the enemy knew was the most important thing of all: He had failed, in that first day, to get into the Schnee Eifel back area. Bleialf, the southern key, was still denied him. And time, time so precious to the Nazi, was ticking on.

The Southern Gateway to St. Vith

From Grosslangenfeld, above the Ihren Valley on the left, to Grosskampenberg on the right, the 424th Infantry that first morning, stretched thin over a six-mile area, took it on the chin all along its portion of the southern sector horseshoe. The 424th not only barred the Pronsfeld–St. Vith highway; its left elements shared in protecting the road to Bleialf, leading into the Schnee Eifel.

The 106th Reconnaissance Troop, attached to the regiment, was on the far left at Grosslangenfeld, in contact with B Troop, 18th Cavalry Squadron, on the right of the 423d Infantry. It barred the Leidenborn–Heckhuscheid–Bleialf–Radscheid road which crosses the Pronsfeld–St. Vith highway on a bald knob at Weissenhof. Cannon Company, next to the troop on the right, overlooked the bare, snow-covered crossroads, halfway between Pronsfeld and Winterspelt, and just north of the latter village B Battery, 820th TD Battalion, blocked the main highway. A platoon of Antitank Company had its guns emplaced on the left flank of Cannon Company, just in front of the 2d Platoon.

The 3d Battalion, south and west of Cannon Company, had L and K Companies abreast from left to right, its outpost line along the road between Heckhuscheid and the Weissenhof road junction. Its main line of resistance ran along the southern edges of the Heckhalenfeld plateau, just north of Heckhuscheid. Company I, in battalion reserve, was defiladed behind the Heckhalenfeld high ground on the edge of the Stein-Kopf, a bare hill mass to the west on the east bank of the Our. Battalion headquarters was also in this vicinity.

Extending the line on the right was the 2d Battalion, with G and F Companies abreast from left to right along the ridge just north of Grosskampenberg. Company G was in contact with Company B, 112th Infantry, the left-flank unit of the 28th Infantry Division, the 106th's right-hand neighbor. E Company, in battalion reserve, was on the edge of Hill 569, on the slopes of the Irsen ravine. Battalion headquarters was at the wood trail crossing by the hamlet of Dackscheid.

The dispositions of the two infantry battalions were not bad; their respective two-company fronts were not over-extended, each had a third company in hand for local reserve, the positions were well echeloned in depth for defense. The left part of the regimental sector was the weak spot.

The 1st Battalion was in reserve back at Steinebrück on the Our, two miles up the Pronsfeld–St. Vith highway. Service Company, at Elcherath, was just off the main highway, one mile and a half northwest of Winterspelt. C Company, 331st Medical Battalion, was up at Steinebrück, and C Company, 81st Engineers, was at Heckhalenfeld.

In direct support of the regiment was the 591st Field Artillery (105). Batteries A and B were in defiladed positions along the Winterspelter ravine on the reverse northern slopes of the Heckhalenfeld high ground, close to the village. C Battery was in the vicinity of Steffeshausen, on the western edge of the Stein-Kopf and some two miles behind the rest of the battalion. Service Battery was at Burg-Reuland on the Our, still farther to the west. This, too, was a good defensive disposition, for not only were the batteries echeloned in depth, but C Battery also was in position to put fire on the right flank well into the 28th Division front.

The 424th Infantry's sector had been the quietest part of the Division front. Sporadic mortar fire had fallen in A Company's area. Three odd conflagrations—one in Service Battery billets which burned one man to death, and one each in regimental headquarters and the engineer billets, had caused some excitement until investigation proved that carelessness rather than sabotage was the cause. And on the night of 13 December outposts reported the noise of considerable enemy vehicular traffic, apparently moving from southwest to northeast along the 3d Battalion front. That was all. Patrols on the night of 15-16 December made no contact.

What the 424th didn't know was that the enemy was methodically building up his strength in the Alf Valley, sheltered by Hill 553 and by two ridges, the Losenseifen and Spielmannsholz, which crop out along the westerly and northwesterly edge of the dense Hofs Wald. This wooded terrain two miles west of Pronsfeld and a bit more than that beyond the outpost line of the 424th, was an ideal concentration area.

The Nazi wanted St. Vith, wanted it badly. So it was that at 1:40 A.M. on the morning of 16 December, a Screaming Meemie mortar concentration came smacking into K Company's sector just west of Heckhuscheid. It was the first heave of the enemy crowbar to free the Grosskampenberg–Heckhuscheid road.

The big barrage came down in the 424th area as it did elsewhere— about 5:30 A.M., in terrorizing amount, disrupting wire communications not only within the regiment and its supporting artillery, but also with Division. Heavy counterbattery fires fell on the 591st Field Artillery positions. Radio and liaison officers were the only means of communication. It was not until 7:45 A.M. that Division got first word from the regiment on the situation.

The 3d Battalion was first hit by the enemy infantry. An estimated company came over Hill 593 in the dawning, infiltrated just below Heckhuscheid and struck K Company, pried its way back to the village into L Company's lines, and reached the company command post. Lt. Albert J. Barnaby, commanding the 1st Platoon, rallied his dazed men, tried to direct fire. The woods, it seemed, were full of Germans and in the confusion no one knew just where to shoot. Barnaby jumped up and began firing his rifle, in plain sight. Answering shots from the snow banks disclosed the *Volksgrenadiers,* and Barnaby's platoon brought down its own fire. He held the platoon together until ordered to withdraw. Later that morning, in a counterattack to break a way back to the surrounded company command post, enemy small-arms fire killed Barnaby.

At the same time that the 3d Battalion was hit, the woods in front of Cannon Company boiled, farther up in the horseshoe. Flashlights twinkled signals, the first waves of attackers stumbled into trip wires setting off the defensive flares and mines. The Weissenhof crossroads blossomed with masses of skirmishers. Tech.Sgt. Irvin Cairns, platoon sergeant of the 2d Platoon, said "the skyline was filled" with the enemy.

They were marching, standing up, bunched. They gaped for targets, they blazed away generally over the area with burp guns. Hopped-up with liquor or drugs they kept coming, in a babble of yells and waving of arms, driven by the screaming *"Marschiert! Marschiert schnell!"* of their cursing noncoms. Easy targets, but there were so many of them.

Cannon Company—it took over from the same outfit in the 23d Infantry in accordance with the "man for man" and "gun for gun" directive, and the 23d men had been used as riflemen—did not have its heavy weapons; they were back at Service Company. Also, much ammunition had been loaned to the 591st Field Artillery. Three .50-caliber, and four heavy .30-caliber machine guns borrowed from the 1st Battalion were all that were available. So most of the company fought as riflemen. Evidently the turnover by 2d Division elements whereby the 106th took what was in the line and gave its own to the outgoing troops was to a great extent responsible for this mix-up.

At this time the first wave of enemy infiltrating up the Alf Valley to hit and drive in B Troop, 18th Cavalry Squadron, on the 423d Infantry flank, overflowed to the west and the 106th Reconnaissance Troop at Grosslangenfeld disintegrated, opening Cannon Company's left flank. The Krauts began pushing in its 2d Platoon.

The right flank of the 424th was hit last, as the enemy welling through the 28th Division sector penetrated the 112th Infantry and ousted its B Company from Lutzkampen, throwing it to the north up the Burg-Reuland road. Forced to the west of Grosskampenberg, this unit called on the 424th for help, and Col. Reid ordered a platoon of G Company over to support it.

A heavy fire fight developed on depleted G Company's front, to the north of Grosskampenberg, and F Company was drawn into the engagement. E Company was committed from reserve by Lt.Col. Leonard Umanoff into the woods below Dackscheid. The enemy infantry was thrown back after a two-hour fire fight; then another artillery barrage dropped and five tanks nosed their way into the picture.

Here is where Lt. Richard H. Hawkes, of E Company, coolly directed the automatic weapons of his platoon on the big tanks pushing through the snow, their commanders peering from open turrets. The concentration made them button up, they lost direction in the snowy fog, and a burst of antitank fire halted them.

Technical Sergeant Glenn D. Risk, of the platoon of Antitank Company on this flank, got one tank even though he was doing his own loading and firing, while Pvt. Gilbert E. Thomas, bazooka man, stopped another. The remainder pulled away. This, for the time being, ended the threat to the right flank.

Things were more serious to the north. By 7:25 I Company had been committed in the 3d Battalion sector to bolster K and L Companies, driven out of their initial positions. A series of counterattacks ensued, supported by violent concentrations from the 591st Field Artillery, and gradually restored the situation. It was tough fighting.

As I Company first deployed over the southern slope of the high ground Lt. William V. Shakespeare, former Notre Dame football star but that day running for Army in a big way as leader of the Weapons Platoon, bagged a German captain of the 116th Panzer Division. The Nazi had a map case full of papers, including Operation Greif and the attack plan of his unit.[8] Crombach, nine miles in air line behind the spot where he had been captured, and two miles southwest of St. Vith, was their day's objective!

With Company I went Capt. Lee Berwick, burly 220-pound battalion S-3. L Company had taken but few prisoners, and he needed identifications, if anyone was to make sense of what this sudden irruption meant. So Berwick went prisoner-hunting.

From three houses on the outskirts of Heckhuscheid enemy fire was sprinkling the edge of the woods. Berwick drew up a skirmish line in the shelter of the trees and led it toward these houses, covered by L Company's Weapons Platoon under Lt. Robert Engstrom. At the same time he sent Lt. Joseph E. Dresselhaus with his platoon of I Company to outflank the place.

Berwick, running out in front, bellowed to the enemy within to surrender. Their fire redoubled. He signaled to the surrounding elements who blazed at the strongpoint from three sides. Again Berwick, out alone, called. And this time the buildings erupted Nazis, hands high, waving anything white they could grab. It seemed they would never stop coming. The bag totalled 107, including two officers, high for the day in the 424th, where in all 193 were gathered in.

As the situation began to stabilize in the 3d Battalion sector, Staff Sgt. George B. Champion led a four-man patrol of Company K into the Heckhuscheid woods to reestablish contact with Company L. Ploughing through the snow and underbrush, Champion flushed a number of *Volksgrenadiers* left behind as the enemy pulled out. Killing four, he marshalled forty prisoners in front of him as he came back.

But Cannon Company was in hard straits up at Eigelscheid. In response to Capt. Joseph Freesland's call for help, Col. Reid called on his 1st Battalion. Lt.Col. Lamar L. Welch, commanding, sent Company C down the Winterspelt road to back up Cannon Company. Reid wanted the entire 1st Battalion. It was only now that he learned Division had it under control. Fortunately, Brig.Gen. Perrin, Assistant Division Commander, was in Winterspelt. After some delay the unit was released without the necessity of getting authorization from St. Vith.

The enemy advancing on Cannon Company were swelling in strength. Personnel carriers rolling in from Grosslangenfeld disgorged wave after wave of infantry, who marched up the road in column of fours. Directly to the front, from Habscheid way, came four tanks surrounded by marching infantry. Ammunition ran short. The company dump was some three hundred yards back of the front line, across a bare patch of snow-covered ground now being churned by artillery concentrations.

Staff Sergeant Ralph J. Murphy three times ran the gantlet to stagger back with bandoleers of ammunition strung over his shoulders. Several other volunteers also brought back loads.

German squad leaders were trilling on whistles. One lone Nazi bugler blared on the advance until the annoyed sharpshooters of Cannon Company finished him off. The tanks got into action within fifty yards of the 2d Platoon positions.

On company orders, the platoon was about to fall back; the enemy couldn't be stopped now. But Lt. Crawford Wheeler, commanding, was still wrenching at a damaged machine gun, trying to get it in firing order, as the lead tank moved in. Someone called to him to get going.

"Well," snapped Wheeler, "somebody's got to stay here and do the job. From now on the rest of you are on your own!"

And Wheeler, turning from the silent gun, grabbed a bazooka and three rounds of precious ammunition. Deliberately he stepped into the open to slug it out with the rumbling behemoth. He died under its point-blank fire.

The Antitank Company platoon established on Cannon Company's left front hung on through the first infiltration from the east. Staff Sgt. Rocco P. DeFelice, though wounded in the first artillery barrage, had insisted on remaining in action with his 57mm antitank gun. When the tanks came scrambling up toward Cannon Company's 2d Platoon, DeFelice held his fire until they got to within 150 yards of his emplacement. Then he opened up and got two in quick succession. A direct hit from the third demolished his gun. DeFelice gathered his detachment and fell back with Cannon Company.

Company C, coming up to support Cannon, deployed north of Hill

551, attempted a counterattack. A group of Nazis, in a nearby house they had hastily organized into a strongpoint, held the company up. Lt. Robert G. McKay jumped to a 60mm mortar, put three rounds neatly on the strongpoint, then stormed it with his platoon, capturing the defenders and releasing twenty Cannon Company men taken prisoners. Lt. Jarrett M. Huddleston, Jr., battalion S-2, up with this platoon, personally accounted for six Krauts.

By this time intense artillery and mortar fire was interdicting the Winterspelt road, holding up the remainder of the 1st Battalion on the outskirts of that village. Calls for the medics were coming from C Company to the front. Pfc. Marshall W. Walker, of the regimental Medical Detachment, with two litters rigged across his jeep hood and another across the back seat, three times raced across the beaten zone safely, to bring his wounded back.

It was too late to save Eigelscheid. C and what was left of Cannon Company fell back on Winterspelt during the afternoon, where the rest of the 1st Battalion was organizing a defensive perimeter after having had a smart brush with some infiltrating enemy from Grosslangenfeld.

Lieutenant Huddleston, battalion S-2, who had gone across country to regimental headquarters at Heckhalenfeld to give Col. Reid the picture of the situation around Winterspelt, returned to report to Welch at his command post now established in the village. Huddleston, having twice traversed enemy-held terrain in his mission, fell into a hot spot.[9]

German voices rang through a window. The staff dove for their weapons, raced outside. As they cleared the building a stick of grenades thrown through the window blew the walls down. Huddleston and Capt. F. K. Davis, Antitank Company, gathered some men and fought their way through. The situation was restored, for the moment at least.

When night fell, the Winterspelt perimeter consisted of Companies C, B and A, from left to right, with Company C, 81st Engineers, on the southwest flank, which position it reached before the next dawn. The engineers had turned out at the first barrage to organize a defensive position on the east side of regimental headquarters at Heckhalenfeld, and were then ordered, about noon, to another position in the woods between Winterspelt and Heckhalenfeld. From there they were moved to Winterspelt, guided in by the aggressive battalion S-2, young Huddleston.

On the right flank, where the first enemy rush had driven Company B, 112th Infantry, up the Burg-Reuland road from Lutzkampen, the arrival of a platoon of G Company, 424th, assisted in supporting its withdrawal. B Company, 112th, was running short of ammunition, and 2d Battalion, 424th, turned over to it five thousand rounds of .30 caliber. The company attached itself to the battalion, all communication with its own regiment having been lost.

The ammunition situation throughout the 424th and its attached units became critical before the day was done. Ammunition trucks coming up from Neuville, the supply point, were held at St. Vith first by the rush of west-bound traffic, later by fear that the roads were cut. According to Lt.Col. Milton S. Glatterer, Division G-4, he called on the regiment for guides, and Master Sgt. Eugene Justice, Tech.Sgt. Thomas McHugh and Pfc. Henry Viele, who had come in with prisoners, took a small-arms ammunition convoy of fifteen trucks to Steinebrück, where the column was split. Ten trucks went to Service Battery at Elcherath, and the remaining five started forward for direct distribution to battalions. They apparently got off the main road, and two turned over on a slippery trail; the remaining three got up into the combat area.

As for bazooka and carbine ammunition, which the entire Division had been calling for, the Neuville dump was completely out of them that morning. Division had started screaming to VIII Corps for additional ammunition before noon. At 1:35 P.M. the answer came that the request was going to Corps G-4 for approval "right away."

The 591st Field Artillery never got additional ammunition that day. By nightfall it had expended 2,622 rounds, practically all its available supply. Seven truckloads of 105mm shells and powder charges were hung up at St. Vith.

That night Col. Alexander D. Reid, who would have wished for more pertinent information from Division on the general situation— Division wished the same, by the way—knew that his left was badly threatened, with communication lost between him and the 423d Infantry. His reserve battalion was committed at Winterspelt, to hold that flank. The 2d and 3d Battalions had restored their lines by dint of sharp local counterattacks. All contact with the 28th Division was gone. And, said Division, the 9th Armored Division would have a combat command down the Winterspelt road early in the morning to attack and relieve that north flank pressure.

Reid's losses were small. The situation seemed far from hopeless. The 424th Infantry combat team had acquitted itself well in its initial action.

As the day ended, the Kraut had not attained his initial objective. The southern route to St. Vith was still obstructed.

The 820th TD Battalion, attached to the 106th, was spread among the various units as previously related—a company here, another there; a platoon at this crossroads, another on that hill. Wherever there was a good potential tank passage, the TDs were emplaced. This is as it should be, but it makes hard delving to record the actions of these detachments, lost in large commands.

Battery A, 820th, was up with the cavalry, as we know. Battery B was on the right flank with the 424th Infantry, and Battery C was in the Schnee Eifel with the 423d. In each sector the field artillerymen with the tiger's head patch of the TDs put up a fight.

There was, for an instance of isolated fighting, the case of Staff Sgt. Joseph J. Schlecht, whose platoon at Prümerberg was being overrun when he personally carried an armful of 3-inch shells to a gun, loaded and trained it himself and knocked out some twenty advancing Krauts. Three times Schlecht toted up his shells under fire, three times he delayed the enemy advance until the platoon was able to disengage.

And there was Sgt. Robert L. Vance, commanding an eight-man outpost squad when the *Volksgrenadiers* came through the snow-bent firs. First, Vance knocked out a five-man spearhead with his submachine gun; then a rocket crew began setting up in the snow, and Vance wiped them out with an M1. A third rush placed three enemy soldiers in the position, and Vance plastered them with hand grenades. His outpost was never overrun that first red day.

One cites these things as examples, not as exceptions. All along the line and back through the shell-plastered areas individuals were rising to the occasion. When the enemy barrage ripped out the phone lines, wire crews of the 106th Signal Company struggled to restore communications. Sgt. Ned F. Rose, working with his crew along the Skyline Drive road from Schönberg into the back areas linking with the 424th Infantry, ran into sniper fire just where the cable had been cut by shell bursts. Two of his men were wounded, but Rose and the remaining soldier coolly spliced the severed strands, relaid the cable along a more protected channel, and then went on to another mission.

The communications system deserves some critical mention. The Division phone net consisted basically of two lines to each regiment and one lateral line from the cavalry headquarters on the north down the line to each regimental command post. At each regimental headquarters a detachment from the 106th Signal Company manned an SCR-193 radio set, linking with a net control station at St. Vith.

At Schönberg the Division forward switching central was set up, channelling the telephone communications back to Division. This net, originally installed by the 2d Infantry Division, was taken over from them. What would seem to have been a serious defect was that, though there were two lines to each regiment from Division, both were laid in the same cable. The same criticism would apply to the lines from infantry regiment back to the supporting artillery; there were two each, but in the same cable. If this were cut, all wire communication was automatically lost.

The 331st Medical Battalion on that first morning shifted from treatment of trenchfoot to gunshot wounds almost immediately. As the wounded came into first-aid stations the wide-strung collecting companies began to move them back.

Company A, at Andler, looking out both for the cavalry and the 422d Infantry, fell back during the morning to Heuem, after Auw had been captured. Its 1st Battalion, 422d Infantry ambulance, coming down loaded, could not get back; the road was barred by an enemy patrol. The ambulance of the 2d Battalion, 422d, driven by Pfc. Andrew Gollin and Pvt. Thomas Fox, coming down the same road behind Schlausenbach in the night, smacked into this patrol and was captured. Oddly enough, the Germans, after loading more casualties into an ambulance, sent it on its way a little later.

Company B, with the 423d Infantry at Buchet, and C Company with the 424th at Steinebrück, handled casualties all day long, part of the time under shell fire. Evacuation to the clearing station at St. Vith was badly impeded by the flow of traffic westward along the road from Schönberg, which got worse as the day went on.

On the morning of 16 December the fourteen ration trucks of Service Company, 423d Infantry, at Halenfeld, were ready to make their daily run back to the dump. In the billets was Mr. Eugene C. Woods, of the American Red Cross. Someone awakened him, rushed him out and told him to take the trucks to St. Vith; Service Company was turning out to fight as infantry.

Woods, with the convoy, got on the road, several times ran the gantlet of enemy patrol fire—apparently they took the Bleialf road—got up to Schönberg, and after more than a day of wandering in the traffic jam turned up at St. Vith, with seven trucks left of his convoy. The others came dribbling back within the next few days.

And there was Lt. John M. Krol, 422d Infantry, who went that morning to Division headquarters to deliver an overlay of minefields in the regimental area, and to obtain information from G-2. Krol was at headquarters when word came in of the German attack. He insisted on returning to his regiment and set off in his jeep with Pfc. Hewett

A. Schoonover, his driver, and Pvt. Donald E. Johnson, a scout, who had accompanied him in.

They got through Schönberg, but south of Auw ran into a Kraut patrol and were captured. Krol suggested to his men they try to escape one by one—he to go last. Both Schoonover and Johnson got away and reported in to the regimental command post later in the day. Krol, whose body was later found, was apparently caught in a burst of our own artillery fire.

NOTES TO CHAPTER 4

[1] Letter to the author, 18 November 1946.

[2] Copies of these plans, picked up in the 423d Infantry positions after the line was retaken, are in the hands of the 106th Infantry Division Association.

[3] Narrative of H Company, 422d Infantry, by Lt. Lewis H. Walker. Thanks are due for this graphic account of the entire Schnee Eifel action, as seen by him.

[4] General Jones and Colonel Craig, who was in the Division CP when the former telephoned Puett, are definite on the point that Puett was instructed to proceed from Schönberg to Andler, thence attacking southeast. The telephone message was not recorded.

[5] S-3 Diary, 423d Infantry, in possession of 106th Infantry Division Association.

[6] Evaluated by regiment as loudspeaker recording; there was no railway line close by.

[7] Capt. F. P. Conroy, 590th Field Artillery, in a letter to the author, 19 October 1946.

[8] Received by G-2, 106th Infantry Division at 1:20 P.M. that day, and immediately translated. VIII Corps was at once informed, says Col. Robert P. Stout, Division G-2. Transcript of translation made is in Appendix I. It is highly probable that this information on Operation Greif was the first intimation VIII Corps, U.S. First Army, 12th Army Group, and SHAEF, in turn, had that Skorzeny's plans (already noted in Daily Periodic Report, G-2, U.S. First Army, 2 December, and in G-2 Estimate No. 37, U.S. First Army, 10 December) had been placed in operation.

[9] Letter, Capt. William Perlman, Company H, 424th Infantry, 13 January 1947.

Chapter 5: The Second Red Day

++

Through the night and into the dawning hours of 17 December the German inrush pressed. Already beginning to get off balance, though probably they didn't know it yet back at Sixth SS Panzer Army headquarters, the weight of I SS Panzer Corps' attack was sliding southward as its thrust toward Elsenborn caromed off the Bütgenbach bastion held by 2d and 99th Divisions.

But from Bütgenbach down to the Schnee Eifel the door was wide, and 1st SS Panzer Division was flowing through into the Büllingen Forest, skirting the Amblève River.

The *Führer* Escort Brigade of Panzers, and the 18th *Volksgrenadier* Division of Fifth Panzer Army were pressing toward Schönberg, with the leading elements of the II SS Panzer Corps of Sixth SS Panzer Army treading on their heels, already hampered by the slow advance. The 150th Panzer Brigade (the American-uniformed and American-equipped element of Operation Greif) should have debouched by dawn from Schönberg and over an already opened St. Vith–Malmedy route if it would do its job of terrorizing infiltration, for Von der Heyde's parachutists were dropping by 4:00 A.M. in the vicinity of the Eupen–Malmedy crossroads in the Hohe Venn marsh country, ten miles behind Bütgenbach. Thus, with the rear areas demoralized, ran the German reasoning, that stubborn northern shoulder must crumble, widening the gap and opening the way to Liège. But the engineers at Auw and the fire of the 589th and 592d Field Artillery Battalions had slowed that rush.

South of the Schnee Eifel elements of 116th Panzer and the entire 62d *Volksgrenadier* Division had slipped into Bleialf, Winterscheid and Winterspelt during the night. Those American outfits in the Schnee were holding things up; they must be definitely bottled up and by-passed. The 116th Panzer should have been in Crombach, west of St. Vith, hours ago. Instead, it, too, delayed in the Eifel, was flowing off its axis of direction toward the southwest as the U. S. 28th Division's positions south of Lutzkampen were brushed aside.

These things, of course, were not known at the 106th Division's command post in old St. Vith, whose narrow streets throughout the night were crowded with increasing traffic and by hordes of refugees whom the MPs tried to keep flowing westward. At the CP the Division Commander and his staff were counting the minutes until CCB, 7th Armored, and CCB, 9th Armored Divisions, would arrive.

Just thirty-six minutes past midnight came a directive from VIII Corps, the gist of which was contained in the sentence, "Troops will be withdrawn from present position only if position becomes completely untenable. In no event will enemy be allowed to penetrate west of line: Holzheim–Setz–Lommersweiler–Maspelt–Leiler–Buckholz . . . which will be held at all costs."

General Middleton's order was about as effective as Canute's attempt to brush back the tide; the 1st SS Panzer Division was already beyond that line, would be more than five miles inside it north of the Our by the next night. But of course, VIII Corps didn't know that. Nobody, in fact, knew anything definite about the enemy front line. But there was the order; it was up to the 106th to carry it out.

When would those armored elements come in?

Contact with CCB, 9th Armored Division, was made less than an hour later and Brig.Gen. William M. Hoge got his orders from Maj. Gen. Jones: "Destroy enemy forces in vicinity of Winterspelt. Extend the left flank of 424th Infantry to the railroad [in the Ihren Valley]. Then withdraw the bulk of your tanks to an assembly area north of the river [Our], prepared to counterattack south or east in case your position is threatened." The busy MPs got orders to clear the way for the expected 7th Armored Division.

With the dawn came increasingly bad news. The 589th Field Artillery Battalion was in trouble getting out; one battery would have to destroy its guns although the 592d was already out and on the road. The 424th Infantry reported the enemy in Winterspelt at 5:45 A.M. but—comforting—"saw advance elements of our armor coming down that way." CCB of the 9th was rolling in.

From VIII Corps came a startling message at 6:50 A.M.: Thirty tanks had broken through the right flank regiment of the 99th Division up to the north; paratroops were dropping near Honstedt.[1] Did the 106th have contact with the 99th at Wereth (two and a half miles inside its "hold at all costs" line)? It did not.

By 6:18 A.M. the 423d was calling for help; the enemy was overrunning Bleialf, approaching Radscheid in force. The regiment had lost communication with Troop B, 18th Cavalry, on its right. The southern penetration was well under way.

All this time the situation of the 422d Infantry was unchanged. But at 8:30 A.M., from the forward switching central at Schönberg, six miles east of St. Vith in the valley behind the 422d, came worse word: "German tanks coming from Andler. Will destroy switchboard." This from the Division Signal Officer, Lt.Col. Earle Williams. Up there the

Schönberg–St. Vith surge was on. The prongs were closing on the Schnee Eifel positions.

Division ordered the 422d and 423d Infantry Regiments to tighten up; the former to withdraw to the line: Bleialf–Auw road, with its right contacting the latter at Radscheid, which would be held by the 423d. The 2d Battalion, 423d, was definitely attached to the 422d, but didn't know it.

Where was CCB, 7th Armored Division?

At 6:36 A.M. the 423d reported the enemy had broken through at Bleialf, was pressing north, over Skyline Drive. From the 424th on the south had already come word that Winterspelt was in German hands. Division ordered all available artillery placed on the town, at 8:30 A.M., at the same time sending word to 2d Battalion, 423d Infantry, to fall back on Schönberg and defend it. CCB, 7th Armored Division, was not even in Vielsalm yet, it now transpired. A frantic message to the MPs to divert a company of the 9th Armored Division's medium tanks toward Schönberg was too late. They had all gone by on the way to Steinebrück, but later in the day a small tank force of this outfit did get up in the northern sector.

These efforts, impeded by the fog of war, were, of course, unavailing. By 8:30 the enemy armored smash from Bleialf northward had linked at Schönberg with the Krauts pushing down from Andler. The Nazi shackles had been sprung around the 422d and 423d Infantry Regiments and their attached units in the Schnee Eifel.

The battered 14th Cavalry Group at 10:20 A.M. announced a patrol up on the Amblève to the north had spotted an enemy tank between Hepscheid and Heppenbach. Its 32d Squadron had seen thirty-one more (evidently the same ones reported by Corps) just south of Bülingen, and an "unknown number" were driving in on Andler, together with an estimated hundred infantrymen; small-arms fire was being received from this group, some of whom were dressed in white snowsuits. The cavalry by 11:00 were pulling out to a final delaying position on the line Wallerode–Born.

A radio direct from the 32d Cavalry Squadron reported it was fighting in Schönberg, having been driven out of Andler. From Col. Williams came word that German infantry in the Our Valley was moving down both sides of the Schönberg road toward Heuem; an extemporized roadblock had knocked out one tank. The Schönberg situation had so definitely deteriorated that the 81st Engineer Battalion was ordered at 9:35 A.M. to establish close-in defense of St. Vith. The 806th Ordnance Company was evacuated.

General Jones, hoping against hope that the 7th Armored would get in, sent word to the 422d and 423d Infantry Regiments at 9:45 A.M. that he expected "to clear out area west of you this afternoon with reinforcements. Withdraw from present positions if they become untenable."

Division Artillery was ready to mark off Schönberg with white phosphorus by 9:45, but Gen. Jones, fearful lest the blasting of the town would block the road for his intended counterattack with the 7th Armored, held his hand for the time being. Later both Division and Corps artillery opened on it.

On the right flank CCB, 9th Armored Division, got into action before noon, deploying upon crossing the Our at Steinebrück. It attacked and drove the enemy from the high ground north of Winterspelt, overlooking the Ihren, stabilizing that situation for the time being as the hard-pressed 424th Infantry clung to the slopes of the Stein-Kopf to the south.

But the Kraut was coming down the St. Vith road now from Schönberg—slowly at first, feeling his way, then gathering momentum.

Be it noted, however, that he was already twenty-four hours behind schedule.

Let's look along the front at the detailed action.

Two Lieutenant Colonels on the St. Vith Road

Up at the Division forward switching central at Schönberg that morning was Lt.Col. Earle Williams, Division Signal Officer; with him was Master Sgt. Clyde F. Foster, wire chief. Enemy fire was falling in the village, the switchboard was frantically trying to clear traffic. Down the valley from Andler came the German tanks.

Williams phoned Division, ordered the board destroyed and its crew to clear out, then took off on the road with Sgt. Foster to try to reestablish some communication. At 9:15 about a half-mile from Heuem scattered mortar and small-arms fire began falling. Foster climbed a pole and cut in on the Division line to report as Williams observed. Then an armored car nosed out of the mist and Foster jumped. The pair got to the jeep and dashed a quarter-mile west where they ran into one of our TDs and a few artillerymen. Col. Williams pressed them into service and Foster again climbed a pole under small-arms fire to cut in. The TD gun opened up and Foster's voice came into the St. Vith board: "Our M-8 knocked out one tank. Getting ready to move out."

Williams pulled his detachment back well west of Heuem, started felling trees for a roadblock. And the 592d Field Artillery in response to his call began spraying both sides of the road between Heuem and Schönberg.

In the meantime another lieutenant colonel was reconnoitering along the Schönberg Road. This was Slayden, Corps assistant G-2, mentioned previously, who at 10:00 A.M. started for the front to see for himself how matters were going.

Slayden worked his way up through the west-bound traffic, past the driven-in cavalrymen to near Heuem, began to receive hostile fire and turned back. At 11:45 he tapped the line, 1,500 yards west of Heuem, told G-3: "I'm the last man between St. Vith and Schönberg. German infantry has reached the point where the road from Schönberg turns north from the Our River. Artillery has one scout car and five jeeps here. Could delay the enemy if we could get artillery fire."

Division told Slayden the 81st Engineers were coming up the road to prepare close-in defense, asked him to see if he could establish any delaying tactics himself. And again the 592d Field Artillery Battalion began putting fire down just west of Heuem.

Slayden joined Williams' detachment, phoned at 12:30 P.M. that the artillery fire was "effective but five hundred yards over." And Williams, at 12:55, called in to report they were three miles out of St. Vith, had sighted three tanks, some thirty infantrymen and an armored car coming at them a half-mile east. Two of the tanks were painted white, the infantrymen wore snow suits.

At 2:10 the little detachment had pulled back to a mile east of St. Vith where the 81st Engineers were getting on the line near Prümerberg, and the three tanks were hovering about five hundred yards away.

What happened then belongs to the story of the 81st and 168th Engineers and the 592d Field Artillery Battalion. To make a long story short, the advance elements of CCB, 7th Armored Division, came rolling in at long last to St. Vith at 3:20 P.M., to be committed piecemeal, bolstering up the engineers' last-ditch defense beginning at 5:45 as dusk was falling on the snow and mist. By that time more enemy tanks were poking about to the north of the town and the Division's Defense Platoon was out on the line. Fritz was knocking at the door.

Already, by 2:45 P.M., Gen. Jones had made another decision based on what he knew up to that time. He ordered both 422d and 423d Infantry Regiments to fall back to the line of the Our, generally between Weppeler on the right and Schönberg on the left. "Schönberg," he told the 422d, "will have to be taken. We can have strength after daylight."

The 422d at 9:30 had reported its 2d Battalion forced to abandon its kitchens and duffel bags, but estimated they had sufficient rations for the entire regiment for the day, together with almost a unit load of ammunition. Its motor pool had been momentarily cut off.

To further complicate matters, the 2d Battalion, 423d Infantry, had by now—2:45 P.M.—joined its own regiment, the broken communications preventing receipt of the earlier Division orders that it be attached to the 422d. In reporting this the 423d calmly announced: "Will hold perimeter. Drop ammunition, food and medical supplies until route open."

At 3:25 the 424th Infantry was ordered to fall back also to the west of the Our, extending the line south generally along the hill masses of the Preisberg and the Hasenknopf to Steinebrück, with CCB, 9th Armored Division, on its left.

The scratch defense force of engineers and reconnaissance elements of CCB, 7th Armored Division, was by nightfall hotly engaged with the enemy spearhead driving in on St. Vith. Two tanks had been knocked out by our artillery fire.

As the night wore on the situation, while serious, was still seemingly under control. The cavalry on the north had been pushed off, or had abandoned, their last delaying position on the Born–Wallerode ridge, however, and were now ordered to retake Born and protect the 7th Armored Division's left flank. In the center the 422d Infantry announced by radio that its three battalions were holding. Only contact with the 423d on its right was by patrols. The withdrawal of the 424th Infantry and CCB, 9th Armored Division, was progressing on the right flank.

As the clock ticked into the morning of 18 December the most pressing situation seemed to be that directly in front of St. Vith. Gen. Jones, who had already requested an air drop of ammunition, rations and medical supplies from VIII Corps for his two encircled regiments, now called on them for another effort.

Let's look farther along the line.

CEYLON'S TEA IS BITTER

We left the 14th Cavalry Group north of the Our, stretched across five miles of wooded hills, from Andler on the south to Hepscheid on the north above the source of the Amblève, along the ridge of the Büllingen Forest. Ceylon, the group's code name, had taken a terrible pounding, would take more today, 17 December. The 18th Squadron had only E Troop (assault gun) and F Company (light tank) intact, its reconnaissance troops having been smashed in the previous day's fighting. The 32d Squadron was better off, though it had lost one complete troop, A, up at Honsfeld during the night.

By dawn it was evident that the enemy armor was rolling in force down the Krinkelt–Büllingen–St. Vith road, as well as westward from Honsfeld. All contact with the 99th Infantry Division had been lost. By 10:20 A.M. a Kraut tank was nosing in on Hepscheid, thirty-one more had been spotted just south of Büllingen, an unknown number were closing in on 32d Squadron's B Troop at Andler, which reported it had no contact with any 106th Division element to the south.

The northern threat was the worst, naturally, from the cavalry viewpoint. Col. Devine decided to fall back to a final delaying position on the line Born–Wallerode, astride the Büllingen–St. Vith road, where his right could be anchored on the Langert Berg hill mass. Moving his command post to the vicinity of Nieder Emmels where the 275th Armored Field Artillery Battalion was supporting him, he sent the 18th Squadron from Medell to Born, with a reconnaissance patrol out at Mirfeld.

The 32d Squadron would pivot back on B Troop now fighting at Andler, supported by F Company (light tank); C and E Troops would move from their Herresbach perimeter through Wereth to an intermediate position at Meyerode.

By noon the 18th Squadron had gotten into Born and group headquarters was established at Nieder Emmels. But the 32d Squadron ran into trouble. Lt. Kenneth Kinsel, of E Troop, reconnoitering the Wereth road, the best though longest way out, ran into a roadblock one mile north of Herresbach. The only way out left for C and E Troops was by a nasty woods trail cutting due west into the Weber Creek ravine to link finally with a secondary road from Heuem to Meyerode.

Troop E took it, sliding and grinding its assault guns on their light tank chassis up and down the slithery slopes; squadron headquarters followed. Troop C, covering the withdrawal, of course found the trail still more churned up into a pudding of snow and mud, but clawed through finally to Meyerode, closing about 11:30 A.M.

Troop B had been in hot conflict since 7:00 o'clock as the tanks moved in—apparently the *Führer* Escort Brigade, with accompanying infantry clad in snow suits. They came down the Our valley from the east; from the southeast along the Auw–Andler road, surrounding two of the troop's reconnaissance teams; and from Manderfeld to the northeast, opening hot fire.

By 7:45 A.M. Capt. Franklin P. Lindsey, Jr., had lost nineteen men and several vehicles. Covered by the platoon leaders' armored cars the troop disengaged, falling back on Schönberg. One cut-off detachment worked its way northwest to Herresbach.

By 8:00 A.M., full daylight, the troop had been forced out of Schönberg. Lindsey pulled up near Heuem, was still debating with himself if he should establish a roadblock lest other Americans falling back might be held up, when the first enemy Mark IV tank poked around the corner, its black-bereted commander leaning out of the open turret. The armored cars barked. T/5 Russell in one, evidently suffering from buck fever, inadvertently slammed an HE shell into his gun instead of armor-piercing. It was a lucky error; bursting near the top of the turret it erased the tank commander and the tank backed off.

Enemy infantrymen came frothing through the woods to the northeast. But B Troop was shaking down now; the cavalrymen opened steady fire. Cpl. Joseph Unger, potting Krauts, found time to yell to his skipper: "Captain, I think I got another one. Paying for myself today—been costing the Government 'til now!"

Here B Troop held out for a while until it got the order to fall back on Meyerode. As it passed north up the road from Atzerath toward Wallerode it went through the light tanks of F Company, which, seemingly—for Capt. Blair declares he didn't know B Troop was out in front of him until it streamed past—had been sitting in its sheltered position since the previous afternoon.

Major John L. Kracke, squadron executive, commanding since the departure of Lt.Col. Ridge the day before, ordered F Company to fall back behind B Troop to Meyerode, outposting on the way the crossroads on the St. Vith–Büllingen highway a mile and a half northeast of the former place, which Blair did, protecting artillery positions and the Division Artillery air-landing strip nearby.

Except for our two lieutenant colonels, Williams and Slayden, and their hodge-podge roadblocking detachment, the Our Valley–St. Vith road was now open to the enemy. The engineers would do something about that, as we shall see later.

By 1:00 P.M. the 32d Squadron was ordered to fall back from Meyerode to the Born–Wallerode line, but had hardly reached the position before it was again ordered by Devine to retreat, this time to Vielsalm. This order is hard to understand. The squadron had made no contact with the enemy on the new line, which was the last commanding ground north of St. Vith. The 106th Division was determined to stick it out at St. Vith. Col. Devine, at 11:25 A.M., in telling Division of his new dispositions on the final delaying line had assured it that he would "Have counterattack force available your orders." Overlay of the delaying position had been received. Our fighter-bombers had begun to come over, had been hitting at the enemy. At 12:20 P.M. 14th Cavalry Group, calling in for the general plan, had been told: "Stay on line where you are. Liaison officer coming to you. One counterattack [CCB 9th AD] has started, but other [CCB 7th AD] not started yet."

But up on the north the spearheads of the 1st SS Panzer Division had been side-slipping in the corridor south of Büllingen. They came down to Amblève, and there swung northwest again to Ligneuville (where incidentally, they captured Service Company, 27th Armored Infantry Battalion, and Service Battery, 16th Armored Field Artillery Battalion, both of CCB, 9th Armored Division, that day). They had also begun to spread southward around the Wolfsbusch forested hill mass towards Recht. And they came across country through Diedenberg toward Born. Always, it seemed, that northern flank was being turned. The 18th Cavalry Squadron fell back toward Poteau, and 14th Cavalry Group moved its command post back to Poteau.

Colonel Devine went reconnoitering that afternoon along the Born–Recht–Poteau road. With him in one car—all his eggs in one basket, it seemed—were his executive, Lt.Col. Augustine D. Dugan; his S-2, Maj. James Worthington; and his S-3, Maj. Lawrence Smith. At the road junction just northeast of Recht they ran into a group of men standing. Dugan was the first to sense anything was wrong and he had his pistol out when a splatter of fire struck the car. Driver and passengers dove into a ditch, scattered on foot.

They all got back to Poteau during the evening, separately. Devine, badly shaken, told Lt.Col. William F. Damon, Jr., commanding 18th Squadron, to take over the group. VIII Corps headquarters at Bastogne had sent for the cavalry commander and Damon went, turning over command to Lt.Col. Ridge of 32d Squadron, who was at the command post. When Dugan returned from the ambush later he assumed command by virtue of seniority.

These things are mentioned in detail because to some extent they account for the seeming vacillation that afternoon of 17 December of the hard-pressed little cavalry group now scattered from hell to breakfast over a nine-mile area. The Division G-3 journal sheds no light on the cavalry move unscreening the northern flank.

So it was that the 32d Squadron, moving past Gut Eidt Farm and over the Kninels Berg into Hunnange, melted into the stream of westbound traffic now cluttering the St. Vith–Sart-lez-St.Vith–Poteau–Vielsalm highway, bumper to bumper, at a one-mile-per-hour pace.

Let's get down to hard facts. Panic, sheer unreasoning panic, flamed that road all day and into the night. Everyone, it seemed, who had any excuse, and many who had none, was going west that day—west from Schönberg, west from St. Vith, too.

Jeeps, trucks, tanks, guns—great lumbering Corps Artillery vehicles that took up almost three-quarters of the road—some of them double-banking. Now and again vehicles were weaving into a third line, now and then they crashed into ditches. All this on a two-lane highway.

And this was what the 7th Armored Division was bucking as it strove —practically the only east-bound element—to get from Vielsalm to St. Vith.[2]

Darkness had come down before the cavalry columns reached Sart-lez-St.Vith; it was after 9:00 o'clock when C Troop got to Poteau, to find Lt.Col. Dugan waiting for them with orders to turn and take Born!

At 5:20 P.M., Division had received another message from 14th Cavalry Group, apparently during the shuffle of command. "Require orders for further action" it read. That was not answered until 9:10 P.M., with a laconic: "Reoccupy Born and protect left flank of 7th Armored Division."

Dugan, at Poteau, was now trying to comply with that order, pulling his outfits of the 32d Squadron out of the tide of stampeded traffic. But B Troop had already gone by toward Vielsalm, which it would reach early next morning; so too with E Troop and F Company.

Dugan did the best he could to scratch up a task force, as enemy flares flickered over the horizon to the north in the general direction of Recht. The Nazi tide was rolling on, it appeared, with nothing up there yet to stop it.

AT BAY IN ST. VITH

Sleepy St. Vith town itself was transformed to a madhouse that morning of 17 December as the Division Commander and staff struggled to maintain control over a situation for which the name "fluid" would be an understatement. G-2 was spotting red arrows of enemy penetration on the situation map as the bad news flickered in, G-4 was striving to move ammunition and rations forward. Division Artillery headquarters was worrying about the 589th Field Artillery. Gen. Jones, his chief of staff and his G-3 were tearing their hair when 7:00 A.M. came and went without word of CCB, 7th Armored Division. CCB, 9th Armored Division, had started rolling through the crooked streets from the north in the early morning, bucking the west-bound traffic the harassed MP platoon was trying to clear for their passage, on the way down to Steinebrück.

And always the sound of the firing in the mountains to the east grew louder. It was soon evident that the most immediate threat of the day would be to St. Vith itself. This was corroborated later as Williams and Slayden on the Schönberg road kept sending in their reports of the enemy's advance step by step down the Our valley.

By 9:35 A.M. Gen. Jones had designated Lt.Col. Thomas J. Riggs, Jr., commanding the 81st Engineer Combat Battalion, as defense commander. Let's see what Riggs had available.

First there was part of his own battalion. Headquarters, and Headquarters and Service Company (fifty men), with the remnants of A Company (sixty-four men) were already on the way back from Heuem, driven out as the enemy approached and having left some of their heaviest equipment behind them despite valiant efforts to save it. They were bound for Sart-lez-St.Vith (Rodt on some maps), four miles west of St. Vith, where they closed before noon. The other companies of this unit were, as we know, attached to the three infantry regiments.

Next Riggs had the 168th Engineer Combat Battalion, Lt.Col. W. L. Nungesser commanding, a Corps unit supporting the 81st. The 168th could muster about half-strength; its battalion headquarters, and Headquarters and Service Company were at Vielsalm, C Company was up at Winterspelt supporting C Company of the 81st with the 424th Infantry, and many men were scattered at schools and on special-duty jobs. Companies A and B between them could muster 358 men, men rusty at bazooka and machine-gun firing.

The Defense Platoon of Division headquarters was available, as was Lt. Joseph Callan's platoon of B Company, 820th TD Battalion. This platoon, originally with the 424th Infantry at Winterspelt, had been shot out the previous day, its guns and prime-movers destroyed. Back at St. Vith now, they had been reequipped with three new guns hurriedly drawn from VIII Corps ordnance people at Bastogne. Unfortunately, they were unequipped with direct-fire telescopes, and one had no sighting apparatus at all.[3]

But up near the Kninels Berg crossroads, not far from Gut Eidt Farm one mile northeast of St. Vith, where the Division Artillery air strip was located, the 592d Field Artillery Battalion had dropped trails at 8:30 A.M., safely out of their dangerous position of the day before in the 422d Infantry sector. Batteries A and C had each lost one howitzer, but the rest of the outfit was intact, and at about 11:00 o'clock its ammunition train came up with three hundred rounds of 155mm ammunition. Its fire support was available.

Riggs' initial plan was to try for a defense astride the Schönberg road somewhere up toward Heuem—these were the orders the 168th Engineers received at 10:30 A.M. Nungesser sent his reconnaissance officer, Lt. I. Balch, hotfooting up to the front. He ran into B Troop, 32d Cavalry, as it was pulling out of its position to move to Meyerode. A cavalry officer told him the enemy was just around the corner.

"And," says Balch, "sure enough he was. But nobody appeared to be doing much about the enemy."

The next decision was to stand two miles from St. Vith, but Riggs, on reconnaissance, found the enemy moving so fast that he picked Prümerberg, one mile east of the city, toward which the engineers were now rolling from Sart-lez-St.Vith. By 1:00 o'clock they were hastily entrenching along a thousand-yard line on both sides of the road.

Headquarters and Service Company of the 81st was on the left side along the east edge of a wooded patch with a field of fire of open ground in front of them. Company B, 168th Engineers—Company A did not arrive until later at night—was on the south of the road in the Bois de St. Vith and on their right. Company A of the 81st extended the flank.

In front of the position the TD platoon was initially set up, commanding the road, and an observation post was established four hundred yards in front of the line where the ubiquitous VIII Corps assistant G-2, Lt.Col. Slayden, who appears to have been having the time of his life that day in the forefront of the fight, set up shop with Lts. Lewthwaite and Souers and Tech.Sgt. Psolka of the 81st. Lt.Col. Patrick of the 820th TD Battalion joined them there.

The sweating engineers, handicapped by lack of entrenching tools, pegged away at their rifle pits, which were dug from five to ten yards apart, set up mortars and machine guns—these were also all too few. It was a race against time, for the Nazis were now pushing through the draw between the Bois de Wallerode and the Muhlenberg, less than two miles away. Had the tanks gotten in before the Prümerberg defense could stop them it would have been just too bad.

But the 592d Field Artillery was on the job. So were their flying artillery observers. Communications were in to the artillery airstrip and Weber had already asked for air observation to register in along the Schönberg road. Shortly after 2:00 o'clock Lt. Alonzo A. Neese, observer, and Lt. George Stafford, pilot, took off in a Cub. Machine-gun fire ripped up at them from five different spots in the woods below. Neese spotted a column of tanks and infantry along the road at a range of 3,500 yards from the battery positions and called for fire.

Battery B of the 592d opened up while the bumbling little observation plane circled amidst the machine-gun bullets from the nests below.

Neese got his bracket and called for fire for effect. The first volley smacked a 155mm HE shell on the lead tank, which went up with a bellow in a belch of red flame. The column halted, the first stab at St. Vith blunted, as B Battery poured fifty rounds into the mess.

But the rising tide could not be stopped forever. It lapped over on each side of the road as the Nazi infantrymen sifted into the woods, and the tanks sought covered routes. They were moving in toward Wallerode on the north and over the woods road from Setz. Things began to happen.

Three enemy tanks pushed cautiously around the bend in front of the 168th Engineer positions, the leading machine running into the snow-covered field where its crew dismounted. Lt. William T. Holland of B Company grabbed a .50-caliber machine gun and wiped them out. A bazooka team, Sgt. James L. Hill firing and Pfc. Martin Connolly loading, opened up on the second as it nosed toward the command post, knocking it out. The third scuttled back.

A Division Defense Platoon antitank gun, barking at more tanks moving up a bit to the northeast, was immediately knocked out. The TDs blazed at them, and the enemy sought cover. Callan's TDs opened up, firing by guess and by gosh since they had no direct sighting apparatus, and though the first shot was high, the tanks sheered off. Behind the invaders could be seen several U.S. 2½-ton trucks, plainly marked, and crammed with Kraut infantrymen.[4] From Slayden's observation post they could be pinpointed, and the group there called for artillery fire. But by this time enemy small-arms fire had begun to fall on the 592d Field Artillery and Lt.Col. Weber, obeying previous orders from Division Artillery headquarters that he get out, had given "March order." The artillery air observation detachment pulled out also.

The observation post had a line to Division air liaison, and linked with a P-47 in the vicinity. The plane made four passes before it located the enemy when a German tanker made the mistake of firing on it. It then strafed the group seven times, starting a fire which disabled one tank and caused considerable casualties to nearby enemy infantry.

As the Division Defense Platoon, an element of the 106th's Headquarters Company, deployed for its part in the day's action Cpl. Werner C. Schnitzer volunteered to man an advance rocket-launcher position in the woods. A burst of small-arms and rocket fire from the infiltrating enemy swept the site, wounding Schnitzer. The first wave of tanks followed close, but Schnitzer clung to his gun until he passed out. He was taken prisoner.

And there were Cpl. Lawrence B. Roberts and Pvt. Floyd L. Black, whose squad was rushed up on the line to find the Germans coming through. The squad fell back to a position between two TD guns and there, together with an unidentified officer and enlisted man, between them manned a .50-caliber machine gun, a rocket launcher, two M1 rifles and a carbine, impeding the tank advance. A Kraut machine gun was rushed up to take them under fire, but the detachment kept picking off the crews. They held for two and a half hours, when the .50-caliber gun stuttered for the last time and died. They got back within the engineer lines.

By 4:00 o'clock the defense position was organized as completely as it could be, under the circumstances. Enemy tanks were moving over the snowy fields up toward Wallerode, where the Defense Platoon skirmished with them. Riggs sent his TD guns to that flank,[5] but only one got in. The 592d was rolling away by this time; it would bivouac that night in the Bois d'Emmels, four miles west of St. Vith. The Germans were closing for another push, now that they had proved the opposition and had some idea of the defensive disposition. And then the chill wind brought rumblings from the west, armored vehicles loomed out of the gloom and dusk behind the engineer position. The 7th Armored had arrived at long last!

The advance elements of CCB, 7th Armored Division, Brig.Gen. Bruce C. Clarke commanding, began coming into St. Vith from Vielsalm, at 5:20 P.M. Gen. Clarke, reporting to Gen. Jones, earlier had been given orders to take over the defense of the town, using his elements piecemeal as they came in, and restore the situation preparatory to a counterattack to the east next morning, to cut through to the surrounded 422d and 423d Infantry Regiments.

Clarke grabbed his first units in—B Troop, 87th Reconnaissance Squadron and a platoon of mediums of the 31st Tank Battalion—and rushed them to Riggs. They went in on the north as night was falling, Headquarters and Service Company, 81st Engineers, being side-slipped south of the road to bolster up that defense.

As the engineers cut across a patch of open ground a German tank, with some infantry, wormed its way through a fire-break lane in the woods and fired on them. A detail of engineers threw a daisy chain of mines across its path, while the rest of the company drove off the infantry with small-arms fire.

Captain Nathan D. Ward, commanding the company, hailed one of the 7th Armored's medium tanks to attack the Nazi. The tank commander at first demurred, then asked Ward, "Are you crazy enough to ride the tank up to the road junction?"

Ward said he guessed he was and jumped on. They nosed over the crest of the hill and the tanks exchanged shots, the first round of 88mm fire knocking Capt. Ward, uninjured, off the Sherman, which then got in three rounds, disabling the enemy's left track. Both tanks then veered off from one another. The engineer company, the pressure relieved, continued across the road to its new position, on the right flank.

For several hours men milled around in the darkness, broken by occasional bursts of machine-gun fire. Then a Kraut combat patrol of some twenty men with automatic weapons rushed the line about 7:00 P.M. and got to within a stone's throw of Riggs' command post before it was stopped. Tracer bullets flared on both sides. Friend and enemy hugged the ground within a few feet of one another throughout the rest of the night.

A quick conference between the commanders concerned resulted in a reorganization. Troop B, 87th Reconnaissance Squadron, held its place on the left; Company B, 38th Armored Infantry, which had now gotten in, took over from the 168th Engineers on the south side of the Schönberg road. Both engineer units were pulled out of the line momentarily and reorganized—its Company A by now had joined the 168th—and went back on the right of the line in the order: Company A of the 81st, Companies A and B of the 168th, with Headquarters and Service Company of the 81st in reserve behind the armored infantry in the center. Again to the right somewhere Company A, 23d Armored Infantry, of the 7th Armored, was feeling its way into position to extend the line to the south. The 275th Armored Field Artillery, originally the 14th Cavalry Group's support, was still in position near Sart-lez-St. Vith and would support the defense. Its commander, when he got into St. Vith that afternoon announced that he was "tired of being pushed around" and was not going to retreat any farther.

This somewhat complicated shifting of front-line positions in the dark was accomplished without much incident, the Krauts being evidently in some confusion themselves as they built up their strength, and content to let matters lie until dawn.

While Riggs' task force was battling only a mile away, there occurred at the highway bridge over the railway skirting the eastern edge of St. Vith one of those serio-comic incidents which sometimes affect the fortunes of war.

Guarding the bridge, which brings the Schönberg road into St. Vith, was Sgt. Thomas Piscatelli, of the 168th Engineers. He and his squad had prepared the bridge for demolition, were standing by in the twilight for orders as their comrades fought on the wooded ridge beyond.

Up to the bridge, according to Lt. Balch of the 168th, who was going by, came an unidentified lieutenant colonel, who ordered Piscatelli to blow the bridge. The sergeant refused, stating he had orders not to do so unless ordered by Riggs or Nungesser. While the argument went on, again according to Balch, a general officer, also unidentified, approached.

"Blow that bridge!" he called.

"No, sir; not without orders from Col. Riggs or my battalion commander."

"I say blow that goddam bridge!"

"But, General, our troops are up there defending on the hill."

"That's nonsense. Any troops up there are either killed or captured by now. Blow that bridge, I say."

What the sergeant then told the general to do is unprintable. The bridge was not blown, of course, and when Riggs heard of the incident he ordered the caps removed from the charges.

The net result of all this was that the Germans got the bridge intact on 21 December, and, later, blew it up themselves to prevent possible counterattacks in their rear.

They Tried to Keep 'Em Rolling

Lieutenant Colonel Kelly's 589th Field Artillery Battalion on Skyline Drive behind Schlausenbach was in a hectic situation during the early morning hours of 17 December. The enemy was building up his infiltration in the woods, was dropping small-arms and mortar fire into the battery positions. The mud and snow was by now churned into an icy mush in which the big 105mm howitzers and their six-by-six prime-movers slid and skidded as the battalion struggled to extricate itself.

Despite all the difficulties, A and B Batteries, as already noted, were slowly worked into road position. But C Battery presented an insoluble problem. Access to the position had been through Laudesfeld to the north and west. Now the enemy was astride this road, was also astride the Auw road barring exit over a trail to the southeast. In addition the howitzers were locked in the mud.

Puett's 2d Battalion, 423d Infantry, since its midnight arrival from Schönberg with orders to assist the artillery withdrawal, had been probing in the woods to the north, east and south of the 589th positions. The place was thick with Krauts, and so far as C Battery was concerned he also had armor dug in along the Laudesfeld road.

By 2:00 A.M. telephonic communication was in with Division. Puett says he asked permission to launch a night attack to relieve C Battery. This was denied and he was told not to get so heavily engaged that he could not break contact. There is no record of this exchange of conversation in the Division G-3 journal, but Gen. Jones remembers instructing Puett not to become too heavily involved. The Division Commander quite naturally hoped to retain control over the only element of his command not yet wholly committed.

Puett attempted to divert enemy attention from C Battery by a patrol in force, but was unsuccessful. The howitzers were pretty well mired in. Puett feels that only by bulldozer and long after daylight could such effort have gotten the guns out. Kelly, who went out with Puett's patrol, was finally convinced that the pieces just couldn't be moved. By this time the infantry battalion was digging in practically through the artillery positions, but on a north-south line through the battalion CP and five hundred yards behind Battery C.

Kelly got Division Artillery—the phone was still working—and asked and received permission to destroy his Battery C pieces. He sent a runner to Service Battery to set trucks up to get the men out. By the time the howitzers were made useless and the C Battery personnel got back to the CP it was 7:00 A.M.

Kelly led them, leaving a forward observer party, to the entrucking point—1,500 yards down Skyline Drive under defilade—to meet his messenger coming back from Service Battery. The Krauts from the south already had Engineer Cutoff between the main highway and the Schönberg road under small-arms fire, and were moving toward Schönberg. Kelly and Battery C were cut off. Capt. Rockwell, the battery commander, begged Kelly to let him try to break out across country by Schönberg—his men were entirely without food or ammunition—and Kelly assented. Later that morning they were gobbled up, and Rockwell himself was killed.

Kelly, after trying to cut over a side road to the rest of the battalion, was bogged down and fired on. He got back to the original command post, where the infantry were now established, and joined Puett.

In the meantime Batteries A and B had rolled over Skyline Drive, turned west over a narrow, one-way woods road down a ravine into the Schönberg road, Engineer Cutoff, passed their Service Battery billet a thousand yards due east of Radscheid, and rolled into their new positions. On the way, one B Battery piece slid off the corduroy in Engineer Cutoff and had to be abandoned.[6] Sporadic enemy shellfire, some of it white phosphorus, was interdicting the highway as they went, but they got through. Every minute counted, for they had to get into action again in support of both Puett's battalion and the 422d Infantry.

The new position, previously selected, was just on the Belgium–

Germany border east of the Bleialf–Schönberg road, a mile and a quarter south of Schönberg. Battery B slid in, dropped trails. It was now nearly 7:00 A.M. Battery A, following, was a little slower. Three pieces got in. Lt. Eric Wood—we've heard of him before—the acting battery commander, was nursing the fourth piece, which had a crippled prime mover. This howitzer was still on the road when firing broke out, evidently only a short distance away. Wood told Sgt. (later Lt.) Barney M. Alford to drop trail on the road for antitank defense.

Service Battery's original position was, as stated, on the Bleialf–Schönberg road, eight hundred yards north of Engineer Cutoff. When the new positions had been selected there appeared no reason why Service should move, so it was still in its little hamlet when hell broke loose at daybreak, as the enemy from the south reached it.

Some forty-odd Kraut infantrymen popped into the locality without the slightest attempt at concealment. When they were fired at by guards from an attic they rushed a house beyond the battery command post and began firing rifle grenades.

At the command post was an armored car of the 820th TD Battalion which had come in during the night. Pfc. Leonard J. Savitskie and his driver jumped into the car and swung its .50-caliber machine gun on the Krauts. An enemy mortar opened up behind the building and Savitskie, with a hand grenade, raced from his car behind the building under small-arms fire, lobbed the grenade and destroyed mortar and crew. The one-man task force then got into his armored car again and resumed his methodic potting at the enemy-occupied building.

Sniper fire drifted in from the hilltop to the east and began to take toll of the personnel at the command post. Savitskie, wounded, lolled back in his open turret. Pfc. Thomas C. Graham of Service Battery, dashing across the open space, took his place at the machine gun. The Service Battery men rallied with bazookas, small arms, machine guns and grenades, in some cases pushing their grenades through holes the Germans inside had made for their rifle grenades.

Twice Graham's gun in the armored car jammed, twice he had the driver pull back while he cleared it, then returned to fight.

Several Krauts, including one officer, surrendered. But the enemy force was building up. Scattered detachments of artillerymen were overrun. It settled down to a battle between the command post occupants and the German house. This harum-scarum battling was the noise that had come to Wood and his one gun on the Schönberg road.

Captain Cagle of Service Battery notified the firing batteries by phone that it was being overrun about the same time. It was 7:15 when the last call came in; tanks and infantry were closing up. "We're done for," was the response to the acting battalion commander's request to hold until a howitzer could be swung around to fire in their support.

Throwing a hail of smoke grenades to cover the evacuation of the command post the Service Battery people piled into the open and over toward the Bleialf road, managing to gather in some abandoned trucks as they went.

So far as the 589th Field Artillery knew, they were now alone in a world of Krauts. There was no defending screen of doughboys, there was no communication with the 422d Infantry whom they were supposed to support. It was time to get out, considered Major Arthur C. Parker, III, battalion executive and now, with Kelly cut off, in command at the firing batteries. He ordered A and B Batteries, individually, to make their way through Schönberg and assemble west of St. Vith.

Lieutenant Wood got two of his three already emplaced Battery A howitzers out. Sergeant Alford was still struggling with the fourth piece just up the road; the howitzer's brakes were not holding and the crew was trying to brace it with boxes. A racing jeep came down to tell of enemy tanks with infantry right behind. Wood told Alford, "March order. You won't be any good against infantry out on the road. Meet me the other side of Schönberg if I get there." Wood then turned to put the last of his three other pieces—it had gotten badly stuck—onto the road and down the cut into Schönberg.

Battery B was having trouble getting out. Small-arms fire was coming down from the woods to the north and east, a tank was rounding the bend to the south. The battery commander ordered the howitzers abandoned and the personnel piled into their trucks and followed Battery A.

Major Elliot Goldstein, acting executive, got a message through by phone to Division at 8:20 A.M.: "Service Battery and one firing battery overrun; unable to get howitzers into position. Tanks one mile from Schönberg coming up road from Bleialf."

Throttles wide, the artillery vehicles roared into the village, over the bridge and turned left on the St. Vith road, one jump ahead of the enemy.

But Eric Wood was still up at the Battery A position, wrestling, together with Sgt. Scannapico and his eleven men of the first section, to get that abominably mired No. 1 piece out. A good half hour elapsed before the grinding prime-mover and howitzer lurched at last in draft out into the highway, T/5 Kroll at the wheel, Scannapico beside him. The remainder of the section were in the big vehicle and as they rolled past him Lt. Wood swung himself into the back—the last man out.

As they rolled for Schönberg, Capt. Arthur C. Brown, commanding B Battery, with Lts. Thomas J. Wright (C Battery) and Euler and the B Battery party, swung in behind them. They had remained in their position to see that all personnel had gotten out (B Battery's pieces were abandoned).

Scannapico's keen eye caught the vision of an enemy tank ahead of them, bulking in the main street as they roared toward it down the steep hill into Schönberg. Wood shouted they would barge through and Kroll's foot pressed down. A hundred feet from the tank he slammed the brake at Wood's order. The officer and the section piled out, Pfc. Campagna with bazooka, the rest with carbines.

They blazed at the tank and it scuttled crab-like away, across the bridge and disappeared toward St. Vith. Wood and his men jumped in their vehicles again, and the truck and piece bumped over the cobbles, across the bridge behind the tank, swung west on the opposite side of the river, while enemy small-arms fire rippled on all sides. Brown's B Battery party followed.

The tank had seemingly disappeared. Scannapico, and Campagna with his bazooka, ran ahead as Wood slowed the vehicle up, to find where it was hiding. They found it, they reported, backed into an alleyway on the right side of the street, where they couldn't bring their bazookas to play.

Again the truck rolled. As it reached the alley mouth Scannapico once again jumped off, fired his carbine point-blank up the alley and as the truck rolled by Campagna let fly from it with his bazooka. The tank remained silent. But Scannapico, running to catch up, was wounded, staggered, was hit a second time by small-arms fire, and killed.

The section picked up speed, cleared the village, seemed to be in the open. It came over a little rise to find a Kraut medium tank barring the road, some seventy-five yards ahead, its cannon and machine guns trained at the truck.

On Wood's command the brakes went on and all jumped for cover an instant before the tank's artillery roared, demolishing the truck cab and mortally wounding Kroll, the driver. Wood and his men crouched in a ditch, near a group of 333d Field Artillery personnel whose truck the enemy tank had apparently smashed just before.

Kraut fire was coming down now from across the river on the left, Kraut infantry were firing from the trees bordering the meadow on the right, and more Krauts came pouring out of Schönberg toward them, while the tank blocked the road. It looked, says one of the group, as if a man couldn't run a yard without being shot to pieces. They were through.

But Eric Wood wasn't through. He dared the fire-swept field, ran unscathed into the woods to the north. The rest surrendered, together with the 333d Field Artillery people, an officer and seven men.

The B Battery party behind all this was caught in the streets of Schönberg. Capt. Brown and his men sought cover, but enemy riflemen opened up on them, burp guns sprayed them. Behind B Battery were about a hundred men of Service Battery, those who had gotten out from their fight and had been picked up by Lt. Wright, executive of C Battery. Burp guns sprayed the column and it disintegrated as the men sought cover. Many were captured; some got free. Of those captured, some sixty, including Wright and Capt. Brown, got away from their captors next day and made their way across country back into CCB, 9th Armored Division, lines to rejoin the 589th a few days later.

Incidentally, Lt. Wright had not been originally captured with the rest of C Battery because as battery executive he had been sent ahead of the battery to the new position.

It was nearly 10:00 o'clock that morning when the bedraggled 589th, its fire power now reduced from twelve guns to three (all that was left of Battery A) had shaken itself free from Schönberg. They had picked up the four operators of the forward switching central, who had stuck to their posts until shelled out. The column got into St. Vith that afternoon, where Service Battery, 590th Field Artillery Battalion, cut off from its own outfit—it had been driven from its billet at Heuem— was joined to it. And the 589th rolled to establish a roadblock to the north. As darkness fell the exhausted artillerymen were pulled into St. Vith to bivouac. Miles to the east, Eric Wood roamed the woods alone in the enemy's midst.

The 589th would seem, by this time, to have pretty much shot its bolt. As it turned out, like John Paul Jones it had "just begun to fight." For it was alerted by midnight, and got on the road in march order, the men dozing as best they could in the icy night, bound for an amazing finale.

Returning to the original 589th Field Artillery position, before dawn Puett's 2d Battalion, 423d Infantry, had made tenuous contact, soon broken, with Cannon Company, 422d Infantry, about 2,500 yards southeast, near Schlausenbach. The patrol accomplishing this discovered three German tanks on the Auw road. By 5:30 A.M. indications pointed to an armored attack forming.

By daybreak, about 7:00 A.M., the three tanks on the Auw road lumbered up. Puett's antitank guns and the M8s of his attached platoon from the 820th TD Battalion, took them under fire at three hundred yards range, got all three, two of them burning up. Four more tanks, with infantrymen riding them, moved up. Some or all of them were knocked out but still more were coming, weaving through their crippled brethren.

At the same time Kraut infantry attacked on the vulnerable left flank; tanks coming from the north were moving in there, too. Wire communication with Division had gone out at 6:45 and now the battalion radio was hit and smashed. Contact with the 422d on the right was lost. Puett decided to fall back on Schönberg. To him, never received, went a message from Division at this time to "defend" Schönberg (now being overrun from north and south). Patrols brought word of the capture of Schönberg and of the fracas with the retreating 589th Field Artillery. Kraut armor, they said, was bumper to bumper on the Schönberg road all the way from the Radscheid junction (Engineer Cutoff) north to the Our valley.

To Puett came an officer from Lt.Col. Lackey's 590th Field Artillery Battalion, in direct support of the 423d Infantry in positions near Hill 575 north of Radscheid, suggesting that the two battalions fall back together on the 423d's Schnee Eifel positions. They did; it was the only thing to do.

The 2d Battalion, 423d Infantry, was a smart unit. It had come through its baptism of fire in good shape and now that the daylight had come to the eerie woods in which it had been fumbling, now that the men had clashed with the Kraut armor and held it, they had really found themselves.

Puett accomplished a daylight withdrawal, one of the most difficult of battlefield maneuvers, in good order, supported by the 590th, down Skyline Drive, past the positions from which the artillerymen had pulled out, and over the Oberlascheid–Halenfeld trail through the top of the Alf ravine into his regiment's sector, contacting Col. Cavender between 10:30 and 11:00 in the morning.

During this withdrawal a detachment of some twenty men of F Company, cut off from their unit, started to infiltrate through the enemy lines. Pfc. Willard T. Roper, acting as lead scout, safely guided the party over the jumbled hills back across the Our and into the Bois de St. Vith. Dodging enemy parties all the way, the group got back into our lines after forty-eight hours of wandering without food or shelter.

Cavender, on Puett's arrival, at once directed him to make part of a perimeter defense, facing west and northwest, and by mid-afternoon the battalion was along the Schnee Eifel slopes, extending from a point eight hundred yards east of Buchet northeast into the Halenfelder Wald some 2,000 yards east of Oberlascheid. The 590th dropped trails in close rear of this position, and slightly west of the 3d Battalion command post. The artillery put part of its personnel into the perimeter close-in defense.

Puett's shift south was unknown to Division until 3:00 P.M., when Cavender's message reporting its arrival, timed 10:51 A.M., finally dribbled through the communications bottleneck, now terrific. Until then Gen. Jones had presumed the 2d Battalion, 423d, to be with the 422d Infantry in accordance with his message to Col. Descheneaux of the latter regiment, sent at 8:18 A.M.

THE 422D INFANTRY

For Descheneaux's regiment, now facing both north as well as east, the trap closed almost painlessly, with harassing artillery fire the principal annoyance. The second day, 17 December, was one of anxiety rather than battle. The German attack pushing down the Our valley and up from Auw into the artillery area and against Puett by-passed the 422d itself. And the drive from the south against the 423d up from Bleialf, which locked the iron ring as it reached Schönberg, was well to Descheneaux's rear.

The 2d Battalion, it will be remembered, had been moved from its pillbox positions to face northward, aligned generally along the Mertesberg heights from Schlausenbach on the left to Hill 636 in the Schnee Eifel.

To its left were L Company and Cannon Company, clinging to the slope between Hill 612 and Schlausenbach after their counterattack of the previous evening.

On its right, and still in the pillbox zone of the old German line, was the 1st Battalion, Companies C, B and A in order from north to south, C Company linked to the right of the 2d Battalion to form a V with its salient apex pointing northeast. On the right again was the 3d Battalion, also in its original positions.

Contact by patrol between the left of the 422d and the right of the 2d Battalion, 423d, was ruptured by the enemy's morning thrust from Auw, and as Puett fell back he left the 422d's western flank in the air. Of that much Descheneaux was certain.

In its hurried previous night move to get into position the 2d Battalion, 422d, had abandoned kitchens and duffel bags; there just wasn't any transportation. Col. Descheneaux, reporting this to Division at

9:30 A.M., stated he would attempt to feed from the kitchens of the other two battalions. "Estimate sufficient rations to last today," he added. "No reserve on hand. Out of communications with motor pool. Doubt their ability to leave bivouac. Almost complete unit load of ammunition on hand. Request immediate action to remedy above situation."

Descheneaux, of course, had no supporting artillery to call on now, with the elimination of the 589th. One gathers that at the time he knew nothing of the 589th's plight, for at 2:25 P.M. he told Division that while he was holding his present position he was "unable to contact artillery." And enemy artillery fire had for the moment cut contact with his 2d Battalion.

Worried now about the 1st Battalion, the 422d commander ordered the 3d Battalion, momentarily not pressed, to form a composite provisional rifle company which would reinforce it. This meant taking half each of I and K Companies, and reduced the 3d Battalion in effect to a one-company front supported by M Company (heavy weapons). Company L, it will be remembered, was in regimental reserve already committed. The enemy did not bother that part of the sector that afternoon, however. Later, this dilution of the 3d Battalion must have seriously affected its efficiency.

In the 1st Battalion part of D Company was organizing a defensive position to protect the rear of the sector. Capt. E. C. Roberts, Jr., company executive, from the slope of Hill 611 southwest of Schlausenbach (not to be confused with Hill 612, directly west) could see the Kraut influx from Bleialf moving up Skyline Drive.

"We had no weapon that could reach them," says Roberts.[7] "We fired a mortar shell with eight increments on it, but we never saw it come down . . . All the night of the 17th we watched to our rear at the artillery fire and our ack-ack firing at the buzz bombs, of which there were many."

While the seriousness of the situation could not have escaped the regimental commander and his staff, most of the men on the fighting line had as yet little knowledge of what was happening around them.

The noise of the fighting to the north, and to the south where their brother regiment, the 423d, was by now engaged in a brutal fight, drifted to them. Patrols had been cut off. The 2d Battalion, separated from their kitchens, tightened their belts, griped and went about their business in the drizzle and mist and soggy snow. That the armored forces were coming to the assistance of the Division had pretty much percolated all along the line. It was a comforting thought. The 1st

Battalion bagged a dozen Kraut prisoners, two of them officers, and learned that the enemy plans were to encircle and capture Schlausenbach.

Communications were bad, and growing worse. When the fitful connections were working, the backlog of messages swamped the operators. The Kraut radio was jamming all the time, too, making radio communication extremely slow.

About 11:00 o'clock communication between Cannon Company's perimeter on the left flank and the regiment was severed. Lt. Clarence A. Husterlid and two men with a walkie-talkie radio attempted to get through to restore communication but were mistaken by Antitank Company men for Krauts and fired on. Husterlid was seriously wounded.

Later Capt. E. Bruce Foster, Cannon Company commander, got through to the regimental command post, and was able to restore communication. From this point he directed fire of the company howitzers on several enemy convoys down the Auw road.

During the night, word from a forward observer came of a hostile concentration in the Auw woods and Cannon Company fire sparked a blaze in the timber, which resulted in a large explosion and burst of flame.

Definite word came from Division some time during the evening: "Supplies to be dropped vicinity (018868) Schlausenbach tonight." The coordinates pinpointed a patch of bare ground in the 3d Battalion area, directly south of the village in a saddle between Hill 611 and the edge of the Schlausenbacher Wald. This was sent from Division at 2:00 P.M. but reached the outfit much later. That was the best possible news, for by this time word of the encirclement was drifting throughout the regiment. Preparations to receive the drop were made.

At 4:10 P.M. Descheneaux had summed up his situation in a message received at St. Vith at 8:40 (which gives some idea of the communications jam):

"Third Battalion (less L Company) and composite companies in original position. They report no activity except enemy cleaning artillery at 035835 [down toward Gondenbrett between the boundaries of the 422d and 423d Infantry Regiments]. Only contact with 423d Infantry is by patrols. 1st Battalion is in original position except one platoon of C Company, withdrawn to close gap between 1st and 2d composition {sic} companies. 3d Battalion, attached to [1st Battalion] is astride the Ridge road vicinity of 035869. No activity reported. 2d Battalion is in position generally along Schlausenbach [word missing]. L Company plus 30 engineers [this would be the 3d Platoon of Company A, 81st Engineers] is at 1st Battalion command post."

Thus we see that the 422d by evening had in reality made some definite shifts, although occupying the same vicinity.

Its right was still anchored in the Siegfried, with the 1st Battalion reinforced by the first "composition" company milked from the 3d Battalion; that latter outfit, now cut down in reality to another "composition" company, was attached to the 1st. A platoon of C Company bridged the gap between the Siegfried position and the 2d Battalion, faced to the north along the high ground immediately in front of Schlausenbach. Inside the V, in the vicinity of Hill 636, a nose jutting from the Schnee Eifel towards Schlausenbach, L Company and the engineer platoon had been gathered.

So the second night came on the 422d Infantry, as red enemy flares went up in the west, north and east. Liaison with the 423d on the south was unsubstantial. Everyone knew that the brother regiment was hard-pressed; but it was holding tight. Shivering, hungry men waited and watched and hoped for an air drop which never materialized. Why it didn't occur we will take up later. It is not good reading.

THE 423D INFANTRY

The upper Alf Valley flamed before dawn 17 December. The 423d Infantry knew it was coming by 2:55 A.M., when Col. Cavender forwarded to Division the statement of a Kraut prisoner that Bleialf would be the target and that two battalions of the 293d Regiment, 10th Luftwaffe Field Division (the Germans at this period of the war were putting their excess flying personnel into ground-troop units), organized as a *Volksgrenadier* division, were at Weinsfeld, four miles southeast of Brandscheid, as reserve for the operation. Artillery and rocket launchers, the prisoner said, were established west of Weinsfeld.

Patrols found armor followed by infantry approaching Bleialf by 3:00 o'clock. At the same time increasingly heavy artillery fire or infiltrating Krauts had cut communication with the supporting 590th Field Artillery. Cavender urgently requested reinforcements and a liaison officer with radio, to link him with the artillery again. An hour later contact with the 424th Infantry on the right was lost. Rockets were blazing into the positions from the hills east of Brandscheid.

Bleialf was assaulted at 6:00 A.M. They cracked it from the railway tunnel, from Muhlenberg and from the Alferberg, ripping passage through the town, splitting Lt.Col. Nagle's task force. The 1st Platoon of B Company, 81st Engineers, which had relieved a platoon of Service Company, 423d Infantry, in Bleialf itself, was overrun. The rest of the engineer company was isolated on a nose north of the town.

Nagle's remaining elements—Service, Antitank, Cannon and Headquarters Companies—were driven back in some disorder up the valley towards Buchet, covered by the fire of Lt. Peter Dughi's platoon of Cannon Company, where they clung to the edge of the Niederlascheid plateau and the east slopes of the Alf. Some stragglers went all the way north to the artillery positions where they were rallied.

Bleialf gained, the enemy immediately pushed north, his main effort —tanks and infantry—rolling up the Schönberg road, a subsidiary effort moving along Skyline Drive. It was this main effort which, as has been related, overran Service Battery, 589th Field Artillery, drove A and B Batteries of that outfit from their second positions. By 8:30 A.M., as we know, it had met at Schönberg the German rush down the Our Valley, sealing the ring about the 422d and 423d Infantry Regiments in the Schnee Eifel.

This drive isolated B Troop, 18th Cavalry Squadron, in its perimeter in Winterscheid, once and for all from the 423d. It was ordered by radio to withdraw to Mützenich and set up flank security for the regiment. [8] We will later see what happened to it.

Cavender, his right flank smashed and rolled into the center rear of his position, adjusted his original center, the 1st Battalion. Company C was pulled from its pillbox positions facing east to extend the right of Company A, just south of Buchet, where it linked with Nagle's left. This brought the 423d's right into a tight arc across the nose of the Schnee Eifel, facing west, south and east.

Up Radscheid way the 590th Field Artillery, which finally withdrew with Puett's battalion to the regimental perimeter, was in the thick of things that morning. Lt.Col. Lackey had been ordered to displace to the vicinity of Schönberg by the Division Artillery commander early in the morning, but finding the Schönberg way blocked and learning of the enemy advance up the Bleialf–Schönberg road, notified the infantry of his intention to close with them and pulled out.

The battalion had been putting down heavy fire in support of the 423d; its last mission in this position was in response to a frantic call at 6:30 A.M. for "Bebe Daniels," code name for a close-in concentration.

The regimental command post of the 423d Infantry at Buchet was threatened by the attack from the rear as Nagle's remnants were forced back from Bleialf. Antitank Company by 7:38 A.M. was fighting practically in the midst of the medics of B Company, 331st Medical Battalion, just northwest of Buchet. The regimental defense platoon was in the fight. Cavender ordered this force to "dig in and fight." He told Division that when driven out he would pull his command post eastward to the 3d Battalion CP in the Siegfried Line.

By 9:00 o'clock the fog of war still hung thick over the rear of the 423d, but Cavender had gotten contact with the 590th Field Artillery and learned something—not all—of the situation. He confidently told Division[9] at 9:03 A.M.—a message that got through in twenty minutes, by the way, in sharp contrast to the two-hour delay of others—"Understand from 590th Field Artillery we have been ordered out. Will protect cut-off and try to tie in with Puett."

Puett, of course, was falling back on Cavender at that time, while Engineer Cutoff was already in enemy hands.

At 9:20 word came from Puett through the 590th, the gist of it contained in the 423d Infantry's S-3 journal.[10]

"General told Puett not to get cut off. We can get back to Lackey [590th Field Artillery] but no further. Division is pulling out. Capt. Statler has AT and CN stragglers at 590th."

A few of our planes were reported by the 3d Battalion at this time, enemy flak thick about them. No one knew just what was happening in the air, and regiment told battalion that it was out of communication with Division and could give no information. About noon four American fighters came in over the Halenfeld road, knocking out two Kraut planes starting to strafe it.

Up in the 3d Battalion sector at 8:30 A.M. a detachment of three guns and some thirty men of Cannon Company, driven back from Bleialf, arrived with one officer. Lt.Col. Klinck turned them over to the artillery liaison officer, Capt. Conroy, who put them in all-around defense of the command post.

With the arrival of Puett's 2d Battalion the situation looked better. It sealed that gaping hole north of Buchet. The 3d Battalion was in good shape, contact with the 422d was close, and the 1st Battalion on the southern nose was holding well. Cavender, reporting the news to Division at 10:51, added: "Will hold perimeter. Drop ammunition, food and medical supplies until route open. We have no artillery."

The last sentence is explainable by the probability that the presence of Lackey's 590th Field Artillery Battalion with Puett's force was not yet established. They came in just about this time. This message did not reach Division until 2:25 P.M.

Troop B, 18th Cavalry, at 1:30 P.M. reported itself at Mützenich, nearly two miles north of Winterscheid, with the 106th Reconnaissance Troop (attached to 424th Infantry), adding "will await orders." Forty-five minutes later the cavalry commander requested permission to proceed to Schönberg and St. Vith. "Cannot reach your CP," he reported.

Cavender, at 3:00 o'clock, told him: "Schönberg situation is unknown. If unable to reach me, act on your own initiative—the Commanding General directs you save all transportation possible."

Division, answering the appeal for an air drop, at 2:35 P.M. asked Cavender for his most essential ammunition needs and the place he wanted it dropped. He called for 81mm mortar, 105mm howitzer shells (Lackey was in, of course), .30 caliber for his machine guns and riflemen, bazooka rounds and hand grenades, to be dropped in a bare patch some eight hundred yards east of Halenfeld.[11]

By 4:00 o'clock the fury of the enemy attack had diminished. The enemy objective—encirclement—had been attained. He was putting his efforts elsewhere. In the 423d area there was time to draw breath, consolidate. To that time the total casualties were 225—approximately 25 each in the battalions, and 150 killed, wounded and missing in the special units which had taken that rocking blow at Bleialf. Still more encouraging had been the belated receipt shortly before 3:00 P.M. of the Division's message to both the 422d and 423d:

"Expect to clear out area west of you this afternoon with reinforcements. Withdraw from present positions if they become untenable. Save all transportation possible."[12]

The regiment was tightened up in a very restricted area. Cavender had pulled his command post back to his 3d Battalion. Anchored to the east in the Siegfried Line, its westward elements were snugged into the high ground rising from the Alf Valley slopes, its southern nose firmly on Hill 570 behind Buchet, both positions with good fields of fire. The 590th Field Artillery still had some ammunition; not much, but all it could take with it from the old positions. And the 422d Infantry to the north was holding firm. Fortunately the 423d's ammunition train had gotten back from St. Vith the night before with a unit load. Only a coordinated attack with strong artillery support could overrun them now, it seemed. Tightening their belts, counting their ammunition, the 423d Infantry waited—waited for the airdrop that never came, waited for that armored counterattack which they hoped would free them.

One gets the impression of confusion about the command post, but an underlying optimism among the regiment at large. No one seemed to have any complete grasp of the situation but all hoped for the best.

The fortunes of war swung more heavily that day against the regiment's two attached units, B Troop, 18th Cavalry Squadron, and B Company, 81st Engineers, both of whom had been cut off during the morning's fighting.

According to the official account of Capt. William J. Hynes, commanding the engineers, B Company, less the 1st Platoon which had been overrun in Bleialf (one squad got back to the infantry), held off the first wave of enemy infantry from their dug-in positions on the heights above the village. They were, however, speedily cut off from the rest of Nagle's task force on their left.

The enemy effort driving north from the railway tunnel also severed their connection with Troop B, 18th Cavalry, on their right, but an armored car got through about noon[13] and Hynes, whose own radio had gone wacky, told the cavalry car to inform the 423d Infantry that he could hold out indefinitely if he could get more ammunition.

Company B clung to its position until 3:00 P.M., while the enemy firing line was building up on its front some seven hundred yards away. Then, their own machine-gun ammunition exhausted, and no more forthcoming, a Kraut assault overran the 2d Platoon and two of its squads surrendered. Hynes, who states he had already gotten word from the cavalry over a walkie-talkie radio left by the armored car, that the troop was withdrawing, now began to fall back to the north, pulling out a squad at a time.

In the wooded hills they found momentary respite. The depleted company—Hynes had three officers and sixty-four men left of his original 169—wandered for an entire day, aiming for Schönberg, which they skirted late on 18 December. Then, blocked on all sides, without sleep for forty-eight hours and with but one meal of C ration during that time, the company surrendered.

The cavalry in its Winterscheid defensive perimeter had been comparatively unmolested. During the night and next morning—and they are emphatic about this—no contact had been made with the engineers on their left.[14] One is at a loss to reconcile the two accounts.

When it pulled out for Mützenich on regimental order[15] at 10:00 A.M. to set up flank security, the troop was in pretty good shape, except for machine guns and mortars of the 1st Platoon, lost during the previous day's fighting.

Mützenich, one and a half miles north of Winterscheid and the same distance northwest of Bleialf, is one of the "sugar-bowl" villages of the region, commanding only the approach from the east. Here the outfit was joined by the remnants of the 106th Reconnaissance Troop (attached to the 424th Infantry), driven out of Grosslangenfeld by the southern irruption. Capt. Million piled in with three other officers, forty-eight men and fourteen vehicles, all that he had been able to extricate. The two forces joined in the defense.

Captain Robert G. Fossland, commanding B Troop, found the Germans moving in force up the Bleialf–Schönberg road out of range of his guns about 2:00 P.M. At the same time an enemy enlisted man from these columns came towards Mützenich under a flag of truce, making contact with Lt. Elmo J. Johnston, 3d Platoon commander. In excellent English he proposed the cavalrymen surrender. The offer refused, he rejoined the enemy.

Three armored cars sent up north to reconnoiter drew heavy mortar fire. Fossland by radio reported to the 423d that Mützenich was undesirable for delaying action, and was told to rejoin in the Buchet–Halenfeld vicinity. This, of course, he could not do with the enemy in force between him and the infantry. Then it was that Fossland, as already related, suggested he fall back via Schönberg and St. Vith and Cavender understandingly left him free, warning him the Schönberg situation was an unknown quantity.

Moving in order 3d, 1st, Headquarters, and 2d Platoons, and trailed by remnants of the 106th Reconnaissance Troop, B Troop started north at 3:00 o'clock in the afternoon. Passing cautiously over the northern secondary road the head of the column reached the junction with the Bleialf–Schönberg road, just north of the 589th Field Artillery positions of the morning, and pushed on. The 1st Platoon, second element in the column, had cleared the junction when a jeep came cutting into the convoy, a jeep filled with armed Krauts!

A 1st Platoon armored car cut loose with a 37mm and the intruder rolled into the ditch in a mess of tangled wreckage and dead bodies.

Just south of Schönberg, Fossland halted the convoy while the leading platoon, the 3d, went in to reconnoiter. Dusk was falling. Three armored cars—Lt. Johnston's the first—followed by the platoon's six jeeps, entered Schönberg, passed unmolested over the Our bridge and turned left toward St. Vith.

Drawn up facing westward was standing a seemingly endless column of American six-by-six cargo trucks, filled with troops. They were Germans; prisoners going to the rear, was the cavalrymen's first reaction. Then it was seen that the entrucked men were armed![16]

Johnston, screaming a warning back to the troop over his radio, sent his car careening down the left of the column, followed by the other two, all three vehicles blazing canister into the trucks as they raked by. Fossland, listening, heard the crackle of fire, heard Sgt. James R. Hartsock, in the second car, announce that he was struck, and the radio went dead.

How far Johnston got will never be definitely known. Somewhere beween Schönberg and Heuem his car was disabled. He was seriously wounded and captured, as was his radio operator; his gunner was killed. Hartsock's car was struck, he and his crew captured.

Sergeant D. L. Rubendall, following in the third armored car, was halted when a Mark IV tank lumbered out of a side road into his path. Rubendall slammed AP shells into the tank, setting the rear ablaze. Its 75 was swinging toward him. Rubendall tried to hurl hand grenades into the open tank turret, then empty shell casings, until his crew got clear. Then he legged it back toward the jeeps.

The jeeps had gotten part of the way behind them, except for the last one, which was able to turn and get back to the troop. But by now the aroused enemy was striking back. The jeep crews scattered, some of them killed, most of them captured. Rubendall and four other men got clear and after wandering over the countryside fell in with the 275th Armored Field Artillery Battalion.

As soon as Captain Fossland heard the fire fight in Schönberg he got the rest of his troop turned around and started back, meeting another American jeep filled with German soldiers carrying bazookas. They swerved off into a woods road and safety. The column, turning west, reached the village of Amelscheid. Here while chains were put on—the road was very muddy—they took stock.

Fossland got through by radio to the 423d Infantry, reported the Schönberg incident. He was told, "St. Vith is in enemy hands. Make your own decision and notify us."[17]

After a conference with Million of the 106th Reconnaissance Troop it was decided to park and destroy vehicles and heavy weapons and try to infiltrate into the American lines. The demolition completed, the troop split up in groups of three or four, aiming at Vielsalm. Fossland lost sight of Million and his men shortly after this.

Some of them made it, others were captured. Captain Fossland and a handful of his men got to Breitfeld, southeast of St. Vith, on the morning of 19 December. There were some troops there—but the fugitives were wary until they heard someone shout in English:

"Where in hell is your helmet, Roy?"

Waving a white undershirt Fossland advanced, to be covered by the Breitfeld men, equally wary of a ruse. Finally identified, they were taken in by the 482d AAA Battalion of CCB, 9th Armored Division.

And while all this was going on Master Sgt. John L. Hall, regimental supply sergeant, was carrying on a war of his own, trying to get through with the food he knew his regiment needed. Hall had been back at St. Vith drawing rations. His convoy got up to Schönberg as the Krauts moved in.

Small-arms fire raked the truck column. Hall got out, grabbed a machine gun and installed himself in a house where he fought it out with the enemy skirmishers until the tanks came rumbling in. Captured, Hall and Pvt. Edgar M. Decker broke away from a careless guard, thumbed a ride to St. Vith, and there the pair obtained additional trucks and rations and started back, this time with an escort of MPs.

The effort, of course, was fruitless. They got up toward Heuem only to meet the German tanks coming down the road. The trucks were destroyed but once more Hall and Decker got away. Back at St. Vith they waited with more rations for a road which would never open.

THE 424TH COMBAT TEAM

There was to be no respite on the Pronsfeld–St. Vith axis that second day, as Manteuffel's right-flank elements pressed in for the kill around the southern nose of the Schnee Eifel. The Winterspelt perimeter on Reid's left flank had been infiltrated during the night and before dawn of 17 December the enemy had an entire company of infantry in the town itself and was dislocating the position. The 1st Battalion, 424th Infantry, and C Company, 81st Engineers, were being pried out to the west, uncovering the Winterspelt–Steinebrück–St. Vith road.

Part of the battalion was smacked back in some confusion, all the way to the east bank of the Our, where it dug in to protect the Steinebrück bridge. Lt. Slutsky, executive of B Company, gathered here some 200-odd men of all units.[18]

As first light broke advance elements of CCB, 9th Armored Division, came rolling over the bridge and through this bridgehead force.

The major portion of the 1st Battalion, driven out of Winterspelt, was being forced up the slopes of the Our Berg.

Pressure on the 3d Battalion in the center was not so great, however, that morning. With I Company outposting its left flank, generally in front of the 591st Field Artillery positions, and L and K Companies in their original dispositions, the battalion held firm.

On the right an enemy assault jumping off from the Grosskampenberg–Heckhuscheid road, hit the 2d Battalion, smacking G Company on the nose, behind a heavy artillery barrage. All three of the rifle companies managed to hold, together with B Company, 112th Infantry, the last element on the right flank, a mile north of Lützkampen.

Here it was that Pfc. Henry S. Litchfield (later Tech.Sgt.) of G Company, rallied his squad when his leader was wounded, found the Krauts coming in from the rear. His BAR man fell wounded and Litchfield, grabbing the piece, personally got ten of the enemy, smashing that particular attack.

Private First Class Harry V. Arvannis, a mortar gunner, propped up his damaged weapon by holding it between his knees while he grasped the barrel with both hands, and lobbed over a shell which wiped out eight of twelve Germans charging his position. Arvannis got two more with his pistol, and while a comrade killed another, he slammed the pistol in the face of the last man, knocking him over.

That sort of fighting continued in the 2d Battalion sector most of the day, in a series of small but violent thrusts and as violent local counter-attacks by the defenders.

Colonel Reid, naturally anxious about his left, informed Division at 7:00 A.M. of the situation and asked specific information on CCB, 9th Armored Division, now on the road down. Reid had sent a guide for it to Steinebrück. It was imperative, Reid told Division, that CCB launch its counterattack "with all possible speed after arrival at Steinebrück." One hour later Reid reported Winterspelt definitely occupied by the enemy, but his other battalion positions unchanged.

It was evident to the regimental commander that the left flank must be firmly refused to the north and anchored down if possible. Looking over the situation, he grabbed Lt. Jarrett M. Huddleston, Jr., S-2 of the 1st Battalion (we've heard of him before and will hear of him again) to do the job. To him he fed piecemeal a company here and a platoon there—"robbing Peter to pay Paul," is the way Reid expresses it. This unofficial "Task Force Huddleston" began to peg down that gap from Auel on the river bank generally along Winterspelter Creek. Reid makes it plain that young Huddleston was in command, regardless of rank of his reinforcement commanders.

Both CCB, 9th Armored Division, and Division Artillery were informed at once of the Winterspelt situation and the village was taken under fire by what supporting artillery could be brought in. The 591st Field Artillery, in direct support, was hammering it already.

By 11:00 o'clock the Winterspelt enemy got into Elcherath and Service Company's area. After a short fight the Service Company pulled out, crossing the Our at Hemmeres, where it left a number of vehicles. Incidentally, the regimental colors, never unpacked, were left behind with the rest of the regimental baggage.

By this time the advance elements of CCB, 9th Armored Division, clearing Steinebrück, had made contact with the enemy on the highway just south of the river.

Reid, with the armor coming up on his left, felt somewhat relieved. His center and right were holding, and south of them, Division told him at 11:00 o'clock, the 112th Infantry, too, was holding fast. The situation was sticky, at best. He could hear the 9th Armored going into action to the north, knew that they were to counterattack toward Winterspelt. He had no details on their progress and his chewed-up 1st Battalion was firmly clinging now to the Our Berg slopes.

The 591st Field Artillery had a busy day, with ammunition the big question mark. Just before Winterspelt fell three trucks managed to get back to Elcherath for ammunition left by the 424th's Cannon Company, but with the Winterspelt road closed the only means of getting ammunition from Service Battery at Burg-Reuland was across country, by jeep. One truckload of howitzer ammunition was hauled in by Pvt. Bill T. Ervin, of B Battery, who ran a Kraut gantlet safely, though his truck was riddled by bullets.

Reid, reporting again to Division at 11:40 A.M., announced his ability to stick to his present position, although he relayed a report from one of the artillery liaison planes that Kraut armor was moving up the Habscheid–Winterspelt road, an estimated thirty minutes' distance from the latter place. This message did not reach Division until 5:30 P.M., and in the meantime Gen. Jones at 3:25 P.M.—with the enemy storming down the Our Valley toward St. Vith and two of his regiments already surrounded—had ordered the 424th to withdraw west of the Our "on line: Stupbach–Auel." Actually, the northern thrust was only four miles from Winterspelt. It was now within the bounds of possibility that another double envelopment would get both the 424th and CCB, 9th Armored, unless they fell back.

The new position was on the steep west bank of the Our, along the Hasenknopf and Our Berg hill masses, split by the Ulf river draining into the Our at Weweler.

Reid planned his withdrawal by echelon under cover of darkness, pulling out his center battalion first. The trickiest part of this maneuver was to get the 591st Field Artillery Battalion's two forward batteries, A and B, away from their Heckhalenfeld position.

The only exit, since the northern route via Winterspelt was in enemy hands, was directly toward the Kraut infantry who had been surging all day against G Company, south of Hill 569. The enemy was less than three hundred yards from the junction of this southern route with the Steffeshausen–Burg-Reuland road over the Stein-Kopf.

At all costs the infantry must hold.

They did, and while C Battery, back at Steffeshausen, took over the battalion missions, Batteries A and B displaced.

The howitzers trundled toward the front, with sporadic Screaming Meemies plastering the snowy slopes of the hill to the west and the crackle of small arms and machine guns rising close from the woods to the east. They made the sharp turn and got away across the ridge into Steffeshausen, thence across the river and west to Gruflange. Arriving near midnight Batteries A and B went into position and then C Battery pulled from its Steffeshausen gun pits to join them. One howitzer got into trouble and had to be abandoned, but next day the battery retrieved it safely.

This bit of leap-frogging in progress, Reid's 3d Battalion fell back, beginning at 7:00 P.M., across country over the Stein-Kopf to take position, after an all night march, along the river from Bracht to Burg-Reuland along the Preisberg nose of the Hasenknopf. The 2d Battalion moved out its vehicles by road, its rifle companies going across country, making use of a Bailey bridge near Weidig, to cross the river and dig in along the Our Berg south of Burg-Reuland. The 1st Battalion got away at the same time, to the Hasenknopf slopes in front of Bracht.

All in all, the 424th Combat Team, it seems, put up a pretty good exhibition of infantry-artillery teamwork during that bitter night of 17-18 December. There was, however, some confusion in the 1st Battalion.

Company C, 81st Engineers, getting back on foot about 9:00 o'clock (its vehicles were back at Bracht), moved northwest, to get into Elcherath in the night. Service Company, 424th Infantry, had been driven out of Elcherath that morning, but the enemy had in turn been pushed out by CCB, 9th Armored Division. CCB had then withdrawn, as we shall see. So the engineers bivouacked in deserted Elcherath that night, between the lines.

Odds and Ends

The faithful medics of the 331st Medical Battalion got it coming and going on 17 December. Company A, which had fallen back to Heuem from Andler when the enemy overran Auw, was pulled into St. Vith during the afternoon ahead of the Our Valley onrush. Here it established a clearing station in place of D Company, which had been moved back to Vielsalm. It also provided a battalion aid post to Riggs' engineer task force defending the town. Company B was sealed off, with the 423d Infantry.

Company C at Steinebrück was under heavy enemy shellfire. It was pulled back to Breitfeld on the St. Vith road during the dark early morning hours, and later to St. Vith itself. The company maintained contact with its supported regiment, the 424th, and carried on evacuation of wounded from battalion aid stations through continuous enemy interdiction fire on the roads. Departure of the 42d Field Hospital unit at St. Vith for Vielsalm further complicated the medics' task as the day went on, for now it was necessary to handle all non-transportable cases at the clearing station.

ARMOR ON THE WINTERSPELT ROAD

Brigadier General William M. Hoge's CCB, 9th Armored Division, rolled confidently to its baptism of fire that morning of 17 December, across the bridge at Steinebrück into Germany to meet the German rush up from Winterspelt.[19]

Originally in VIII Corps reserve, prepared to counterattack in the old 2d Infantry Division sector now taken over by the 106th, CCB of the 9th Armored was fairly familiar with the terrain.

At Gen. Jones' command post in the welter of confusion of that first day the only definite information he could pass to Hoge was that Auw had been taken. There was, perhaps naturally, but little information on the magnitude or objectives of the German attack.[20] CCB, 9th Armored, Jones told Hoge, would proceed to Manderfeld to restore the line. Later it was proposed he move to St. Vith, thence east on Schönberg.

This order, as we know, was later rescinded by Jones when informed that CCB, 7th Armored Division, was also at his orders and would arrive in the St. Vith area at 7:00 A.M., 17 December.

Hoge, returning from the CP, got his command rolling shortly after midnight, arriving in St. Vith shortly after daybreak. Here he received the mission to take the high ground south of the Our at Steinebrück, prepared to attack Winterspelt on Division order.

Speculation on what would have happened had CCB, 9th Armored, gone on its original mission brings one to the conclusion that the situation would not have been changed very much. Doubtless the enemy attack down the Our Valley would have been thwarted for the moment. Sepp Dietrich's Sixth SS Panzer Army might have been delayed more seriously than it actually was. On the other hand, Manteuffel's 62d *Volksgrenadier* and 116th Panzer Divisions developing up through Winterspelt had already knocked the 1st Battalion, 424th Infantry, out of position and, without the arrival of CCB, 9th Armored, at Steinebrück, would have had an open road to St. Vith. One comes right back to the point that the non-arrival of CCB, 7th Armored Division, at 7:00 A.M. that morning was the crux of the situation.

Hoge's advance guard met the enemy just south of Steinebrück, bucking numerous stragglers on the way.[21] The 27th Armored Infantry Battalion with a platoon of medium tanks, supported by the fire of the 16th Armored Field Artillery Battalion, and by Corps artillery, attacked south up the Brüssel Berg at noon. By 3:30 P.M. the Krauts in Elcherath had been driven out and the armored troops were holding that vicinity.

Preparations were made for another assault—on Winterspelt, with the 14th Tank Battalion coming through the opening made by the 27th Armored Infantry Battalion, but the attack was called off by Division order.

The armor, Perrin told Hoge, was to withdraw to defensive positions that night west of the Our, on the right of the 424th Infantry at Auel, up north to Weppeler.

The enemy, for the time being rocked back on the Winterspelt road, apparently did not put much pressure on the withdrawing armor of Hoge; he was still pressing the 424th Infantry to the south to get elbow room. So CCB, 9th Armored Division, as night fell found itself back across the river, withdrawing by echelon.

It was a long line for Hoge to hold—three miles of winding river bank. The 27th Armored Infantry (less Company A), anchored its center on the pear-shaped knob of Hill 470 stretched from Weppeler to Steinebrück, where Troop D, 89th Cavalry, held a small sector. Scattered elements of the 1st Battalion, 424th Infantry, rallied by the 9th Armored, temporarily continued the line to the south where Company A, 27th Armored Infantry, held across the river from Auel, contacting the right of the 424th.

Hoge's force was itself split. At Gen. Jones' order he had sent two companies of the 14th Tank Battalion with Company A, 811th TD Battalion and a detachment of Battery B, 482d AAA Battalion, up north when he came in to attempt to stop the northern rush to St. Vith. This task force got up somewhere in the neighborhood of Wallerode, astride the Amblève–St. Vith highway, messing up one of the spearheads of the 1st SS Panzer Division which they met just north of St. Vith, but had no influence on the Kraut drive eastward from Schönberg. It would hold out up there until relieved by the 7th Armored Division after dark next day.

Further embarrassment to Hoge's operations was caused during the day by the northern drive which hit his supply trains at Ligneuville, capturing the service units of the 27th Armored Infantry and the 16th Armored Field Artillery Battalions.

NOTES TO CHAPTER 5

[1] Not identified; may be Honsfeld. The air drop was in fact along the axis Eupen–Monschau.

[2] Much has been made and always will be made of this tide of American soldiers crowding the roads in pell-mell rout. There is no doubt in the author's mind that a portion of the panic-stricken mob must have consisted of 106th Division personnel. The area contained, however, many Corps installations and units, both service and combat, most of the latter being artillery. These began moving westward, either with or without orders. In addition, service trains of the 106th Division, its attached units and corps units, bound to dumps to obtain supplies of ammunition and rations, were west-bound on their lawful missions on 16, 17 and 18 December. Little impetus would be necessary to spread panic amidst such heterogeneous traffic under the conditions.

[3] Lt.Col. John F. DeV. Patrick, commanding 820th TD Battalion, to the author, 7 February 1947.

[4] *Ibid.*

[5] These may have been a platoon of the 811th TD Battalion, of CCB, 9th Armored Division which was in the vicinity. Col. Patrick of the 820th TD Battalion states his platoon (Callan's) did not withdraw until nightfall; German tanks later overran the spot. Patrick also notes the presence in the vicinity of a battery of 4.5-inch guns, which he states withdrew as the action began.

[6] Colonel Craig remembers seeing this piece when he inspected the terrain 9 February 1945. However, Major Parker is under the impression that this piece was recovered in time to be emplaced in the next position; that B Battery had four pieces in the second position.

[7] Letter to the author, 18 November 1946.

[8] Troop B narrative, in possession of 106th Infantry Division Association.

[9] Message book in possession of 106th Infantry Division Association.

[10] In possession of 106th Infantry Division Association.

[11] Division G-3 Journal notes at 1:45 P.M., message No. 436: "To 423d Infantry—supplies will be dropped vicinity Buchet (992838) tonight." The messages quoted above are to be found in 423d Infantry S-3 journal and message book carbons in possession of 106th Infantry Division Association. The basic point is that both Division and regiment expected an air drop would be made.

[12] G-3 journal notes this "out" at 0945 (9:45 A.M.). The message as received (now in possession of 106th Infantry Division Association), bears Division message center notation indicating time filed of 1240 (12:40 P.M.), signature time 0944 (9:44 A.M.), with remark that it was sent by radio. Time of receipt is not noted, and record is lacking from 423d Infantry S-3 journal. It must have been received prior to the 423d Infantry's message to Troop B, 18th Cavalry, mentioning the Division Commander's directive to "save all transportation possible."

[13] Troop B's official narrative flatly refutes Hynes' story of contact at any time.

[14] "The 423d Infantry had told the cavalrymen that engineers of the 81st Engineer Combat Battalion were in the Bleialf vicinity, but constant searching patrols failed to make

contact with these engineers, and the CP coordinates were visited and found vacant. Contact was not made . . . contact to the left (north) again failed during the morning . . ." (Troop B narrative, in possession of 106th Infantry Division Association.)

15 *Ibid.* There is no record of this order in the fragmentary 423d Infantry S-3 journal and messages in possession of the 106th Infantry Division Association.

16 In all probability this was the 150th Panzer Brigade.

17 No record of this exchange of communication is extant. There would be no reason for the 423d at this time—before 5:30 P.M.—to believe that St. Vith had been captured. Capt. Fossland is definite about the conversation.

18 Letter, Pfc. Clinton H. Wilber, B Company, 424th Infantry, to Secretary, 106th Infantry Division Association, 21 September 1946.

19 CCB, 9th Armored Division, consisted of the following elements:
    27th Armored Infantry Battalion
    14th Tank Battalion (Medium)
    16th Armored Field Artillery Battalion
    D Troop, 89th Cavalry Reconnaissance Squadron (with a platoon each of assault guns and light tanks from E Troop and F Company)
    B Company, 9th Armored Engineer Battalion
    B Company, 2d Armored Medical Battalion
    C Company, 131st Maintenance Battalion
    B Battery, 482d AAA Battalion (SP)
    A Company, 811th TD Battalion (SP)
    Detachment 489th Ambulance Company

20 General Hoge to the author, 19 December 1946.

21 *Ibid.*

Chapter 6: The Third Day

The 1st SS Panzer Division was romping north of St. Vith, probing westward and southwestward—Amblève, Born, through the gap at Kaiserbaracke between the Wolfsbusch and the Bois de Born towards Poteau, down the Ligneuville–St. Vith highway. Behind it came the 12th SS Panzer, pushed off balance from its repelled thrust to Büllingen.

Treading on their toes, their vehicles packed bumper to bumper on the roads from Losheim, more of Sepp Dietrich's Sixth SS Panzer Army was striving for an opening. The 2d and 9th SS Panzer Divisions of the blocked-off II Panzer Corps were shoving. The Our Valley road was jammed with the 150th Panzer Brigade. The 18th *Volksgrenadiers* were buzzing around the north and rear of the 422d Infantry, were clearing up through the Büllingen Forest.

From Prüm and Pronsfeld, around the southern nose of the Schnee Eifel the tide of Manteuffel's Fifth Panzer Army's right was swirling. The 62d *Volksgrenadier* and 116th Panzer Divisions, and the *Führer* Escort Brigade, were striking across the Our in the 28th Infantry Division's area, had licked northward to seal off the 423d Infantry Regiment by the drive from Bleialf to Schönberg, were pressing close beyond Winterspelt. Farther south the going was good for the Fifth Panzer Army.

All of which, statistically expressed, meant that on the north the Nazi advance elements raced some fifteen miles through the original lines of the 99th Infantry Division and the 14th Cavalry Group to positions six miles northwest and in rear of St. Vith. On the south they had penetrated through the 28th Infantry Division positions some eleven miles, to arrive fifteen miles southwest and in rear of St. Vith.

The situation of the 106th Infantry Division was already beginning to resemble a peninsula lapped on both sides by angry waters; the isolated Schnee Eifel elements of the Division an islet at its tip, around which foamed the rising tide.

But until and unless St. Vith was taken, the hammer blow of the Sixth SS Panzer Army could not fall. Sepp Dietrich, now thirty-six hours behind his schedule, bit his fingernails in rage. His paratroopers were down behind the *verdammte Amerikaner,* but his terrorists of the 150th Panzer Brigade, in U. S. uniform, were blocked from the slashing drive through tackle which would bring them behind that Büllingen nose up north. He was like a fighter jabbing with his left while trying to get his right arm free from a clinch.

St. Vith must fall today—18 December.

Thus the enemy situation.

In St. Vith itself the 106th Infantry Division command post hummed all through the night and the early morning hours of 18 December, while the thin line of defenders in the Prümerberg a mile to the east hung on.

General Jones' problem was simple in expression, difficult in execution. The VIII Corps had ordered him to hold. His left flank was being rolled in, his right flank penetrated, his two center regiments surrounded. With the aid of CCB, 9th Armored Division, the right-flank situation was in process of stabilization along the Our. CCB, 7th Armored, was bolstering the defense of St. Vith proper. The rest of the 7th Armored Division, he knew, was coming in on his left. It might, if its flank were protected and the line St. Vith–Born could be held, restore the entire situation to the north.

The most pressing element of the problem was to get the 422d and 423d Infantry Regiments out of their encirclement. To do that the enemy in the immediate front, along the axis St. Vith–Schönberg, must be destroyed. If the two regiments could assist in this destruction and at the same time get out of their predicament, so much the better. So, to the 423d and 424th went this message at 2:15 A.M., by radio:

"Panzer regimental combat team on Eimerscheid–Schönberg–St. Vith road, head near St. Vith. Your[1] mission is to destroy by fire from dug-in positions south of Schönberg–St. Vith road. Ammunition, food and water will be dropped. When mission accomplished, move to area St. Vith–Wallerode–Weppeler, organize and move to west."

A basic criticism of this order is that it was sent to both regiments as separate units held under Division control, although they were cut off from all but uncertain radio contact. Without becoming too much of a Monday-morning quarterback, this writer believes that the order should have designated a common commander for what was a sizable task force (six battalions of infantry and a battalion of field artillery). Col. Cavender was the senior officer present in the Schnee Eifel.

Throughout the remainder of the action, however, until communication was at last severed, Division dealt with both infantry regiments as separate units.[2]

At 2.00 A.M. the Division Artillery command post was pulled out of St. Vith, to be established somewhere to the west, either at Poteau or at Vielsalm. Brig.Gen. McMahon, Division Artillery Commander, stayed with Division at St. Vith. The remnants of the 589th and the 592d Battalions, now somewhere west of Sart-lez-St.Vith, were to be gathered up by Col. Malin Craig, Jr., artillery executive officer, and established in new positions in support of St. Vith. Later on in the day the Division command post would also withdraw, it was decided, to Vielsalm, nine miles to the west.

It was 4:35 A.M. when Division requested First Army Air Section (IX TAC) to drop a specified amount of small-arms, machine-gun and bazooka ammunition at the designated points for each regiment (changed in the case of the 422d to a point in the Schlausenbacher Wald one mile southeast of the village on a woods road).

There is no record of the original call for an air drop of food and ammunition in the G-3 journal. We know it was done, and that Division expected it to come during the night.[3]

When the 423d Infantry's request for specified amounts of ammunition and for medical supplies, delayed in teletype transmission for nearly twelve hours, came in, these were also relayed to IX TAC, at 5:50 and 6:20 A.M. The 423d Infantry was told to display a fifty-foot-square orange panel at the drop point.

In the meantime there was trouble with the 14th Cavalry Group which at midnight had attempted to beg off its mission to retake Born. At 4:20 A.M. word came from Division rear echelon at Vielsalm that the group had reported in there. Its orders to retake Born and protect the left flank of the 7th Armored Division were at once reiterated. To assist the cavalrymen in getting back through the tangle of traffic VIII Corps was asked and granted priority to the cavalry east-bound on roads, over everything but the 7th Armored Division.

VIII Corps Artillery was assisting things along the Schönberg road, in response to Division's call, by putting eighty rounds of 155mm interdiction fire per hour along it from Setz to Schönberg.

By 8:25 A.M. the 14th Cavalry Group had reported enemy at Recht and Poteau, and things were warming up in front of St. Vith, where Riggs' force was becoming heavily engaged. CCB, 7th Armored, and CCB, 9th Armored, were holding from north of St. Vith to Auel, the 424th Infantry was stretched generally south of that. The 112th Infantry of the 28th Division was floating in air somewhere on the south, in the vicinity of Weiswampach. All, it seemed, were looking over their shoulder. One cannot blame them.

As afternoon drew on the situation became gloomier. The enemy on the north was gaining ground, the artillery Headquarters Battery was clawed at Poteau, the attacks on St. Vith became heavier. Back at Vielsalm in the rear echelon G-4 was being swamped with requests for rations, ammunition and gasoline.

The armored elements and the cavalry group were in desperate need of fuel. G-4 was told to provide twenty thousand gallons. He was also called on to produce two thousand rounds of 76mm armor-piercing shell for the armored outfits and two thousand rounds of 105mm for the divisional howitzers. The St. Vith defenders were calling for twelve truckloads of small-arms ammunition.

And, Division told G-4 at 2:42 P.M., "Continue to drop ammunition, food and medical supplies to 422d and 423d Regiments."

Continue? The drop hadn't started.

Nevertheless, since Division didn't know that, it sent word again to the 423d Infantry (communication with 422d was out) that an air drop was coming—next day, this time—along the path they were to take in moving on Schönberg. "You will advise 422d Infantry," the message added.

The Division command post evacuated St. Vith, opening at Vielsalm at 6:00 P.M.

But St. Vith did not fall.

ACTION AT POTEAU

Poteau, a tiny hamlet on the St. Vith–Vielsalm highway, five miles west of the former and exactly halfway between the two towns, will be long remembered by the 106th and the 14th Cavalry Group. The 7th Armored Division also has some memories of Poteau, but theirs is another story.

Poteau flared early on the morning of 18 December as the Germans, driving down from the northeast, tangled with the traffic flow jamming the highway linking St. Vith with the west. So far as the 106th Infantry Division is concerned, the story of Poteau is a story of cavalry, field artillery and headquarters units in two independent meeting engagements in the foggy dawn.

Here, the night before, had come the command post of the battered 14th Cavalry Group, and here in the pre-dawn fog and blackout Lt.Col. Dugan of that outfit had pulled C Troop, 32d Squadron, out of the traffic tangle. Now he was wrestling with the job of patching up a task force to retake Born, six miles to the northeast, and protect the left flank of the 7th Armored Division.

Approaching Poteau from St. Vith was Headquarters and Headquarters Battery, 106th Division Artillery, a column of some twenty-
five vehicles of all kinds, led by Col. Malin Craig, Jr., the artillery
executive. Craig had been ordered by Brigadier General McMahon, the
artillery commander, to move the command post either to Poteau or to
Vielsalm, conforming with Division, and on the way to pick up and re-
assign the tattered 589th and the 592d Field Artillery Battalions, which
had been moved back from the St. Vith area when the attack closed in
on the previous evening.

Craig had found the 589th and its remaining three howitzers pulled
up on the road just west of Schlommefurth, the exhausted artillerymen
huddled asleep in their vehicles. Telling them to go into position five
hundred yards farther on, facing northeast, when it became light enough
to see, Craig and his headquarters outfit moved on. He had not found
the mediums, the 592d Field Artillery, and when the creeping traffic
finally ground to a halt just before dawn with his lead vehicle about
half a mile from Poteau itself, Craig decided to set up a temporary command post until the traffic cleared.

Instructing the next senior present, Lt.Col. Burtis L. Fayram, artillery
S-3, to set up, parking the vehicles facing the road, so they could get
out in either direction, Craig then went east again to hunt for the 592d
Field Artillery.

The situation was uncertain. No one knew for sure where the enemy
might be. The jammed traffic piled up on the forest-lined road, while
over the trees flares from time to time lighted the sky to the northwest.
Rumors ran that the enemy was also to the south.

Poteau consists of a handful of houses huddled at a combined road
junction and railway crossing. The road from St. Vith turns sharp right
just two hundred yards south of the hamlet, passes over the St. Vith–
Vielsalm railway, here entering a deep cutting, then turns left again,
west-bound. The road coming down from Born and Recht makes a side
curve to the west to join the St. Vith–Vielsalm highway immediately
north of the bridge over the railway. While surrounded by forests, the
hamlet and road junction actually stand in a cleared belt about a
hundred yards wide on each side.

Dugan's efforts to turn the cavalry vehicles out of the west-bound
traffic into the sharp V of the Recht road appear to have been one of
the causes of the traffic halt. He got C Troop, 32d Squadron, with its
head pointing northeast towards Recht, the rest of the column around
the V. He gathered four light tanks and a platoon of assault guns from
the 18th Squadron with it, put the whole under Major Mayes—we remember him in the fighting north of Manderfeld two days previous—

and this Task Force, Mayes No. 2, he ordered to occupy the high ground in the vicinity of Born.

Somewhere in this melée was also mixed a light-tank company of the 7th Armored Division, according to Capt. Charles Martin, commanding C Troop. This outfit, says Martin, "had been chased out of Recht and said the town was in flames."[4]

The column started up the road toward Recht. As it did its head was blasted by bazooka fire, mortars, small arms and machine guns. A light tank and an armored car flamed. C Troop attempted to deploy through abandoned howitzers and TD guns. Two enemy tanks loomed on the Recht road in front. A group of C Troop people, Lt. Herron, Staff Sgt. Alfred W. Enlow, Sgt. Daniel Ruse and Cpl. J. Kolododzkie, tried unsuccessfully to man an abandoned TD gun. They then got bazookas and the enemy tanks sheered off.

At the crossroads confusion was worse than when the firing started. The light tanks spurted up and went on their way to Vielsalm,[5] and such individual vehicles as could clawed out of the traffic to make a getaway, both to east and west.

The cavalrymen of Task Force Mayes gradually built up a firing line about three hundred yards north of the Poteau houses, supported by fire of the .50-caliber machine guns of the armored cars and by mortars they emplaced in the houses, firing through holes cut in the roofs.

For some reason the enemy did not at once press his attack in force. Instead he moved some infantrymen north and northwest into the woods of Der Hau, apparently with the objective of taking Mont Legros and seizing the high ground immediately bordering the St. Vith–Vielsalm highway, here running through a cutting all the way to Petit-Thier —an ideal setting to slaughter passing traffic. To the eastward, too, he started to infiltrate south. We will come to that in describing what happened to Division Artillery's Headquarters Battery.

While cavalrymen fought, the long column on the road began to move again, the refugee elements east of the road junction scooting past as Task Force Mayes held the road open.

It was an odd, piecemeal fight in the snowy fields north of Poteau— more a series of quick, short skirmishes than any heavy drive. The oddest of these was, perhaps, when a group of men in American uniforms materialized out of the fog about one of the abandoned assault guns of E Troop, 18th Squadron. Sgt. John S. Meyers took a five-man patrol out to investigate. Their boots didn't look right to Meyers. He had seen just such boots on dead Krauts, and when one of them hailed him in English with a shout: "We are E Company!" he knew it wasn't right. It's "troop," not "company" in the cavalry.[6] Meyers, falling flat on the ground, covered them. One began firing at the patrol and then, at the signal of Captain Meadows, commanding the real E Troop, a light tank smacked the group of disguised Germans with a round of canister, killing all of them.[7]

Through this morning of milled-up fighting Lt.Col. Dugan, unlit cigar in mouth, circulated among the little clumps of 14th Group cavalry soldiers, grinning, encouraging, advising.

By noon, the probing ceased. The Krauts had diagnosed the strength opposing them, kept lapping over to the west. The job of holding them was too big. No reinforcements arrived. Back in Vielsalm as the rest of the group, mostly elements of the 32d Squadron, rallied from their all-night withdrawal, they were being formed into another task force under Major Kracke. But when they tried to buck the west-bound stream, they had hard going. Some time between 8:00 and 9:00 o'clock Lt.Col. Ridge, commanding the 32d Squadron, had given up. "It won't work," he said. So Task Force Mayes was on its own.

It was touch-and-go when they finally made a dash for Vielsalm. The road was now empty. In three armored cars, two jeeps and one light tank the cavalry ran the gantlet, taking heavy but badly directed small-arms fire as they raced through the long stretch of sunken road between Poteau and Petit-Thier.

At 1:00 P.M. that day the group was attached to the 7th Armored Division. Colonel Devine and several of his officers, including Ridge, were relieved of command and the shattered remnants were incorporated into a provisional cavalry squadron under Lt.Col. William F. Damon, Jr., originally commanding the 18th Squadron. So far as the 106th Division is concerned, the story of the 14th Cavalry group ends here, though as part of the 7th Armored the provisional squadron later fought on the south flank of the Division and acquitted itself well. CCA, 7th Armored Division, moved up to Poteau, momentarily plugged the gap. The hard-fighting 275th Armored Field Artillery Battalion, which had been supporting the 14th Cavalry Group and was now assisting in the defense of St. Vith, was also attached to the 7th Armored this day.

And now we come back to the Headquarters Battery, 106th Division Artillery.

The artillery Headquarters Battery lagged, it seems, after Craig left; his orders to pull off the road and set up station were apparently disregarded. A motorcyclist in U.S. uniform weaved through traffic from Poteau going east, then returned in about five minutes. Halting about a hundred yards beyond the battery column the rider dropped a flare, spurted off.[8]

The bright light blazed in the dawn mist, then died. And as it died mortar shells began dropping on the road and panic seems to have struck the battery.

Most officers and men dove for cover. Captain Harold R. Dann, the battery commander, attempted to break out machine guns from the vehicles, but they had been badly stowed. Part of the battery personnel and some staff officers, led by Lt.Col. Fayram, worked their way into the woods to the south when a truck coming from Poteau sped past, its driver calling that there were two Kraut tanks at the road junction.

Craig, still looking for the 592d Field Artillery, had gotten back to Sart-lez-St.Vith, where he met General McMahon. They heard the firing to the northwest. It was now about 7:00 A.M. and beginning to get light. As they scoured the vicinity for the artillery and a good route, some fugitives from Poteau reported the enemy were there. This was about 8:30 A.M.

McMahon and Craig determined to get the artillery out. The former moved via Hinderhausen, to run into sniper fire just beyond; the latter moved back the way he had come. Craig found the 592d this time, in the woods just east of Schlommefurth, and ordered them to pull out to the southwest through Hinderhausen. Then he sped west again toward Poteau. On the way he passed the three-gun 589th trundling for safety, already warned by Lt. Ronald C. Johnson, of his party.

Craig found the site of the Headquarters Battery a mass of confusion. The vehicles, still unturned on the road, lay between two stretches of open land between the woods reaching down north from the railway cutting. Down these clearings machine-gun and small-arms fire was sweeping. At least half the personnel had gone. Lieutenants Mool and Kaulitz and Warrant Officer Stults were trying to get the vehicles turned around. Craig and Lt. Albert C. Martin, 590th Field Artillery, now assistant S-3 of the artillery, tore in to get the outfit out. Craig stopped a battery commander of the 592d Field Artillery, at Schlomme-furth, from burning a disabled tractor—it would have blocked the road for all the other vehicles west of it.

Everyone who could drive was put at a wheel. All the vehicles except three were rolled east toward Sart-lez-St.Vith, the last ones running a gantlet of determined fire. Craig wheeled the last jeep out. He wondered why it had no pick-up, then discovered that it was hauling a trailer!

At Sart-lez-St.Vith Lt. Johnson was directing traffic to the Hinderhausen road. All the artillery that could roll came through, including the 589th and 592d. Martin worried about the last vehicles of Headquarters Battery—there were now four unaccounted for—and said he'd go back and see what was happening. In a jeep driven by Sgt. Kuka he dashed up the road. He passed the last vehicle of Headquarters Battery—why, nobody knows. The jeep got almost to the open space immediately east of Poteau when three German infantrymen on the road opened fire on it.

Sergeant Kuka rammed the jeep into a sharp turn. It swung on the proverbial dime, and at the moment a Kraut bullet got Martin. Hurled out of the jeep by centrifugal force, he yelled to Kuka to "keep going."

The sergeant stepped on it, with the reports of Martin's automatic ringing in his ears. Several days later they found Lieutenant Martin's body. Near it lay three dead Germans.

The two artillery battalions and what still remained of Headquarters Battery rolled to Bovigny, where the battalions went into position. The rest went on to Vielsalm where they joined Division headquarters and started functioning again.

Fayram and his party, who had decamped from the Poteau fight, wandered on foot south through the woods to the vicinity of Oberst Crombach, where they found a corps outfit, a battery of the 771st Field Artillery Battalion, hurriedly going into march order, and joined it. From there, as it turned out, they would poke all the way to Namur where Craig, sent hunting them, found them and took them back with him to Vielsalm the night of 19-20 December.

Exception to this was a small group headed by Major Lester S. Smyth, who was S-1 and S-4 of the artillery. They wandered west to Burtonville where the command post of CCR, 7th Armored Division, was now setting up, and from there got back to Division headquarters in Vielsalm by 1:00 P.M. that day.

The worst repercussion of this episode was felt by the 592d Field Artillery. Emplaced at Bovigny, it was pulled back to Ottré through a misunderstanding, and bivouacked there for the night. CWO James B. Bennett was sent to Marche to get gasoline. Arriving during the night of 18-19 December, he ran into Lt.Col. Fayram. As a result Bennett came back to the battalion with instructions to move "to the west, toward Laroche and Marche."

Lieutenant Colonel Richard E. Weber, Jr., commanding, considered this order to be legitimate—Fayram, it will be remembered, was S-3 of Division Artillery—and the battalion went wandering all the way to Rosée, across the Meuse, six miles west of Dinant, before the error was rectified. As a result the Division was minus the services of its medium artillery battalion for three critical days.

It is somewhat remarkable that Weber, the artillery battalion commander, should have been so obsessed by these peculiar instructions from Fayram that he rolled his outfit clear out of the Division's rear boundary without further check. It does not jibe with his previous disinclination to withdraw in the Schnee Eifel during the hottest sort of action, nor with the skillful, daring and rapid return he later made into the battle zone.

Lieutenant Colonel Fayram, after an investigation, was relieved.

The 589th Field Artillery became victim of another doubtful order. Everyone seemed to be giving orders on that debatable ground that day. It got to Bovigny, went into a position in readiness, when Col. Herbert W. Kruger, commanding the 174th FA Group of VIII Corps Artillery, commandeered its services to protect the movement of his group of five battalions, then withdrawing from Bovigny through Chérain to the southwest. Enemy tanks, it was said, were in Chérain. The battalion and its three guns fiddled between Courtil and Bovigny, though the tanks never materialized. Major Arthur C. Parker, now commanding the 589th, was ordered by Kruger to consider himself attached to the 174th Group, "VOCG VIII Corps."

Service Battery, 590th Field Artillery, now attached to the 589th, was sent over to the 592d to get all impedimenta away from the threatened attack, and it followed that outfit in its will-o'-the-wisp move through Dinant.

All in all, the action at Poteau had a far-reaching effect on the future operations of 106th Division Artillery.

WORKSHOP BEGINS TO GRIND

To get the picture around St. Vith on 18 December one must examine the mission, dispositions and previous movements of Brig.Gen. (later Maj.Gen.) Robert W. Hasbrouck's 7th Armored Division— "Workshop" in ETO's military code. The 7th, hurriedly transferred from Ninth to First Army when the Ardennes avalanche started sliding, moved from Scherpenseel, Germany, down into VIII Corps jurisdiction. On the way it was hampered by the enemy jab around the Büllingen nose and had two clashes with the Krauts.

The 7th Armored was alerted for a move southward to VIII Corps, the routes and time unspecified, at 5:30 P.M., 16 December. The Division Commander was given no information by Ninth Army as to the tactical situation. Certainly Hasbrouck never dreamed that anyone expected him to be in St. Vith by 7:00 o'clock the next morning. Some time elapsed before the route situation was clarified; at last Hasbrouck was told he would move in two columns, the western one to start at midnight, 16-17 December, the eastern one at 8:00 A.M., 17 December.

Hasbrouck directed CCA over the western route. His artillery, which, when the movement order was received, was in active support of the 84th Infantry Division, could not be disengaged in time to move with its normal combat command, so the artillery would move with CCR along the eastern route.

Three times the western movement orders were changed. First the Division was told it should start on the west road at 2:00 o'clock on the morning of 17 December, instead of at midnight 16-17 December. Then the movement was held up again, until 3:30 A.M. Finally when the column started it was halted again for another hour. Evidently First Army was having troubles of its own in clearing the passage.

It was sixty-five miles from the starting point of Hasbrouck's western column to the proposed concentration area in the vicinity of Vielsalm. Since daylight did not come until well after 7:00 o'clock, the first three hours of the move were in pitch dark; one can assume the column didn't travel at a rate faster than about eight miles an hour in that period.

Only when the western armor had gotten into the VIII Corps zone and met streams of civilian refugees, saw German parachutes hanging here and there in the trees and began to buck American vehicles rolling west did the officers and men of the 7th Armored realize that something momentous was happening.

The east column, which got away without delay, ran into the enemy first south of Malmedy. CCR got by after a sharp brush, but the artillery was rerouted over to the westward to fall in behind the other column. CCR had another engagement at Stavelot before it could continue.

It was 11:00 A.M., 17 December, when CCB, leading the western column, rolled into its assembly area at Vielsalm to find orders waiting it from General Clarke, who had already gotten into St. Vith, to proceed to that town.

The armored column plunged into the maelstrom of traffic fleeing from St. Vith. The leading vehicles bucked, dodged, halted and ground on again, into the almost indescribable confusion on the highway. Traffic control was nil. The MP Platoon of the 106th was trying to handle traffic on the eastern side of St. Vith. Major Raymond P. Riniski, assistant G-4 of the 106th, states that he was unable to get through to Vielsalm until dark, and then only on foot, as the 7th Armored going east and the Division and Corps transport going west tangled. Riniski at Vielsalm asked Corps for more MPs but got none until the next day when two jeeploads arrived.

All this, of course, did not help CCB of the 7th. Arguments, threats, sometimes the physical hurling of offending vehicles into the ditch, got the command along, literally inch by inch, until its leading elements hit St. Vith at 5:30 P.M., to be rushed into the line.

As for the rest of the Division, General Hasbrouck at Vielsalm, where he had set up his command post in the afternoon, received a telephoned order from G-3, VIII Corps, at 4:15 P.M.: "Waimes and Malmedy[9] have been taken. You should take steps to protect anything passing these points."

CCA was now moving south and east of Vielsalm, under Colonel Dwight A. Rosebaum, to the vicinity of Beho. CCR, commanded by Lt.Col. Robert B. Jones, bivouacked that night near Vielsalm, except for two companies of the 17th Tank Battalion which had been engaged in the day, during the movement, and were now, apparently, somewhere in the vicinity of Recht.

This was the situation on the morning of 18 December when, after 7:00 o'clock, Hasbrouck received a letter of instructions from VIII Corps, establishing the respective zones of action. The 7th Armored, less CCB, was responsible north of the boundary line: Gouvy–St. Vith (exclusive). The 106th, with CCB of the 7th and CCB of the 9th Armored Divisions attached, was responsible for St. Vith and the southern zone.

Hasbrouck by this time had of course been in touch with Jones, and was filled in on the situation as far as the 106th could ascertain it. One thing alone was sure—the north flank was wide open, the 14th Cavalry Group shattered. The first thing to do, to borrow an expression from Field Marshal Montgomery, was to "tidy things up."

So Hasbrouck ordered CCA to attack and take Poteau. Rosebaum's advance guard, consisting of C Company, 48th Armored Infantry Battalion, and C Company, 40th Tank Battalion, moved out at 10:10 A.M., via St. Vith–Sart-lez-St.Vith, contacted the enemy southeast of Poteau and by 3:20 P.M. was trying to fight its way into Poteau itself.

Kraut resistance—infantry and tanks—was strong, and it was not until 5:00 P.M. and dusk that the place was definitely in our hands. CCA consolidated the position.

CCR in the meantime had received orders to establish a defensive line in the vicinity of Petit-Thier, two miles west of Poteau on the St. Vith–Vielsalm highway, and by nightfall was astride the road, facing northeast, with elements of the 814th TD Battalion supporting the roadblock.

As rumors of an enemy advance from the south came in, Lt.Col. Jones established another defensive position just beyond Neuville, a mile and a half southeast of Vielsalm.

Summing up the situation of the north flank that night, the 7th Armored Division, less CCB, was establishing itself generally along an eleven-mile arc stretching from Vielsalm to St. Vith; a somewhat tenuous, much overextended arc, if you will, but one held by fresh, veteran troops, highly mobile.

As Hasbrouck took stock of his situation that evening he received VIII Corps' famous "all costs" letter of instruction dated 16 December, mentioned much earlier:

"1. Troops will be withdrawn from present positions only as positions become completely untenable.

"2. In no event will enemy be allowed to penetrate west of line: Holzheim–Setz–Lommersweiler–Maspelt–Lieler–Bockholz–Lellingen–Masseler–Bourscheid–Colmar–Meisemberg–Ernzen–Beidweiler–Wecker–Mertert . . . which will be held at all costs."

The G-3 journal of 7th Armored Division notes this with the terse comment, "Our positions were already in rear of the line to be held at all costs."[10]

HOLDING ST. VITH

Combat Command B, 7th Armored Division, attached to the 106th Infantry Division and slipped into action piecemeal east of St. Vith during the evening and night of 17 December, consisted of the 31st Tank Battalion, 23d Armored Infantry Battalion, 38th Armored Infantry Battalion (less Company C), Company B, 33d Engineer Battalion, 87th Reconnaissance Squadron (less assault gun and light tank elements), and Company A, 814th TD Battalion (reinforced).

At dawn on 18 December the defensive position at Prümerberg from north to south consisted of Troop B, 87th Reconnaissance Squadron, Company B, 38th Armored Infantry, Company A, 81st Engineers, the 168th Engineer Battalion (A and B Companies only), Headquarters Company, 81st Engineers, and Company A, 23d Armored Infantry.[11]

The line ran from the St. Vith–Amblève road on the north to the southern end of the Schleid Berg woods near Neidingen. North of that line the rest of the 87th Reconnaissance Squadron was engaged in a running defensive fight up near Hunnange, in front of it somewhere a two-company detachment of the 9th Armored Division's 14th Tank Battalion. South of the defensive position the 23d Armored Infantry was making contact with the left of CCB, 9th Armored Division, somewhere between Dreihütten and the Our River.

The whole situation was a catch-as-catch-can effort, building up on the original thin position of the 81st and 168th Engineers.

Four different attacks were launched against the position after dawn. The first three, minor in significance, were beaten back handily. The fourth, an estimated company of infantry supported by one Tiger tank, crashed against Company A, 81st Engineers. Lt. Paul E. Rutledge, the acting commander, out in front of his company observing mortar fire, was wounded during the third attack and in this final one was killed by a shell fragment.

"He stayed out in front right to the end, his silver bar on his helmet shining just a little too bright; that's probably what got him," says one eyewitness.[12]

The tank rumbled up to within point-blank range of the position, but was finally knocked out by a Sherman of the 7th Armored Division. The Krauts came in howling in English.[13] Shouts of "You Yankee bastards! Kill those Yankee sons of bitches!" reverberated as they made their way into Company A's lines just north of the secondary road coming in from Schlierbach.

Artillery and mortar fire delivered close in finally broke the enemy's spirit and the invaders were driven out.

The positions in the woods ran along the lines of fire breaks which crisscrossed the timber in a series of lanes. It must be remembered that like all European forests, which are highly cultivated, underbrush is unusually rare, and the trees are more regularly spaced than in our American woods. Hence, although giving no clear field of fire, individuals may be seen easily in daylight moving between the trees.

At about 3:00 P.M. another attack of company strength came crashing through the trees against the left flank of Company A, 81st Engineers, driving it back to the next successive fire line. Two squads of Krauts got through while behind them the enemy began building up his small-arms and automatic-weapons fire.

Riggs, with the provisional platoon of Headquarters and Service Company, 81st Engineers, counterattacked up the hill, while on the left B Troop, 87th Reconnaissance Squadron, closed to the right, Company A, 38th Armored Infantry filling its place.

It was nightfall before the original line was regained and the position once more consolidated. No further attacks were received that night, the only change in disposition being to fill a gap between the 168th Engineers and Company A, 23d Armored Infantry, on the right, by the provisional platoon mentioned above.

The day's fighting had cost the cavalry troop some forty officers and men, while both the 81st Engineers and Company A, 23d Armored Infantry, lost approximately twenty per cent of their existing strength.

Nungesser's A and B Companies, 168th Engineers, holding a 600-yard front from the Schlierbach road south along the edge of the woods, were also considerably pushed around during the day.

The 275th Armored Field Artillery Battalion maintained its close support of the St. Vith defense sector, assisting materially in the repulse of the attacking waves during the day.

Up on the left flank in the "no man's land" northeast of St. Vith that afternoon, where anything might, and did, happen, a detachment of the 634th AAA Battalion, consisting of one Bofors gun and a machine gun, attempted to displace under heavy small-arms fire. In the midst of the turmoil a Kraut tank hove around the edge of a bit of woods. Pvt. James E. Hefner opened on the tank with a machine gun.

While the Bofors was being dragged to safety Hefner squatted behind his .50-caliber machine gun, sent a stream of bullets which glanced from the tank like hail off a tin roof. The long 88 swung around to bear, bellowed once. Hefner died.

But the Bofors gun got away to fight again.

CCB, 9TH ARMORED DIVISION

By dawn of 18 December Hoge's combat command was north and west of the Our along a thinly held line from Weppeler to Auel, the units in contact with the enemy being from north to south: B Company, 27th Armored Infantry, D Troop, 89th Cavalry Reconnaissance Squadron, the provisional company of elements of the 1st Battalion, 424th Infantry, and Company A, 27th Armored Infantry.

The 14th Tank Battalion, less the two companies up in the north, was maneuvering to close the gap thus developed between the St. Vith defense force and the left flank of CCB, 9th Armored.

The enemy, once he was fully convinced that the armor had withdrawn, probed again up from Winterspelt, and, gathering strength, stormed down the road to Steinebrück to take the bridge over the Our, which the sappers of Company B, 9th Armored Engineer Battalion, blew in his face.

But with his left flank wide open, and the attacks on St. Vith developing, Hoge's position was untenable, particularly as the Krauts had good observation into the river valley from the heights of the Brüssel-Berg. During the morning Hoge had no contact, either, with the 424th Infantry on his right. So CCB disengaged again.

Company A, 27th Armored Infantry, was withdrawn from the right to a position in the vicinity of Maspelt, where it dug in. C Company established a covering position some 500 yards southeast of Neidingen, and the two left flank units disengaged, falling back behind it to establish a new defensive position along the Neidingen ridge, joining with the St. Vith defense force on the north.

Company C then withdrew in turn to the new position. All this was accomplished with the close support of the 16th Armored Field Artillery Battalion.

Company A on the right maintained its Maspelt position, echeloned well southeast of the remainder of the command, and during late afternoon patrols from the 424th Infantry on the south made contact with it, once more linking the remaining elements of the Division.

It was during this withdrawal that Staff Sgt. Fred N. Grossman, 634th AAA Battalion, commanding a two-gun detachment of the coast artillerymen originally assigned to protect the Steinebrück bridge, but now assisting in the ground defense, rallied a group of thirty disorganized infantrymen coming back to the Our, re-formed them and established a skirmish line, then reported the position.

Later Grossman, reconnoitering around one of his gun sections, was asked by a tank officer to locate the range and position of a Kraut concentration. Grossman opened up and adjusted with a burst of HE on the spot, neutralizing enemy fire and pointing out the target by his shell bursts, enabling the tanker in turn to bring down accurate fire.

ENGINEERS' LUCK

We left C Company, 81st Engineer Battalion (less its 3d Platoon which had hitch-hiked through the night to St. Vith), bivouacking in deserted Elcherath the night of 17-18 December, the only element of the 106th Division—though they didn't realize it at the time—east of the Our and not surrounded. Before dawn the enemy barrage began pounding the village and the Brüssel-Berg north of it as the Krauts prepared for their advance north from Winterspelt toward Steinebrück on the St. Vith road. Machine-gun fire could be heard from the northeast of Elcherath and it was quite evident that egress northward was barred.

So C Company moved west, striking the little village of Hemmeres on the river. Hemmeres, through which Service Company, 424th Infantry, had pulled for safety the day before, was also deserted. But in the village were the vehicles of Service Company, abandoned when its personnel escaped over the footbridge which was the only link with the west bank.

Lieutenant Maier, acting company commander, decided that an effort should be made to save these trucks. Incidentally, of course, there was the very practical thought that if the engineers could get the vehicles out, they would ride, not walk, those last two miles to Bracht where the company was supposed to rendezvous.

Hostile artillery fire was falling nearby, but seemingly the enemy had not noticed the outfit. Maier picked drivers, lined up three trucks to try to ford the stream.

The first truck splashed heavily into the river, ploughed, bogged down in the mud. The second truck fared no better. But the third one —engineers' luck—got through, plugged its way up the rather steep west bank to safe standing.

This truck had a winch and cable on it. The rest—except for the task of Private First Class Reynolds, who volunteered to wade waist-deep each time into the icy water to retrieve the cable and attach it to the nose of each succeeding truck—was simple.

They had to drive the trucks across a field and through a piece of woods before they hit the road, but by 8:30 A.M. they had all gotten to Bracht. And later in the day the somewhat red-faced Service Company, 424th Infantry, was presented with its trucks. One more score for the ubiquitous engineers.

THE SOUTHERN FLANK

To get proper perspective on the operations of Reid's 424th Infantry and its supporting artillery battalion, the 591st Field Artillery, that day of 18 December, one must take a bird's-eye view of the 28th Division situation, particularly of its left-flank regiment, the 112th Infantry.

The Kraut assault had driven in all along the 28th Division's front. In the 112th Infantry sector all three battalions had been forced back on the Our River line, one prong dislocating, as we have already learned, its left flank element, B Company, from the Lützkampen area and throwing it into the 424th Infantry area where the company was attached for the moment to the 2d Battalion. A major prong had smashed between the 112th and its brother regiment on the right, the 110th Infantry.

After dark on 17 December the 28th Division had ordered the 112th to take up defensive positions west of the Our, and thus, at dawn of 18 December, we find the regiment occupying a line generally between Beiler and Weiswampach, two miles west of the Our, with both flanks in the air. A gap of some two miles separated it from the right flank of the 424th, a gap filled with German patrols probing for soft spots through which the 116th Panzer Division was trying to slice a combat team, its 156th *Panzergrenadier* and 60th Panzer Regiments.

Reid, organizing on the line the Preisberg–Weweler–the Our Berg, that morning, himself had both flanks in the air.

He had no contact, of course, with the 112th on his right, and there was a sort of no man's land between him and his partner of yesterday, CCB, 9th Armored Division. The enemy, with good observation from the high ground east of the Our, was putting down heavy artillery concentrations, particularly in the vicinity of Bracht, in the 1st Battalion sector, and around Grufflingen, junction of the highways up which any reinforcement and supply from the west must come in that area.

Uppermost in the regimental commander's mind was the necessity for keeping the road open at Burg-Reuland for the counterattack of the 9th Armored, if and when that should materialize. That road now afforded the only remaining passage across the Ulf and the Our into the Schnee Eifel.

The new defensive position had the still somewhat disorganized 1st Battalion on the north, with the 3d Battalion in the center to the junction of the Ulf and the Our, while the 2d Battalion lay south of the Ulf.

The 3d Battalion appears to have come through its trying fights of the previous days in good shape. It dug in near Bracht with I and L Companies on the line and K Company in reserve. The 2d Battalion, south of the Ulf, not only held the Our line but also sent patrols south and southwest in an effort to contact the 112th Infantry.

The 591st Field Artillery Battalion, in the vicinity of Grufflingen, continued to give close support to the regiment. A platoon of Cannon Company, 424th Infantry, all that appears to have been left of that outfit, was adopted by Lt.Col. Philip Hoover, commanding the 591st, and organized into a fourth battery under Lt. Buedington, executive officer of Cannon Company. Attached for two days, this extemporized battery accomplished yeoman work.

The 424th had no difficulty in holding its position during that day; the enemy's main weight was still east of the Our. As soon as the engineers had come in from their trek they were set to work on preparing the four Our River bridges in the regimental sector for demolition. Two of these were blown that night.

During the morning contact was finally made on the left flank with Company A, 27th Armored Infantry (itself well out beyond the rest of its unit), but it was not until 6:00 P.M. that Reid received word, through a liaison officer, of the dispositions of the 112th Infantry on his right. He knew the regiment was consolidating in the vicinity of Weiswampach, and at once sent word to Division—a message, by the way, not received until 6:00 o'clock the next morning.

The 112th, according to the information Reid received, was cut off entirely from its division and feared that supply by air might be necessitated; the regiment asked that the 106th transmit news of its situation to the 28th Division. Reid at once sent an officer of his own to Weiswampach, in an effort to clarify the situation and, as he told Division, "explore possibility of 112th Infantry changing disposition to close the gap presently existing [between it and the 424th]."

FETTERED IN THE HILLS

The clock was just ushering in 18 December when Cavender of the 423d Infantry managed to get in touch with Descheneaux of the 422d Infantry to relay the message Division had sent that previous afternoon and Cavender now—almost twelve hours later—had just received. This, it will be recalled, ordered both regiments to withdraw to the line of the Our.

Since the time that message was filed both regiments had reported their encirclement, had indicated their ability to hold in place if supplied, and messages had passed concerning air drop of food and ammunition. Both colonels agreed to disregard this now superannuated order.

But about 4:00 A.M. they received Gen. Jones' radio order of 2:15 A.M. to attack the Germans in the Our Valley in the vicinity of Schönberg.[14]

Descheneaux of the 422d was in his command post when the message came in. With him were Master Sgt. Alpheus A. Loewenguth and Tech. Sgt. T. Wayne Black, respectively the operations and intelligence sergeants.

Descheneaux weighed the import of the message, bowed his head into his arms and almost sobbed: "My poor men—they'll be cut to pieces."[15]

Cold men stirred their numb joints in the wet snow and dreary, windswept hills as both regimental commanders, after deciding among themselves that each would move at dawn, issued their orders. According to Col. Cavender, they agreed that the 423d would move first, the 422d following. However, there appears to have been no further synchronization of effort.

Thick fog and rain blanketed the woods as the 422d Infantry moved from its positions as silently as possible, in column of battalions, on foot. Only a few jeeps were utilized as the various elements moved generally south through the Schlausenbacher Wald across the old front.

The regimental motor transport apparently never moved from its original position around Hill 576, in bulk, though a motor column, apparently light elements, under Capt. E. Bruce Foster started to get out on the morning of 18 December, following a circuitous route eastward toward the 1st Battalion area, thence south and west, to end up in bivouac somewhere northeast of Bleialf—in the woods a thousand yards north of Oberlascheid near the regimental bivouac. Survivors' memories are vague about the actual location.

The cross-country push northwest of the major foot elements started at 9:00 A.M., the 2d Battalion leading, with F Company in advance. The route was over a woods road across Hill 611, between Oberlascheid and Schlausenbach, thence westerly down into a Y-shaped draw, the source of the Alf River, and on to a point in a fairly narrow ravine south of the Skyline Drive ridge one mile north of Oberlascheid. Here it was determined to bivouac for the night, preparatory to attacking toward Schönberg the following morning.

The last elements of the 422d cleared the original positions shortly after noon, herding their German prisoners of war before them.

The actual distance to the new assembly area was just three miles, but it seemed like fifty to tired, hungry men, burdened with weapons and ammunition, splashing, slipping and sliding in mud and slush through the ghostly forest. Marching was hot work; discarded overcoats littered the trails, coats men would have almost sold their souls for that night.

The going was bad, the trails conflicting. Part of the regiment lost its way. Actually some of the leading elements overshot the area. F Company, in the lead, crossed Skyline Drive, got down into the Ihren valley and finally linked up with the 3d Battalion, 423d Infantry, whose fortunes it shared from that time. Cannon Company, with its vehicles, took the woods trail southwest into the tip of the Alf ravine, and at Halenfeld ran into the 423d column. Later it rejoined the regiment.

Other detachments retraced their steps to pile at last into the now overcrowded ravine where the regiment found itself huddled that night in an intermixture of units which never did get fully straightened out.

The 422d had taken a pretty heavy pounding for two days, but at least its elements had been dug in under some protection. Now they were floundering in the open over terrain unknown to most of them. The fact that the enemy was unaware, for several hours, of the move, speaks well for the discipline displayed. The route reconnaissance and liaison, however, left much to be desired.

The regiment took it in stride, the men generally in good humor. All knew that the 422d had not given an inch of ground since the attack first started; it was leaving now only because Division had so ordered. All felt that a counterattack was coming to relieve them.

" . . . Visibility was limited to a few hundred feet," says one participant.[16] His outfit moved in single file in the march. "We abandoned everything except our weapons and ammunition . . . Ammunition was very low and there was no food or water. There was no straggling. Stops were made every few minutes as the advance guard searched every foot of the terrain ahead. No shots were fired in the vicinity of the column where I was . . . "

Only on the right flank in late afternoon, was there any enemy opposition to the march. There C Company had several skirmishes with tanks poking about in the vicinity of Hill 612, just west of Schlausenbach.[17]

No one, it seemed, was absolutely sure of their position. The lack of reconnaissance is apparent. And some officers were beginning to feel that it had been unwise to evacuate their previous positions. In the 2d Battalion, Lt. Elmer F. Lange of H Company had returned that morning to the old Siegfried Line and found that it was still unoccupied by the Germans. When Lt.Col. Scales heard this he expressed the wish that the regiment had stayed put,[18] to fight it out in well dispersed protected dispositions.

Colonel Descheneaux, arriving in the ravine, asked Scales, "Where in hell are we?"[19]

That night, while the 422d shivered in its bivouac and indefatigable Father Cavanaugh, regimental chaplain, made his cheering rounds, Col. Descheneaux held officers' call.

The regiment, Descheneaux told them, would advance next morning, seizing Hill 504 above Schönberg—1st Battalion on the right, 2d Battalion on the left, 3d Battalion in reserve. It would capture Schönberg and Heuem in turn and move west to meet American armor coming to the rescue.[20]

Tomorrow, despite the fact that no air drop had yet materialized and, in this thick weather, might be still further delayed, would be another day. And tomorrow the 422d Infantry would take the offensive.

We turn to the brother regiment, the 423d, from whose area all that day had come the grumble of heavy fighting.

The 423d moved from its perimeter defense with its western element, the 2d Battalion, leading. Behind it came the 3d; the 1st brought up the rear. All regimental transport accompanied. The proposed route was via Halenfeld–Oberlascheid–Radscheid–Engineer Cutoff–Schönberg.[21]

Puett's 2d Battalion moved out at 10:00 A.M. in order: E, F, H and G Companies. Meeting enemy fire about noon at Radscheid as they debouched into Skyline Drive, E Company deployed to the left in an attempt to push the enemy south and clear the road. Machine-gun, mortar and rocket fire at first pinned the company down—the country was very open—so the energetic Puett promptly deployed F Company on the right, supporting the action with a machine-gun platoon and the 81mm mortars of H Company (heavy weapons).

Here it was that an H Company weapons-carrier, leading one of the platoon convoys, ran smack into a German roadblock covered by an 88. The first round smashed the front of the vehicle, partly overturning it. Pfcs. Robert G. Fischer and Paul D. Spencer wrenched at its machine gun, got it into action, and while a third man raced up the trail to warn the following trucks, the two men actually drove the Kraut gun crew away, silenced two supporting machine guns.

Companies E and F, taking heavy punishment, attacked down astride Skyline Drive and took the high ground on the western edge of Radscheid, while G Company, committed at 1:45 P.M., smashed into the Cutoff ravine, advancing to the Bleialf–Schönberg road.

As soon as the fire fight developed Puett called on regiment for a counterattack. The enemy was being rapidly reinforced from Bleialf, so he recommended a drive against the Kraut right (east) flank, in that direction.

But as the march started Cavender had received word from Division countermanding the orders to take up positions south of Schönberg and directing an advance directly against the town.[22] Accordingly Cavender ordered Lt.Col. Earl F. Klinck's 3d Battalion, now in Oberlascheid where it could have been utilized at the time Puett called for the counterattack, to push on for Schönberg, keeping to the right of the 2d Battalion.[23]

So the 3d Battalion moved past the embattled 2d, took the right fork at Oberlascheid to Skyline Drive, jogged left and right, and headed northwest over the secondary road leading to Hill 504 directly southwest of and overlooking Schönberg. We will see in a moment what happened to it.

Puett's battalion was putting up a magnificent aggressive fight against greatly superior numbers. On the way down the previous day he had run across an abandoned truckload of 81mm mortar shell, mostly white phosphorus, and he put it to good use now. Several groups of Krauts were crisped as the battalion fought on; seventy-five were counted in one draw alone, all badly burned.

During the desperate fighting at the end of the Cutoff, T/4 William K. Dientsbach and T/5 Clyde E. Watters, pocketed by a German rush, were captured, dragged to the road and forced to ride the hood of a captured American jeep. The Kraut driver rushed them up a side trail past an American roadblock, but the two men, yelling "Germans!" threw themselves off the jeep into the ditch. A volley from the roadblock killed the enemy driver; his three companions surrendered.

Lackey's 590th Field Artillery Battalion, from its positions still in the original perimeter, suported the attack with several concentrations, but Lackey had to insist on use of his howitzers for high-priority missions only; ammunition was limited (he was down to three hundred rounds by afternoon) and the prospect of heavy fighting ahead loomed large. Battery A supported Puett. The other batteries were in march order. Radio communication failed, however, and the confused situation rendered the artillery support almost useless.

It was about dusk when Cavender committed the 1st Battalion on Puett's left, southwest down the draw of Düren Creek toward Bleialf, but the attack made little progress against a now thoroughly aroused and capable enemy.

Incidentally, some time during the late afternoon hopes were raised in the 423d command post when a rumor reached them that the 9th Armored had retaken Bleialf. Cavender radioed Division for confirmation, asking that any 423d personnel remaining there be picked up and that he be notified. This message is noted by Division two days later![24]

By nightfall the 2d Battalion had doggedly consolidated its position and dug in after a day of desperate fighting. It had suffered some three hundred casualties, including sixteen officers; the 81mm mortar ammunition was expended, only two rounds per piece of 60mm mortar stuff remained. Five heavy and four light machine guns had been knocked out. The machine-gun ammunition totted up to but 375 rounds per gun remaining.

Klinck's 3d Battalion had received the regimental order[25] to move out at 8:15 A.M. and crossed the initial point hard on the heels of the 2d Battalion.

Company L led, followed by K, the battalion Headquarters Company, and I Company. The heavy-weapons platoons were seeded through the column with the rifle companies as they had set up in the original positions. Behind it in the Siegfried Line the outfit left a shell consisting of one squad per platoon, to withdraw at 12:30 P.M. under the battalion executive; a good, workmanlike withdrawal plan.

It was some time between 12:30 and 1:00 P.M. that the regimental order to change direction and move on Schönberg came direct to L Company. The rest of the column conformed.

The route northwest had not been previously reconnoitered.[26] Klinck's battalion topped the Skyline Drive, disappeared down the northwestern slopes of Hill 536. The sound of heavy firing drifted back shortly, but all contact and communication between Klinck and regiment was soon lost for the remainder of the afternoon.[27] Actual contact with the enemy was first made as the advance guard crossed the Ihren at the international boundary.

At about 2:30 P.M. word was passed back to Klinck in the middle of his battalion column that L Company, in contact with the enemy, was being pinned down by heavy fire both from anti-aircraft artillery and small arms. The battalion commander at once put K Company into the fight on L's right.

The two companies were thus deployed on the northwestern slopes of Hill 536, and within a few hundred yards of the Bleialf–Schönberg road.

Reinforced by part of M Company (heavy weapons), they attacked, brushing aside the first enemy resistance, though remaining under heavy artillery fire.

Gradually they worked their way forward under increasing opposition, until L Company's left platoon had gotten astride the highway, cutting enemy communication between Schönberg and Bleialf. By nightfall the battalion had consolidated its position a scant half mile south of Schönberg. Here in the dark a large portion of F Company, 422d Infantry—the outfit which had overshot its regimental bivouac area a mile and a half to the southeast—came drifting in, as did[28] part of F Company, 423d, of Puett's battalion fighting below Radscheid. Two TD vehicles also found their way into his perimeter.

Klinck sent two runners back to regiment to report the situation while he dug in. Evidently they never got through. He had been unable to get in touch with the remainder of the 422d, although K Company had been instructed to gain contact.[29]

The 1st Battalion, 423d Infantry, was the last to pull out for the advance on Schönberg. Lt.Col. William H. Craig had orders to follow the 3d Battalion, providing the rear guard. His order of march was in two columns on the edges of the road, with battalion transportation between.

Headquarters and A Companies made up the right-hand column from front to rear, C and D Companies were on the left hand. B Company followed as rear guard.[30] Since there was no danger of air attack through that heavy fog, no criticism can be made of this somewhat serried formation.

Behind it the 1st Battalion, like the 3d, left a crust in its old positions, which would withdraw an hour and a half after the rear guard cleared the initial point.

Only one mile had been covered, which would place the head of the column between Halenfeld and Oberlascheid, when the fighting up ahead brought the march to a halt. Craig pulled men and vehicles off the road; B Company set up a rearward defense. Here they sat, joined later by the defensive crust behind them, until 4:00 o'clock when Craig received orders to commit his battalion on the left of the 2d.

Companies C and A in line from right to left, supported each by a platoon of D (heavy weapons) Company's machine guns and with the 81mm mortars in general support, deployed over Hill 546 just south of Oberlascheid, fought their way in the falling dusk into the Düren Creek ravine and across to the heights two thousand yards beyond.

As they went down into the valley the enemy caught them with mortar and machine-gun fire. C Company attempted to encircle the opposition on the right, capturing an 88 emplaced on the hillside, but by 6:00 o'clock had lost thirty men. Further advance became impossible. By 10:00 o'clock at night, with the rifle companies virtually out of ammunition, they withdrew toward Oberlascheid and the battalion dug in and prepared to hold.

Under the conditions it is rather surprising that this assault, really a night attack over unknown terrain, made any advance at all.[31]

Company C lost heavily in this action; Company A to a lesser extent. Company B, protecting the rear, did not become engaged.

While all these things were going on the 590th Field Artillery Battalion, entirely without protection in its original positions, displaced at 4:00 P.M. for Oberlascheid, where Lackey put his howitzers in firing position facing northwest.[32]

At dark Colonel Cavender displaced his command post from Oberlascheid, where he had been during the day, to Hill 575, north of the Radscheid crossroads (initial command post of 590th Field Artillery Battalion in the Schnee Eifel positions).

Here the situation was reviewed. As matters stood from the regimental viewpoint, two battalions were engaged (1st and 2d) and one (3d) was lost somewhere forward. Nothing had been heard from the 422d Infantry; its present whereabouts were unknown.

Cavender decided[33] to send a patrol forward to locate his 3d Battalion and also, if possible, the 422d Infantry. Kelly asked and received permission to accompany it. The patrol started forward at 10:00 P.M. in two jeeps, one of them laying wire. They found Klinck's battalion, with its vehicles behind it bogged on the side of Hill 536 just north of the headwaters of the Ihren; motors just couldn't make it through the mud up that hillside.

Here Kelly talked to Klinck and also to Captain Stewart, commanding F Company, 422d Infantry, but the latter could give no news at all of his regiment.

A futile search up Skyline Drive toward Auw, flushed only a Kraut sentinel whom they killed; the party returned to Cavender's command post and Kelly reported.[34]

About this time the erratic radio contact between Division and regiment was opened again, through persistent enemy jamming. Cavender learned that a food and ammunition drop would be made at the bend of the Schönberg road near his present 3d Battalion position.

More to the point, Division, in language somewhat bombastic—almost hysterical, in fact—ordered the 423d to attack Schönberg. As recollected by Lt.Col. Frederick Nagle, executive officer of the regiment, the message read: "Attack Schonberg, do maximum damage to enemy there, then attack towards St. Vith. This mission is of gravest importance to the nation. Good luck. Brock."[35]

Colonel Cavender had this message in his hand when he came up to the 3d Battalion command post a short time later, to investigate for himself. Cavender's decision was to disengage his 2d and 1st Battalions immediately and concentrate in the 3d Battalion area for an attack on Schönberg in the morning.

Analysis of Col. Cavender's decisions and orders for that afternoon and night is in order, particularly his decision with respect to Puett when the latter called for a counterattack. Division had ordered Cavender to attack Schönberg. His leading battalion (2d) had run into a fire fight which, of necessity, because it was involved with an enemy coming up from Bleialf, was dragging it to the left rear of its axis. But until that enemy in the left rear was taken care of, Cavender could not expect to hit Schönberg unimpeded.

Yet he left that battalion to its own resources, pushing the next and nearest effective unit (3d) northward toward the objective (Schönberg), permitting his rear battalion (1st) to remain halted in a perimeter defense, although unthreatened in fact, for approximately four hours.[36] When he did commit it in support of the 2d Battalion darkness was falling and the enemy strength was such that at best stalemate only could be effected.

One might speculate on what would have happened had Cavender at once committed the 3d Battalion in support of the 2d, and pushed the 1st Battalion on toward Schönberg. As alternative he might have committed the 1st Battalion in support of the 2d immediately on Puett's call, the while sending the 3d toward Schönberg.

The best to have been expected in either case would have been successful concentration of the entire regiment along the Bleialf–Schönberg road before darkness fell that afternoon. The worst that could have occurred would have been what actually happened—one battalion on the out-skirts of Schönberg; but at least the Bleialf enemy would have been blocked.

Cavender's final decision of the night, given the situation in which he now found himself, was, on the other hand, the one appropriate course which would further the mission: To cast the dice once more in what as all at the conference now began to realize, was a long-shot gamble on the fortune of war.

He had to concentrate somewhere. His 3d Battalion was nearest to the objective. True, he would have to abandon his transport; no more vehicles could get through the mud in the valley beyond. But, were he to call back the 3d Battalion and concentrate in the Radscheid area he would not only be leaving the objective but also he would be remaining in a situation in which the enemy had already shown superior force. Furthermore, there was the question of that coming air drop. That would be to the north.

So the orders went out and exhausted men with sleep-seared eyes struggled to their feet and stumbled heavily northward through the night.

The artillery went first; the prime movers could pull the howitzers to the one position available—on the bare northern nose of Hill 575, five hundred yards north of Radscheid crossroads on Skyline Drive. Then Cannon Company went sliding down past them into the Ihren Valley. Puett's gallant, decimated 2d Battalion unhooked itself from the Cutoff and followed. Craig's 1st Battalion began to untangle itself from the steep ravine below Oberlascheid, leaving Company A to cover the move; Craig's job was to protect the regimental rear, closing the perimeter behind Lackey's howitzers.

Cavender, in messages back to Division—they were not received until next morning—reiterated the critical situation in which he found himself.[37]

In the 1st and 2d Battalion areas grim-faced medics—officers and men—watched their comrades melt into the night. Then they turned to continue their task of caring for the wounded piled up in the bleak and overcrowded first-aid stations. For there was no transportation. The regiment was leaving its wounded.

The scenes were shifting for the finale.

NOTES TO CHAPTER 6

[1] "Our" is the manifestly incorrect word in the G-3 journal.

[2] General Jones, in conversation with the author, 21 January 1947, stated that he did not designate a common commander of the Schnee Eifel forces because of the uncertainty of the situation at that time.

[3] Message No. 436, 106th Infantry Division G-3 journal, 17 December. Also statement of Lt.Col. Josiah H. Towne, AC, attached to VIII Corps, who relates that he received the call from the 106th Division on 17 December and relayed it—a request for food and ammunition for two regimental combat teams—to Col. Myers, A-3 of IX Fighter Command, who in turn relayed it to IX Tactical Air Command. What happened after that is another story, which will be taken up at the proper time.

[4] This was probably a company of the 17th Tank Battalion, part of Combat Command Reserve, 7th Armored Division.

[5] According to Capt. Martin.

[6] Except for the light tank companies.

[7] Probably—we don't know, of course—part of the disguised 150th Panzer Brigade.

[8] One of Skorzeny's terrorists?

[9] Erroneous information. Corps, at this time must have been in quite a dither. 7th Armored Division G-3 journal notes after it—"Read after our column was cut at and south of Malmedy."

[10] At this time only the 424th CT and CCB, 9th Armored Division, south of St. Vith, were still east of this line, as they clung to the west bank of the Our.

[11] Riggs says Company A; 7th Armored Division overlay for that day says Company B.

[12] Capt. Harold M. Harmon, 81st Engineer Battalion.

[13] Unit of 150th Panzer Brigade?

[14] Repeated for the reader's benefit: "To 422 and 423 Infs: Panzer regtl CT on Eimerscheid–Schönberg–St. Vith rd, head near St. Vith. Your mission is to destroy by fire from dug in positions S of Schönberg–St. Vith rd. Am, food and water will be dropped. When mission accomplished, move to area St. Vith–Wallerode–Weppeler. Organize and move to W."

[15] Letter of Tech.Sgt. Black to the author, 17 October 46.

[16] Capt. E. C. Roberts, Jr., of D Company.

[17] Lt. William P. Doheny, C Company, 422d Infantry, to the author.

[18] Walker, *op. cit.*

[19] *Ibid.*

[20] *Ibid.*

[21] The Cutoff so frequently mentioned was a 500-yard-long woods trail connecting the Schönberg–Bleialf road and Skyline Drive over the hills between Bleialf and Auw. Widened and corduroyed by the Division engineers, it shortened the distance between Schönberg and Radscheid by two miles, and obviated use of the dangerous hairpin turn over bare Hill 539 at Justenschlag, nicknamed Purple Heart Corner by the 106th because it was always under desultory interdiction fire from German 88s. The Cutoff ran from a sharp bend in the Schönberg–Bleialf road three-quarters of a mile southwest of Radscheid, up a steep ravine, to debouch on Skyline Drive at the southern outskirts of the village of Radscheid itself.

[22] Narrative of CO, 423d Infantry, in possession of 106th Infantry Division Association. There is no record of any such order in Division G-3 journal. Apparently it was transmitted by radio.

[23] Cavender says the order was to "move to the right of the 2d and endeavor to cut the Bleialf–Schönberg road." Klinck (narrative of CO, 3d Battalion, 423d Infantry, in possession of 106th Infantry Division Association) says the regimental S-3 brought the order direct to his leading element, L Company, "to advance by a different route with mission to cut the Bleialf–Schönberg road and await further orders."

[24] Message No. 587, G-3 journal, 106th Infantry Division, in 201300A.

[25] ". . . in substance a coordinated attack with 422d Infantry to seize high ground east of Schönberg and destroy enemy panzer columns on Auw–Schönberg–St. Vith road." Narrative of CO, 3d Battalion, 423d Infantry.

[26] Narrative of Lt.Col. T. Paine Kelly, commanding 589th Field Artillery Battalion. Kelly, it will be remembered, when cut off from his outfit the previous day, came down into the 423d Infantry area with Puett's battalion and the artillery. His narrative, from the viewpoint of an impartial observer, has been of great value in reconstructing the Schnee Eifel action.

[27] *Ibid.*

[28] Says Klinck.

[29] Not surprising, since the 422d instead of being on the right of and generally abreast of Klinck, was now southeast of this position. Klinck's battalion was far in advance.

[30] Narrative of Major Carl E. Cosby, executive and later commanding 1st Battalion, 423d Infantry, in possession of 106th Infantry Division Association.

[31] Kelly is of opinion that the attack became disorganized; it probably did.

[32] No firing was done from these positions.

[33] Says Kelly, who was present.

[34] Kelly narrative. (The patrol must have been at one point within five hundred yards of the 422d bivouac. R.E.D.)

[35] Lt.Col. Charlie A. Brock, G-3, 106th Infantry Division. No record of this message has been found in the Division G-3 journal.
    Kelly, among others, considers this appeal to patriotism to have been "slightly insulting and totally unnecessary." Cavender, who says he received it about 10:00 P.M. merely notes that the order stated "it was of the utmost importance that I seize Schönberg." Puett mentions it as the "for the good of the nation" message; both he and Kelly refer to it as having been somewhat garbled.
    The picture at Division, as given in the G-3 journal, is covered by the following message:
    "No. 512, *out 182100A.* To 423 Inf: Supplies for you and 422 Inf will be dropped at bend in road one-half mile south of Schönberg (995880) on 19 Dec. You will advise 422 Inf.
    "No. 515A [badly out of place in file. R.E.D.] *out 190555A.* To G-3 Air, VIII Corps

(call taken by Major Norman): A 50-ft square of orange panel will be displayed at (P962867) instead of prearranged bend in road for dropping supplies for 423 Inf." [This would indicate some unrecorded exchange of conversation between Division and regiment. The coordinates given pinpoint an open area six hundred yards south of the 3d Battalion position. R.E.D.]

[36] Since the regiment was marching over narrow woods trails, in column of twos, deployment for action would necessarily be very slow in any event.

[37] As listed in the Division G-3 journal these messages contradict to some extent eyewitness accounts, unless one disregards the alleged date time. For the record, they follow:

"No. 525, in 190230A, dated 181220A. From 423 Inf: 3d Bn position facing W along Schönberg–Bleialf rd at (957874). 2d and 1st Bns have been heavily engaged astride road S Radscheid. Remainder of CP being moved to vicinity 3d Bn.

"No. 526, in 190355A, dated 181220A. From 423 Inf: 590 FA has three hundred rounds; casualties moderate; out of contact with 422 Inf. Med supplies and evacuation critical. Motors lost. Urgent escape route be opened. If unable to reach drop point, will display panel.

"No. 527, in 190600A, dated 181535A. From 423 Inf: Head 3d Bn at (960864). 422 Inf cross country on [right?] with head at Oberlascheid. 2d and 1st Bns clearing out enemy from woods SW of Radscheid. Need am, food and water."

Checked against the trend of eyewitness accounts, and in view of the other apparent errors of transcription, it is believed that these messages should run in sequence: 527, 525, 526; and that the date time on the two last should be 182220 instead of 181220. The information contained in them clicks with the situation as known at the 423d Infantry command post some time after 10:00 o'clock that night.

Chapter 7: The Fourth Day

Sepp Dietrich's Sixth SS Panzer Army was not doing so well at dawn of 19 December. The 12th SS Panzer Division was butting its head against the Büllingen shoulder, the 1st SS Panzer was poking in the area Stavelot–Stoumont but was meeting increasing resistance southward between Vielsalm and St. Vith as the 7th Armored Division's CCA built up its screen from Vielsalm east through Recht.

It was all very well for Kramer, Chief of Staff of the Sixth SS Panzer Army to reiterate "The principle was to hold the reins loose . . . I never worry about my flanks!" But the fact was that the corridor between Büllingen–Stoumont on the north and Vielsalm–St. Vith on the south was only seven miles wide.

And the Yankees at St. Vith were still astride of the one main road through the mountains. Furthermore, though perhaps Sepp Dietrich and his chief of staff might not have known it, the Krauts fighting in that part of the Our Valley were still worried about that force they had bottled up in the Schnee Eifel.

That day at Schönberg German medical officers worked only on American surgical cases. They told a captured American doctor who was working in the dressing station with them that if they had to retire all patients would be left under the American care.[1]

South of St. Vith Manteuffel's Fifth Panzer Army was progressing in fine shape. That didn't help Sepp Dietrich's disposition much, either, for there was intense jealousy between the *Wehrmacht* and the SS.

Manteuffel's panzers and infantry were rolling toward Houffalize and Bastogne, had already reached Clervaux. Only on his northern flank were the combat teams of the 116th Panzer and 62d *Volksgrenadier* Divisions being seriously impeded southeast and south of St. Vith.

And there it was again: St. Vith. St. Vith, which was to have been taken on 16 December! All in all a pretty hot potato to pass up to Field Marshal Walther Von Model, of Army Group B, the overall commander of the forces engaged in the Ardennes.

Coming back to our side of the picture, on 19 December Generals Jones and Hasbrouck at their command posts in Vielsalm were trying to stem the tide. Hasbrouck was responsible north of St. Vith. The fog of war hung heavy over Vielsalm as scraps and bits of information were reported, as rumors of enemy thrusts from the north, the east and the south drifted in.

VIII Corps was closing down at Bastogne as the hostile tide welled nearer, opening its command post at Neufchâteau.

Our St. Vith peninsula was now sticking out still farther into the enemy tide, the Schnee Eifel islet in front of it. The Krauts were twenty-four miles inside the old lines on the north, sixteen miles north-west, and in rear, of St. Vith. On the south the flood was twenty miles southwest, and in rear, and still flowing freely. Inside that area we were facing three ways; no man knew when we might be battling back to back.

So far as concerns the 106th, two vital questions loomed. Most im-portant, of course, was the situation of the 422d and 423d Infantry Regiments up in the hills, behind the iron curtain. During the early morning the three messages noted above came in[2] so late that they threw no real light on the day's situation.

At 6:10 A.M. Division, reiterating previous instructions, sent a radio to the 423d Infantry: "Display 50-foot panel orange at (P962867) [the previously agreed-on drop point]. Make every attempt to establish contact with 422d Inf in regard to dropped supplies."

There was no answer. There would be none, though the message was repeated every fifteen minutes all through that day and night.

It was 2:30 P.M. when Division queried VIII Corps: "Please advise at once if supplies were dropped to units this division in vicinity Schön-berg." And it was 10:00 o'clock at night that VIII Corps radioed back the shocking information: "Supplies have not been dropped. Will be dropped tomorrow weather permitting."

That was that. Someone, it seemed, had blundered. It's about time that we look into this air-drop business. We won't find much. The only evidence is the statement of Lt.Col. Josiah T. Towne, AC, attached to VIII Corps. He handled the initial request of Division,[3] for an air drop of ammunition and food for the surrounded outfits, sent in on 17 December.

Towne states that the message was forwarded through IX Fighter Command to the IX Tactical Air Command, which apparently, he alleges, ruled that the request must be handled through ground chan-nels, and forwarded it to G-4, First Army. Then, further alleges Towne, someone in First Army G-4 office, ostensibly because the request had not come through "proper channels"—direct from G-4, VIII Crops—held it for twenty-four hours, telling no one of his action. When the red tape was straightened out weather over target and base had closed down.[4]

When it is considered that such an air drop would have had to be made by Troop Carrier Command from bases in Britain, and in view of the amount of supplies necessary, it is hardly possible that under the best conditions the drop could have been carried out before some time during the day and night of 18 December.

Weather conditions over the target on 18 December were not too bad. Though the fog over the Schnee Eifel was heavy that morning, P-47s were operating in the Stavelot–Stoumont area, twenty miles away; they thoroughly strafed a Kraut panzer column near Andrimont. American Thunderbolts were over the Schnee Eifel on the 17th, 18th and 19th. Kelly remembers seeing those on the 19th and wondering if the long expected drop was coming.

Weather conditions over the base that day are not known. The author, himself in the Lorient area of Brittany during 17-19 December, knows from personal experience that fine weather existed midway between base and target on 17 December, that it was misty during the morning of 18 December but cleared up by noon, and that on 19 December rain and fog were so bad between Lorient and Paris that it is doubtful if any cross-Channel lift could have been attempted.

Which is prelude to the author's opinion that a drop might have been made on 18 December, the planes being vectored in by instrument if necessary. In justice to these brave men of the 422d and 423d Infantry whose hopes were raised by the *ignis fatuus* of an air drop, and in justice to the Troop Carrier Command which always tried its best in emergency to bring in supplies to beleaguered troops, it is the author's considered opinion that a Congressional investigation into this business is called for.

Towne's comment on 16 January 1945 is: "Somebody in First Army should be court-martialed for the delay which was involved."

In the early morning word was received from the 424th Infantry on the south, of the 112th Infantry's withdrawal to the Weiswampach area and of its isolation from the rest of its division. Gen. Jones sent Lt.Col. Slayden down to that area. Slayden found the regiment still further pulled in, its command post at Huldange. After conferring with Col. Nelson, commanding the 112th, Slayden returned with the recommendation that Jones assume command of the isolated regiment. Hasbrouck, to whose command post Nelson had come that morning, made the same recommendation.

The 106th's commander already knew that the Krauts were deep in 28th Division territory that day, for Lt. Jack McGuire, commanding the MP Platoon, had been sent down to reconnoiter the Houffalize–Bastogne highway for possible withdrawal, and had run into them at Houffalize.

McGuire and Sgt. Robert Cramer in their jeep came around the hairpin turn just north of Houffalize, ran past the park along the river on the flat, to find a German tank scrambling in circles like a wounded crab, at the road junction before the steep climb to the south.

They had just time to realize what it was when the tank's guns let go. While it was having trouble with a tread, there was nothing wrong with its fire power and the two Americans ducked their jeep around a corner. Two hours passed before they could get away. Then McGuire, reporting, begged a bazooka team to bag the tank. They returned to find it gone. But a Kraut staff car—a Lincoln Zephyr, by the way—came swirling up the road, and the MP group knocked it out, killing the three officer passengers and the driver.

Now, with the McGuire incident in mind, Jones informed Corps at 4:00 P.M.: "I have assumed control of 112th Infantry of the 28th Infantry Division and its attached units and will coordinate defense of that sector." Gen. Jones then sent his second in command, Gen. Perrin, down to coordinate the dispositions of the 112th and its supporting 229th Field Artillery Battalion and ensure that it linked with the 424th Infantry in what was now rapidly becoming a bulb-shaped defensive sector, some eleven miles from north to south and ten miles deep in enemy-infested terrain, with its western base on the Salm River.

In the center the St. Vith defenders were standing fast. Liaison between CCB, 9th Armored Division, and the left flank of the 424th Infantry was not all that it should be—a gap showed up generally south of Dreihütten as the enemy began infiltrating across the river between Steinebrück and Auel, supported by heavy artillery fire. But the 424th was trying to maintain contact.

And in front of all these things the tragedy of the Schnee Eifel reached its climax.

END OF THE ROAD

Behind the saddle of Hill 536 athwart the high nose over Schönberg, the 423d Infantry huddled at daybreak 19 December. Over the saddle and barely visible through the mist to the outposts of the 3d Battalion lay Schönberg town, half a mile northward, in a fold of the Our Valley. Men gnawed at what K rations remained, cursed the lack of drinking water, stirred their chilled bones.

Puett's 2d Battalion had gathered in the night, was on the reverse slopes of the hill to the right. Craig's 1st Battalion, less Company A which had been left as covering force, was slightly behind the others. Company A should have been in by this time, but runners had not found it. It would never join; it had missed the way in the night, had turned eastward and bivouacked beyond Oberslascheid. Its story will come later.

The 423d was at about half fighting strength. The 1st Battalion could muster two depleted rifle companies, the battered but still cocky 2d Battalion had lost nearly fifty percent of its personnel. (Puett had 19 officers and 405 men left). The 3d was in fairly good shape. Ammunition, except for caliber .30, was practically nonexistent. On the slope behind them across the trickling Ihren and its mud bed, Lackey's 590th Field Artillery Battalion had less than three hundred rounds for its howitzers, sufficient for one good, hard blow.

After visiting Klinck's battalion long before dawn, Cavender had discussed the situation with his battalion commanders, had decided on his scheme of attack which he formally announced at 8:30 A.M. While he was speaking the 1st Battalion was moving forward beyond the 2d for its jumpoff position. The 422d Infantry was somewhere; no one knew exactly where.

The regiment was to attack in column of battalions echeloned to the right-rear—3d, 1st, 2d. To Klinck on the left fell the main effort. The main effort would have been better made, perhaps, on the right, but the battalions were not disposed that way, and the 3d Battalion was the only one strong enough for the task. Time of attack: 10:00 A.M.

Precise, formal, Cavender, his order given, glanced at his watch to coordinate the time: "It is now exactly 9:00 o'clock."

The group stiffened to attention to salute. Then—"It sounded like every tree in the forest had been simultaneously blasted from its roots," says Kelly—a Kraut battery salvo fell almost in their midst, mortally wounding Lieutenant Colonel Craig and scattering all to cover. The salvo opened a concentration of all calibers, coming from Schönberg, which swept the area.

Nagle, the regimental executive, hustling around the area despite the wound he had received at Bleialf, after the first terrific burst of fire ran across a huddled and bewildered group of soldiers from a headquarters unit. The first sergeant didn't seem to know what to do with them, despite Nagle's reiterated orders to scatter them under cover, get them moving on.

Then out of the woods stalked one lone, large Negro soldier, tommygun nonchalantly tucked under an arm bearing a corporal's chevrons.

"Colonel, sir," he reported, "you-all seem to be alone here. I'm from the 333d Field.[5] Anything you want me to do?"

"Get this platoon organized, corporal. Move north, covering the flank."

"Yes, sir!"

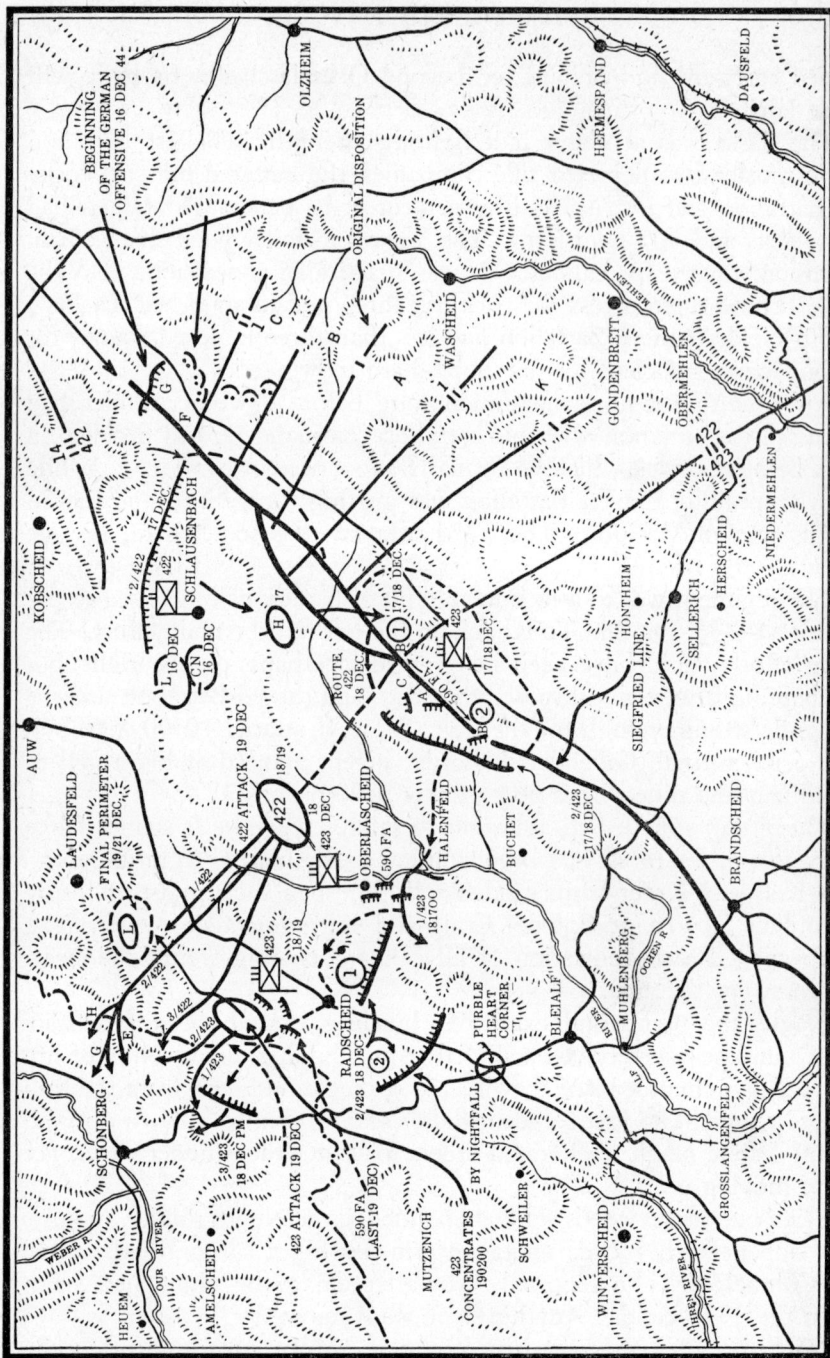

Map 5: The Tragedy of the Schnee Eifel.

And as Nagle went his way the platoon, fighting men once more, was creeping forward, well scattered, under the booming voice of one corporal who knew he was in command and knew his business—leadership. Nagle never saw him again. It's too bad one doesn't have that man's name.[6]

The barrage pounded in for some thirty minutes, then lifted.

Shouts rose from over the valley to the rear. Lackey, on the way from the conference to his guns, with Kelly, could see a wave of Germans overrun his positions. The 590th was through. Cavender urged on his attack. It was all or nothing now, with the enemy from Bleialf attacking the rear.

Klinck's 3d Battalion jumped off smartly. Capt. J. S. Huyatt's L Company, moving up the Schönberg road with two platoons in attack, the third in reserve, supported by a machine-gun platoon of M (heavy weapons) Company, ran smack into heavy 88 and 40mm antiaircraft artillery fire; they were blocked, pinned down. A Sherman tank nosed around the hillside, and L Company breathed easier; the rescuing armor had arrived at last. Then the tank, as it came abreast of the company line, raked it with all its guns.[7]

The tank passed on, but from the reserve platoon in the rear the crackle of rifle fire rose. German infantry, more of the Bleialf crowd, in about company strength, were attacking. Huyatt pulled out part of his advance elements to repel this, became involved in a whirl-about fight, counterattacked, fought his company up a hillside and actually drove the enemy off with many casualties.

Then Huyatt took stock. He had thirty men still on their feet, together with fifteen of the machine gunners. Although in walkie-talkie contact with the battalion, the company was completely cut off physically. They dug in. The encroaching Krauts came back, ammunition began to give out. At 1:30 P.M. a German rush from all sides captured what was left, some thirty-two in all.

When L Company was hit, Lt.Col. Klinck had committed I Company to relieve the pressure and close the gap with K Company, still moving toward Schönberg. The two companies actually got to the outskirts of Schönberg, but without artillery support were at the mercy of the enemy fire—some of it now direct.

By 3:00 o'clock in the afternoon Klinck could go no farther. He pulled the remnants of his infantrymen up on the slopes of Hill 504 off the Schönberg road and held, while groups of mop-up Kraut armored infantry flitted on his flanks, cutting off stragglers, getting closer every moment.

The 1st Battalion was messed up from the start. The wounding of their battalion commander, Craig, delayed the attack order. The first barrage broke up D (heavy weapons) Company, killing the company commander, two platoon leaders, and many men. Major Carl H. Cosby, battalion executive, assumed command, heard the 2d Battalion behind him preparing to move off, and started for the line of departure.

On the way a regimental staff officer tagged C Company for regimental reserve. So Cosby's "battalion," when it launched its attack, consisted of one rifle company—B—and the battalion command post group. This latter was soon separated from the company in the thick woods. Company B got to a clearing, fought its way to the Schönberg road, ran into direct 40mm antiaircraft fire which halted it, and was then surrounded and overrun by tanks. Cosby and a small group of his men joined K Company of the 3d Battalion. The 1st Battalion had ceased to exist by noon.

Puett's 2d Battalion, sideslipping to the east some five hundred yards, moved out in good order on the right and rear of the 1st Battalion, and pushed on until abreast of it, with a deep draw between the units. Puett could hear the heavy firing on his left, and from his position on Hill 504 could see Schönberg.

Puett—remember that he was in reserve—felt that he could attack to good effect and sent word to regiment. Communication was broken, however, and at 2:00 o'clock, having gotten no answer the aggressive Puett decided to attack Schönberg by circling to the east.

The battalion moved down into the ravine of Linne Creek, which empties into the Our a thousand yards east of Schönberg. As the leading elements deployed into the draw they came under a blaze of heavy small-arms fire from the other side. The crackle ran along the right rear.

Shaken, the battalion attempted to re-form to meet the new enemy, only to discover that they were being attacked by the 422d Infantry.

Inside of five minutes the error had been rectified, but the damage was done; both outfits were badly disorganized.

Thus Cavender, as the clocked ticked toward 4:00 o'clock, found his regiment with one battalion wiped out, another—Puett's—entirely out of his control, while the remnants of Klinck's 3d, with which he was, were being swept by waves of artillery and small-arms fire as they clung to the Schönberg hill.

To complete the picture we must go back to the morning, take a peek at the enemy, and also note the dispositions of the 422d Infantry, which we had left crowded in its bivouac area just south of the Skyline Drive.

There can be no doubt that by early morning all German units in close contact with the Schnee Eifel positions knew that the American units had moved out, and were threatening Schönberg and the Our Valley road, so essential to them. On the northwest they had been attacked all the previous day south of the town (3d Battalion, 423d Infantry), on the southwest the Bleialf German forces had been fighting below Radscheid (2d and later 1st Battalions, 423d) and on the northeast tank detachments reconnoitering from Auw had had brushes with an infantry force moving northwest (1st Battalion, 422d). Certainly one can assume that by now the Kraut patrols had also gotten into the abandoned Siegfried Line positions.

During the night German patrols had been weaving in and out of the area, had effectively prevented contact between the two regiments.

The threat to Schönberg must be eliminated. So it was that as dawn broke we find the German artillery opening on the regimental assembly areas, and both infantry and artillery—particularly antiaircraft artillery—so emplaced as to immediately resist any American advance, while both tanks and infantry pushed in aggressively.

The fact that, to protect their line of communications from our Air Forces, the Krauts had rushed large quantities of antiaircraft artillery into the area, was of immediate value to local German commanders, who poured flak on both regiments.

Descheneaux's plan of attack for the 422d was an advance with 1st and 2d Battalions in line, echeloned to the right, and Thompson's 3d Battalion, already emasculated by the draft of men to form the two "provisional" companies noted previously, in reserve.

Moving out at approximately 7:30 A.M., the battalions, already in some confusion of mixed units, crossed Skyline Drive to come under enemy fire about 9:00 A.M.[8]

The 1st Battalion, on the right—its original commander, Lt.Col. Thomas Kent, had been killed and Major William P. Moon, Jr., was in command—was at once hit by 88s and machine guns. Company C, with two platoons in line and one in support, was raked by this fire as it crossed the bare knob just north of the highway and five hundred yards south of the beginning of Ihren Creek. Its forward movement was broken up, its 1st Platoon alone managing to push on the high ground north of the creek. Descheneaux, joining them there, halted their advance to coordinate with his left.

The remainder of the company, badly disorganized, broke up, the 2d Platoon drifting to the east, under Lt. Robert R. Wessels, a few of the remainder seeping westward to run into the parked transport of the 423d in its mud-packed valley, by now overrun by the enemy.

Companies A and B never got out of the assembly area, for Kraut tanks materialized from the direction of Auw, pinned them down with fire and then moved in for the kill. Remnants of Company A got into the 2d Battalion zone, on the left, but B Company was destroyed.

Exit 1st Battalion, 422d Infantry.[9]

Lieutenant Colonel William D. Scales' 2d Battalion, though scotched by the fire raking the assembly area, got away in good style, G and E Companies abreast from right to left, and H Company in close support (F, it will be remembered, had been lost the night before and was now with Klinck's 3d Battalion, 423d Infantry, together with a machine-gun platoon of H). They crossed Skyline Drive, up to the high ground won by C Company's 1st Platoon, and pushed on.

They reached the open ground overlooking the Our Valley, east of the Linne ravine. To the west a thousand yards was Schönberg. Below them motor vehicles, bumper to bumper, packed the Schönberg–Andler road. "Friendly vehicles," someone decided, "don't fire on them." And G Company plunged northwestward toward the objective.

Small-arms fire ripped from the far side of the ravine. And as the advance paused the "friendly" vehicles sprayed the open hillside with fire. They were Kraut flak half-tracks! Scales, Major Ouellette, his executive; Capt. Jacobs, H Company commander, and headquarters were down in front with G Company. Up the slope was H Company, which began to take the Krauts below with machine-gun and mortar fire. Lt. Emmitt Harman, trying to assist a wounded noncom, was killed, as was Lt. George E. Hammond, who like Harman had been standing erect, observing and correcting mortar fire. The flak guns, at that range, were deadly; all of H Company's machine guns and two of its mortars were knocked out by direct hits. Tech.Sgt. Samuel F. Baxter, rushing in to clear one of these guns when it jammed, was killed by one of these direct hits. Pfc. Joe D. Beneditto, crawling back to his gun to complete its destruction, was badly wounded (he would die later in the Christmas Eve bombing of the POWs at Gerolstein). Staff Sgt. Almond, who had called down his mortar fire on himself up in the Schnee Eifel that first red day, raced and rolled a hundred yards downhill successfully to silence a Kraut machine gun yammering at them. These are a few of the acts of raw courage accomplished on that bare hillside.

The mortar men of H Company, too, in that mad half-hour, played their part. Corporals Edward W. Dorn, Andres H. Madsen, Jr., Irvin E. Brough and Robert I. Snovel, Jr., scored three hits in eleven rounds on the enemy SPs, knocking two out of action, crippling the third, before the enemy fire smashed their pieces.

What was left of H Company, under Lt. Lewis H. Walker, himself twice wounded, fell back over the slope to momentary shelter. Up from the ravine to join them came fragments of E Company, badly disorganized now, and stragglers from various units.[10]

Walker got the outfit back into a patch of woods a thousand yards west of Laudesfeld, found he had 199 men from fifteen different units, including Wessels' 2d Platoon, C Company.

Cut off from the remainder of the regiment, with Krauts on all sides, with rumors of surrender flying, Walker took stock. Across a dip three hundred yards to the south Lt. Hartley, the battalion's S-2, recognized Hill 575 and the regimental motor pool. Staff Sgt. Pearsall went out to reconnoiter; it was still held by Americans. The group, dodging Kraut machine-gun bullets, made their way safely into its perimeter.

Here, too, would come later what was left of G Company, some 150-odd men, which Capt. Kielmeyer had held under control, falling back from the debacle in the Linne ravine.

And that's what happened to the 2d Battalion.

Lieutenant Colonel Donald F. Thompson's depleted 3d Battalion, the left element of the regiment, came up to the high ground to the west of the 2d, plunged down into the Linne Creek ravine, saw armed men moving on the other side and opened up—on Puett's 2d Battalion, 423d. At this time both outfits were receiving cross fire from the Germans who had taken Lackey's field artillery and held Hill 536 to the left rear.

As the two outfits milled around in reorganization, Puett joined forces with Descheneaux, at the same time sending out patrols down the ravine toward the Our, to try to find a covered route to Schönberg.

The patrols reported back about 2:30 P.M., with word that 1,500 yards to the right some thirty-odd Kraut tanks and self-propelled guns were massed, that there was strong armor to the front in the valley, and that more artillery was coming in across the river enfilading their present position.

Descheneaux was pulling his forces into a perimeter defense; he could go neither forward nor back. Machine-gun fire was sweeping the hill, a steady stream of wounded were being carried into the dressing station beside the command post—pitiful men with staring eyes, for whom there was no food, dressings nor blankets.

Puett, obstinate, went out himself to reconnoiter the situation. While he was gone Descheneaux pondered. There was no more machine-gun ammunition, there was no food or water, his remaining battalion fragments were melting before his eyes. Kelly and Lackey, artillerymen without guns, had made their way to him from the 423d, and he knew that Cavender was ringed round, that the artillery was gone.

"The situation was hopeless," says Kelly, "but some of us were in favor of holding out until dark and attempting to get out in small parties. I thought that had been decided upon and went to dig a slit trench when Descheneaux sent out the white flag. If his command post hadn't been the regimental aid station he could have stood it a while longer—he had been right up with the leading elements in the attack that morning. It's just as well, I guess, that he surrendered—it was just a question of time and we weren't even a threat."

Descheneaux decided—with bitter heart. He sent out a white flag, ordered firing ceased and weapons destroyed.

The flag had gone when Puett came back. He demanded permission to try to cut his way out with his battalion, but Descheneaux said no. It would only make matters worse, now. Puett told his men any could go who wanted to, and between fifty and one hundred drifted away.

It was over. And just about that time—4:00 o'clock—Cavender of the 423d, in the midst of his own parched remnants, a thousand yards to the west, had come to the same conclusion, put up the white flag and ordered all arms destroyed.

Nagle it was on whom Descheneaux placed the onus of arranging for the 422d's surrender. With a soldier who could speak German the executive officer moved cautiously out of the perimeter until he ran into a group of Kraut ack-ack men about a 20mm gun, waved and got to a Nazi major.

"That was the hardest thing I ever had to do," says Nagle.[11] "The worst part was coming back and telling the men how and where they should surrender. Many of them didn't understand it; they wanted to fight on."

What had started out, in theory, as a coordinated attack by two regiments of infantry and one battalion of field artillery had in fact ended in a tragedy of futile efforts by brave, bewildered men. One cannot but deplore Division's continued decision to handle its two cut-off regiments by remote control, the while one wonders at the fog of war which evidently blanketed the regiments one from another all during their approach from the Schnee Eifel positions toward Schönberg.

The regiments in their perimeter defenses in the Schnee Eifel, despite the dwindling of all ammunition (except .30 caliber), and of medical supplies and rations, could have lasted for several days. Supplied by air they could have continued indefinitely, necessitating a co-ordinated enemy attack on the stronghold, costly and time-consuming.

Offensive action in the open, over ground they had not reconnoitered, against an enemy whose strength and dispositions (except that he was all around them) were unknown, and lacking ammunition for their artillery, mortars and heavy machine guns, was something to be attempted only in desperation.

On the other hand it was essential that every effort now be made, desperate as it might seem, to break up the Our Valley assault rolling in on St. Vith. The fact that the 422d and 423d Infantry had to be removed from their Schnee Eifel Siegfried Line positions to attack Schönberg is just one more proof of the fallacy in initially choosing positions which were not situated to bar an enemy counterattack.

What was needed under the circumstances, was one resolute, clear-headed commander on the spot in the Schnee Eifel, who could have taken the responsibility of running a coordinated show and who was not hampered by a hold-the-Siegfried-Line order. And that, it seemed, lacked.

If, however, the proposed attack on Schönberg was in itself a dismal failure, the net result was a definite contribution to the defense of St. Vith; one more factor of delay. For until the threat to the Our Valley irruption was erased, Sepp Dietrich's left flank could not concentrate in force in front of the Prümerberg.

Of this the Yanks in the Schnee Eifel may be proud.

AND THE AFTERMATH

When the 422d and 423d Infantry surrendered on that fatal afternoon of 19 December, there still remained in the Schnee Eifel woods and crags a residue—as the Germans found out. This residue can be classified in three categories.

First there were those who, breaking up into little groups or individually, fought, bit, clawed and sneaked their way back to the American lines. Second, those who rallied into a large group and fought on for nearly forty-eight more hours until they, too, surrendered. And finally there were those who, wandering in the woods, cut off from all hope, nevertheless fought on in guerrilla war for weeks until, so far as is known, every last man of them was hunted down and killed.

There is record of the first two classes and we will follow them. The last we know of only through hearsay, and their story is so fantastic that it might be classified as fiction if we did not know that through all this war, as in past wars, not only is truth stranger than fiction but also that men exist who refuse to accept the dictates of fate, and stop fighting only when the breath of life leaves their bodies.

Let's look first at those who fought and got back.

When Company A, 423d Infantry, lost its way in the early morning hours of 19 December, after pulling out from its covering position for the 1st Battalion south of Radscheid, it ended up in Oberlascheid. Here too came Lt. Ivan H. Long and his regimental Intelligence and Reconnaissance Platoon, who had been holding a roadblock on the outskirts of Radscheid.

Long, finding his platoon alone in a world of Krauts that morning, had previously run into a detachment of F Company, 422d Infantry, dug in just south of Radscheid. The Lord only knows how they had wandered down there. He determined to get on north to the regiment, with his vehicles, but when warned by one of the regimental medicos in the village that he couldn't make it, and artillery fire began dropping into the position, he wrecked his transport and led his men northeast to get out of range.

This brought him to Oberlascheid, where he found Major Sanda B. Helms, S-4, and Capt. Nauman of Company A organizing a perimeter defense with some flotsam and jetsam of both regiments and some 820th TD men.

At noon it was decided to break out, taking a wide swing to the northeast—seemingly the only way open—flanking Schönberg, and joining the regiment. As they started, a German 88 which had rolled up nearby opened on them. The outfit broke up. Nauman led Company A north, and ran into a strong force of Germans—this would be the enemy striking across Skyline Drive from Auw and smashing in the right of the 422d—and after a short fight they were gobbled up, except for Lt. Harold A. McKinley's platoon in the rear.

Long and McKinley joined forces, some forty men in all. They hid in the woods by day, moved at night by compass, edging due west all the time, and finally dribbled into St. Vith on 21 December, where they were thawed out, fed, rearmed and took their place with Riggs' engineer defense force.

Individual and small-group escapes were many. Perhaps the most amazing was that of Capt. Edward H. Murray, First Sgt. Wallace D. Rifleman and Pvt. Dickerson, of Company G, 423d Infantry.

When Puett told his 2d Battalion they were free to attempt to save themselves as the white flag came up near Schönberg, Captain Murray, his topkick and the private started off together. They, too, hid by day and travelled by night, creeping past enemy bivouacs. They sneaked past Setz, crossed the Our and worked north, ran into a Kraut sentinel in the Bois de Wallerode on their last lap.

Murray stabbed him but the blow was not fatal and the German began to scream. Dickerson grabbed him by the neck and Murray stabbed again, this time finishing the work, but also slashing the private's hands badly.

The trio got into the 7th Armored Division's lines; Dickerson went to the hospital and the captain and first sergeant fought with the 7th. Murray was badly wounded by a shell fragment and hospitalized. Rifleman later joined the 424th; we shall hear of him again.

Cannon Company, Antitank Company and Headquarters Company, 422d Infantry, who found themselves jammed south of Skyline Drive behind the Hill 570 ridge, with the motor park, never got into action. Anxiously they waited for word to advance. Finally in late afternoon they saw a large group of men on the road, which fugitives told them were men of their own regiment, now prisoners.

Captain E. Bruce Foster, commanding the special units, had heard the baseless rumor previously mentioned, that the 9th Armored had recaptured Bleialf. He now asked for a volunteer patrol to get through to Bleialf and make contact with the 9th.

Three jeeploads of volunteers, under Lt. Irvin Juster, started down the road. Just on the outskirts of Bleialf a large force of Germans debouched from the village. Cpl. Troy H. Kimmel, who had a .50-caliber machine gun in his jeep, shot it out with them until his ammunition belt was empty. The patrol, some twelve men in all, then discarded its vehicles and took cover. They attempted to climb a hill along the Düren ravine slope, but were finally surrounded and captured.[12]

According to Tech.Sgt. T. Wayne Black,[13] the motor column now took off, apparently following Juster's patrol. It must have moved down toward Niederlascheid, motors roaring and vehicles careening over the rough trails, with 88 shells crashing overhead and in the trees. It got to a village "about three kilometers east of Bleialf" (perhaps Buchet) when the road was found to be mined. The column ground to a stop. A handful of Germans popped out, the column surrendered. The Germans rearmed the Kraut prisoners to which the 422d had still hung on, and the respective roles were reversed.

When the tide of battle had overflowed the 422d Infantry's right and its assembly area, the fragments of the 2d Battalion, as we have said, found themselves, with scattered remnants of other outfits, washed back to the east into the original regimental rear echelon and motor park. This was situated southwest of Laudesfeld, by Hill 576, where two side roads meet jutting north from Skyline Drive.

Here a detachment of the 634th AAA Battalion had been established and a defensive perimeter had been organized. Amazingly, it seems, this islet had been untouched by all the previous fighting. About this nucleus now rallied the debris from the Schönberg fight—infantrymen, engineers, artillerymen. Here came Major Albert A. Ouellette, 2d Battalion executive; here, too, Major Moon, commander of the 1st Battalion, found himself. They prepared to stick it out.

By late afternoon there were approximately five hundred men in the force, all with plenty of small-arms ammunition, and with the not inconsiderable fire power of some twenty .50-caliber machine guns. There was still some food; enough was gathered up to deliver two scant hot meals for every man for the next two days. By nightfall the position was fairly well organized.

Patrols established the fact that the two regiments had surrendered, and that the outfit was surrounded, though the enemy fire at first appears not to have been too heavy.

But that night Kraut artillery began to plaster the position as the enemy discovered that there was still some organized resistance. The Germans pressed closer. During the next day patrolling was simple. A man would stand up, a burst of fire would follow; contact had been made.

Casualties were surprisingly few—the men had learned to take cover. And the Kraut began to play cat-and-mouse with what he evidently felt was a plum which would fall into his hand without unnecessary casualties.

Loudspeakers blared from the German lines all through the day of the 20th. "Berlin Betty" cooed persuasively into their radio, which was still working.

From the loudspeakers came American jazz intermingled with hearty invitations to come in for hot showers, warm beds and hotcakes for breakfast.

Gaunt-faced, hungry and dirty men received the solicitations as might be expected from American fighting men. Major Gaylord G. Fridline, MC, regimental surgeon, tells of seeing one man sitting in a ditch, tears of rage streaking his muddy cheeks while the German loudspeaker rasped. Every few moments the man would bellow "Blow it out, you German son of a bitch!"

"There wasn't much we could do about it," summed up another survivor in a group interview later. "It just made us awful mad. It sounded as if the bastards were all around us." They were. Some kept cheering their comrades—probably cheering themselves too—as they murmured: "They'll get through to us, all right. We'll get out yet."

But Staff Sgt. Richard A. Thomas, of H Company, after listening to that rasping loudspeaker a while, decided that something *could* be done about it. He rounded up a few volunteers with hand grenades and they wormed their way across the valley to the knoll where the enemy sound-truck stood. "Berlin Betty's" playful reference to the joys of playing baseball in a POW camp ended with the wham of a well directed grenade.[14]

And so the long day of 20 December passed. A heavy machine-gun section set up on the hill commanded Skyline Drive, and cross fires had been arranged. It was after noon that a German reconnaissance car flying a white flag came down the road from Laudesfeld. In it was a German medical officer from Schönberg and a captured 423d Infantry medic.

The officers's first proposal was astounding to his hearers. Would the Americans consider a truce so that the Germans could evacuate wounded, both Kraut and Yankee, over the roadnet to Schönberg? It was all rather apologetic and sportsmanlike, but as his sharp eyes took in the situation he added another suggestion. Perhaps the Americans would consider surrender.

Ouellette decided to send Lt. Houghton, D Company, over to make sure the Germans had nothing up their sleeves. He would assent to the transfer of wounded. And a "suspend fire" order went out until Houghton came back, about 6:30 P.M. He brought word of artillery trained on the position and of troops poised to rush in after a preparation; the Germans had given him opportunity to see their strength and had set 11:00 P.M. as deadline.

A conference of officers was called. Capt. Kielmeyer and Lt. Walker recommended holding out for two days more, but the others felt that without artillery further resistance would only cause needless loss of life and would not affect the tactical situation. The 634th AAA's radio had reported to Division they were still holding out, but so far nothing had been heard in answer.

At 11:00 o'clock a German officer turned up as hostage to continue the "suspend fire" order and to dicker further on surrender. Ouellette

finally agreed to surrender at 8:00 A.M. next day, provided a truce
would be kept until that time. After some argument, because, the
German said, he could not guarantee against attacks from another
enemy division bearing down from the north, the compact was made.

That night those men who so desired were told they were on their
own. Many drifted off, but small-arms fire in the distance told its story
of interception.[15]

Weapons were destroyed and all ammunition buried in the mud.
The motor pool men cut tires, ripped out ignition wiring, stuffed sand
in gas tanks. Everything was done which would render the equipment
useless.

And at 8:00 o'clock the next morning, 21 December, Ouellette and
his garrison threw in the sponge. The last organized resistance in the
Schnee Eifel had ended.

At least so thought Field Marshal Model, *Obergruppenführer* Sepp
Dietrich and the sharp-visaged Rex Degrelle, the Belgian traitor who
commanded the wolves of the Wallonian SS Division of Belgian Nazis.
All three, with their respective staffs, moved into the little village of
Meyerode, six miles northeast of St. Vith by direct line on 22 December.
Sepp Dietrich took up his quarters in the house of the *Bürgermeister*,
Jean Pauels.

"POWERFUL . . . AND BRAVE OF SPIRIT."

And Jean Pauels and his neighbors tell a fantastic story.

It has to do with a tradition that has grown up in that war-wracked
Ardennes village of 52 homes and 280 inhabitants; the tradition of an
American officer—young, big-framed, bold-hearted, who, so the story
goes, gathered about him American stragglers from the Schnee Eifel
and from 20 December until a few days before the Americans threw
the Germans out for the last time, waged guerrilla warfare in the grim
pine woods.

As they tell it in Meyerode[16] when the Germans poured through the
Büllingen Forest and swept down the Malmedy–St. Vith highway,
brushing back the 14th Cavalry Group, two bands of American soldiers
were engulfed behind them.

The larger one—the Germans told the Meyerode folk there were 120
of them—fought for several days on the Adesberg, Hill 523, north of
the village, whence they several times raided the Malmedy–St. Vith road.
It was Christmas Day or thereabouts that a Kraut task force with artillery support finally rounded them up.

But, on the afternoon of 18 December, as Meyerode recalls it, had begun something else again. For it was late that afternoon when Peter Maraite went into the woods southeast of Meyerode to cut a Christmas tree. And by a six-way trail crossing one mile away from the village he ran into two armed Americans.

Neither could speak the other's language, but Maraite convinced the two wet, cold and tired Americans that he was a friend, and on his invitation the trio slipped back to the house, where the woodsman's wife pressed hot coffee on the pair and daughter Eva hustled quietly over to the home of Jean Schroder, who spoke English. There were Germans all around the village now, although none had as yet been billetted in homes, so the watchdog was put out to give warning if prowlers should come, and behind closed doors, while the women rustled up hot supper, the Americans and the Belgian burghers held confab.

One of the newcomers was an officer, with single silver bars; a big young man with confident, smiling face. He "said funny things, which made us laugh," notes Peter Maraite. Both were cheerful and determined. The soldier, a small man, was armed with a rifle, not a carbine; the officer had his pistol, and a map.

The officer told them he and his companion had broken away from a small group who had been surrounded near Schönberg. He was going to try to get back to St. Vith. He was also concerned with the fate of his men "who were all very good and loyal men to whom he owed all possible care."

When the villagers assured him that the country between them and St. Vith was full of Germans the officer wasn't disturbed. He said very calmly that he would "either fight his way back to his own outfit or, if that proved to be absolutely impossible, would collect American stragglers, of whom he had seen some in the woods, and start a small war of his own. It couldn't start too soon to suit him; he hoped that he might meet SS men that night—he and his friend would take good care of them."

But the Maraites persuaded them to stay the night, and start at dawn next day. They oriented the officer on the countryside, showed him where they knew German bivouacs to be, explained landmarks. All these things he noted on his map. They dried their clothing, cleaned their weapons, and slept that night in the Maraites' own double bed.

They needed the sleep, apparently, for they slept through the explosion of a V-bomb which dropped nearby. And before dawn the Maraites woke them up, fed them breakfast, gave them sandwiches "well buttered, with plenty of meat therein." Peter Maraite put them on their way, "accompanied by our prayers."

And, beginning 20 December, things began to happen in those woods to the east and southeast, behind the German lines in the dense Omerscheid area of the southern stretches of Büllingen Forest. Daily, bursts of small-arms fire, with sometimes the wham of a mortar, came on the cold air to the ears of the peasants huddled in their homes.

When the weather cleared around Christmas, and the Allied air forces began to take their toll of the German columns, fighter-bombers continually strafed the highways, particularly the roads from St. Vith to Schönberg and to Malmedy. So German daylight movements were routed through the two secondary roads in the woods below Meyerode.

Traffic coming westward down the Our Valley turned off the highway just above Andler, passing through Herresbach and thence to Meyerode, whence it moved south again, if St. Vith-bound, back to the highway, joining it in the Bois de Wallerode, two and a half miles in airline from St. Vith. This latter route was split into two narrow one-way lanes through the woods trails. Traffic north and west of Meyerode flowed at night only, from the village over the secondary bare road across the Adesberg to Amblève. And to keep the woods network passable, the Meyerode village six-horse snow plow was pressed into continuous use. There was no other way; the snow was now three feet deep.

It was an ingenious network, efficiently planned for maximum protection from the air. But, as the Krauts found out, no provision had been made for ground protection.

And the Meyerode people began to notice that never did a small body of Germans, nor a transport column, pass from the vicinity into those woods roads, that one of those mysterious bursts of fire did not follow. Large forces came and went at will, however. And the Krauts issued orders strictly forbidding civilian movement into the woods.

Chance words dropped by the Germans, unguarded outbursts of wrath from both officers and men of the staff detachments billeted in the village, plus the evidence of their own eyes, were gradually pieced together.

Sepp Dietrich himself, quartered in the *Bürgermeister's* house, began to thunder about American "criminal scoundrels and bandits." The Krauts were nervous, itchy. Working parties went out only under heavy guard. Daily, wounded men came in from the easterly woods, some hobbling, some carried by their comrades. Over the hot stoves Kraut orderlies growled and gossiped. The *verdammte Freischütz,* it seemed, flitted like ghosts through the trees and hid in snow banks. A man travelling those woods never knew when a bullet would come singing through his brain.

Meyerode is small, and soon, from the patches of conversation, from the whispered exchange of gossip, all knew of the Maraites' visitors. From the daily crackle of small arms on the winter air, the burghers of Meyerode built up a theory. The theory was that out in the forest a small organized group of Americans roamed. They were armed, they had medium mortars, they took constant, irritating toll of the Germans. No Americans were ever brought back by the searching patrols that now went into the woods daily, so it was assumed that they brought no man back alive.

And all the stories added up one way: That these Americans were led by a young officer, "very big and powerful of body and brave of spirit." He kept his wolf pack going, it was said, by sheer will power. How they existed during those winter weeks, no one knew. There was an abandoned American dump at a trail crossing just a mile south of Meyerode, in which—after the Germans had gone—the villagers found quantities of mortar ammunition still remaining. Perhaps the American rovers found K rations, too. Perhaps they subsisted on what they might find on Germans they killed. Most probably they lived on horse meat. German horse-drawn artillery and transport had many casualties.

When the invasion ebbed, the people of Meyerode began to comb those woods. The *Bürgermeister* first sent two competent woodsmen, his cousin August Pauels and Servatius Maraite, to search. They found burned-out, gutted German vehicles strewn from Meyerode to Herresbach, and down the southern road to the St. Vith highway. They found German graves; they also found some unburied German dead; two hundred was the estimated toll. And they found a few American dead.

They found, in particular, in a dense thicket just off the southern road, a thousand yards below the six-way crossroads where Peter Maraite met the two Americans on 18 December, the body of an American officer. He was a big man, "with single silver bars upon his shoulders." Near him lay the bodies of seven German soldiers. That no live German had later visited the spot, the villagers agree, was evidenced by the fact that the American officer still had in his pocketbook four thousand Belgian francs.

That man, say the American Graves Registration people who passed through the area later and collected our dead, was Lt. Eric F. Wood, Jr., 589th Field Artillery Battalion. Eric Wood, of whom we last heard when he broke for liberty six thousand yards southeast of Meyerode on the morning of 17 December; Eric Wood, whose indomitable spirit had gotten Battery A through its first ordeal in the Schnee Eifel.

And, careful check of records and statements of eyewitnesses shows

that the only officer of the 106th Infantry Division unaccounted for—
this is, neither dead, nor alive as a free man or a prisoner of war—from
16 December 1944, was Lt. Eric Wood.

That's the story.

Powerful . . . and brave of spirit.

ST. VITH HOLDS OUT

Returning to the immediate situation on 19 December, we find CCA,
7th Armored Division, consolidating along the general arc Poteau–
Recht–Gut Eidt Farm. Here, just northwest of St. Vith, it linked with
the left of CCB, 7th Armored Division, which was, we recall, attached
to the 106th Division.

Combat Command A continued to find strong resistance in the vicinity of Poteau, where enemy tanks scrabbled about without making any
definite thrust. A roadblock was established at Sart-lez-St.Vith against
enemy penetration.

Closer to Vielsalm CCR, 7th Armored, was establishing itself as
secondary defense. Hasbrouck was taking no chances on another enemy
breakthrough.

In front of St. Vith the elements of CCB, including our engineers of
the 106th, the 81st and 168th, solidified the defense of the town and its
road net. That morning the line ran north to south: C Company, 23d
Armored Infantry; Companies A and B, 38th Armored Infantry; B
Troop, 87th Reconnaissance Squadron; Company A, 81st Engineers;
Nungesser's 168th Engineers (Companies A and B); Headquarters and
Service Company, 81st Engineers; and on the right flank the rest of the
23d Armored Infantry.

The Krauts made no coordinated attacks on the defense that day,
though all indications pointed to a massing for another thrust. An
incessant artillery fire hailed down, taking a heavy toll. Tree bursts
did the most damage, despite the efforts of the defenders to cover their
foxholes with logs and earth.

The indefatigable Lt.Col. Riggs, who up to that time had commanded
the defense task force, under the direction of Gen. Clarke of CCB, was
replaced by Lt.Col. Fuller, commanding CCB's 38th Armored Infantry
Battalion; Riggs became his executive officer.

The methodical Kraut in this area, as we have said, was too much
occupied with reducing the Schönberg threat that day to drive at this
irritating brake to his progress.

Farther south the enemy was crossing the Our in some force between
Steinebrück, Hemmeres and Auel, despite the efforts of the attenuated

CCB, 9th Armored Division, to hold him. While its left was in contact with the right of the St. Vith defense force near Breitfeld, Hoge's right, Company A, 27th Armored Infantry, was pushed back from Maspelt.

This left a considerable gap between CCB, 9th Armored, and the 424th Infantry. Hoge asked the 424th Infantry to plug this gap in the Maspelt area, but the regiment could not do it. As a result, during the night the enemy infiltrated up the railway line from Steinebrück, between Hasselbach and Lommersweiler, grabbing Neidingen.

Reid's 424th Infantry that day had some trouble up by Bracht, as the enemy pressure started to build up on the Hasenknopf. It was the 62d *Volksgrenadier* Division as identified by prisoners later taken from the 182d and 190th Regiments. Despite Reid's efforts he could not make contact with the 9th Armored. His patrols to the south during the day could not find the 112th Infantry either, although he sent one motor patrol seven miles down the west bank of the Our.

Reid's general line was now fairly firmly established on the heights between Bracht and the Our Berg, through Burg Reuland, but, as he reported to Division at 3:00 P.M., from his command post at Gruflingen (Gruflange), his regiment was now down to fifty percent efficiency from the previous fighting—with both flanks in the air—and he had prepared plans for withdrawal though determined to hold out as long as he could.

On the night of the 19th Reid sent Lt. Robert S. Logan, S-3 of Lt.Col. Orville Hewitt's 2d Battalion, toward Beiler with a strong combat patrol, contacting outposts of the 112th Infantry's 1st Battalion.

One gathers that the 424th and its supporting artillery, the 591st Field Artillery Battalion, were attending to their knitting.

The Keystone Regiment Falls In

Nelson's 112th Infantry and the 229th Field Artillery Battalion had received orders from the 28th Infantry Division at midnight, 18-19 December, to withdraw to Troisvierges, three and a half miles west of its Weiswampach–Beiler position and thence fight a delaying action falling back on Bastogne. But as its after-action report notes, "In the absence of information on the enemy, orders were issued to the battalions to move during the night to the vicinity of Huldange, where the 229th Field Artillery Battalion was now located, and prepare to move from there to the Troisvierges–Bastogne line." The move started at 6:00 A.M. and was completed by 1:30 in the afternoon.

Then followed Slayden's visit to the regiment, and the order of the 106th attaching it, which was received by Col. Nelson at 5:45 P.M.

In the meantime B Company, which had been fighting with the 424th Infantry, returned to regimental control.

A Kraut push from the south was turned back and the day ended with the 112th dug in in its Huldange positions. Here Gen. Perrin came down to organize the southern flank. Perrin directed the regiment to seize the Beiler Berg, a ridge commanding the Our Valley, and also tie definitely in with the right flank of the 424th.

The 112th Infantry and the 229th Field Artillery Battalion had become members of the family.

NOTES TO CHAPTER 7

[1] Narrative of Lt. Michael E. Connolly, MC, 589th Field Artillery Battalion, in possession of 106th Infantry Division Association.

[2] See note 37, page 132, *supra*.

[3] See note 3, page 130, *supra*.

[4] Section VIII, Annex No. 2, G-4 Report, *U.S. First Army Report of Operations, 1 August 1944-22 February 1945*, contains the following on the subject:
"By the afternoon [17 December] two RCTs of the 106th Infantry Division had been completely cut off and calls were received for preparations for supply by air, which were promptly set in motion. . . ."
". . . Confirmation was received [18 December] that air resupply for the 106th Infantry Division was needed. However, a combination of the weather, and difficulties of communication and of getting accurate drop locations delayed the project. . . . [Page 120.]
"The situation remained fluid throughout the day [20 December] . . . two regiments of the 106th Infantry Division however were completely cut off and the matter of air supply continued to be impossible." [Page 121.]

[5] 333d Field Artillery Battalion (155s), part of 333d Field Artillery Group, VIII Corps. This unit was overrun in its positions near Schönberg, losing ten of its twelve pieces.

[6] Lieutenant Colonel Nagle to the author, 4 December 1946.

[7] One more score for the 150th Panzer Brigade.

[8] There is some conflict of opinion as to when the actual attack order reached the battalion commanders. Lt.Col. Donald F. Thompson, commanding the 3d Battalion, which was directly under the regimental commander's control, states that contact with the 1st and 2d Battalions was lost when his unit moved on Schönberg at daybreak, on Descheneaux's order, but that shortly afterwards he got in touch with the 2d Battalion.
He received the attack order at approximately 9:00 A.M., and soon after regained contact with the 1st Battalion about a thousand yards away to the right. (Letter to the author, 8 October 1946.)

[9] The account of Capt. E. C. Roberts, Jr., of D Company, differs sharply here from the above, which is a résumé of all other narratives noted. Says Roberts:
". . . As dawn came Company A jumped off first, supported by D Company machine guns. The mortars were set up on the edge of the woods to fire on targets of opportunity. They had very few rounds of ammo left. B Company followed and then C, in successive waves. The attack was going well until about 9:30 A.M. when three German Mark IVs hit us in the right flank coming down the road from Auw. We had no antitank guns and were unable to stop them at long range. They sensed our attack was coming from the woods and began firing 88s into the trees.
"Major Moon ordered the rest of the battalion to move out of the woods to the left down a draw where we would have some cover. . . . I took the mortar platoon and the company headquarters out of the woods as ordered. There were in the group altogether about three hundred men. Major Moon had led the staff out during the attack and had reached and crossed the road just as the tanks began firing on the attackers.

"The draw in which we were turned sharply to the right and went toward the road, getting smaller and smaller as it went. Small groups of men were trying to cross the road when the tanks began filling the opening of the draw with fire . . . Another tank pulled up behind us and began to fire at the other end. The slaughter at the end of the valley by the road was bad."

Roberts, with First Sgt. Edward Olicki, rushed to the top of the hill with a bazooka. One of the tanks was only seventy-five yards away, with a dozen Kraut infantrymen around it.

"We loaded and got ready to fire," continues Roberts. "When I saw several of our own men walking toward the tanks with their hands up, I saw it was useless to fire because I was sure they would kill all those men. We broke up our weapons (no ammunition now) and surrendered. There were about 250 in this group I guess."

10 Walker, *op. cit.*

11 Lt.Col. Nagle to the author, 3 December 1946.

12 Letter, Lt. Irvin Juster to the author, 11 October 1946.

13 Letter to the author, 17 October 1946.

14 Walker, *op. cit.*

15 Walker, *op. cit.*

16 Affidavits of Jean Pauels, *Bürgermeister* of Meyerode, Belgium; Peter Pauels; Peter, Anna Maria and Eva Maraite; Servatius Maraite and Jean Schroder: supporting recommendation for award of Medal of Honor.

Chapter 8: The Fifth Day

+++

The German timetable was sadly disrupted by this time. Sepp Dietrich's II Panzer Corps was still trying to come through the bottleneck down from Losheim. The Our Valley road through Schönberg, open now that the menace in the Schnee Eifel had been eliminated, was nevertheless cluttered up by the transport jammed back for miles.

Until St. Vith was taken and the northerly roadnet freed, II Panzer Corps could not operate. And its weight, plus the drive of its predecessor, I Panzer Corps, now definitely sagging southward, was pressing on the right wing of Manteuffel's Fifth Panzer Army below, itself prevented from northwest movement by the St. Vith barrier.

So, as we reconstruct the operation, 116th Panzer Division, following the path of least resistance, as happens in any large-scale military operation of this kind, was moving west by south, together with the 340th *Volksgrenadiers,* while the 62d *Volksgrenadiers* were concentrating on the southern flank of the St. Vith defense force.

The St. Vith picture, from the enemy viewpoint, was not at all improved by the fact that aggressive armor (7th Armored Division) was building up a ring of steel from the Salm River west to St. Vith. The reduction of this salient was of first priority; steps were taken.

Covered by the dense screen of the Bois de St. Vith a task force of armor and infantry was concentrating for a final coordinated blow at the Prümerberg position. Build-up of artillery strength in direct support was also in progress. As diversion, and to further test the American strength locally, small thrusts were to be made along the line from Neidingen south. In particular, the possibility of a penetration westward generally from Maspelt into the Bois de Thommen, where the defense appeared to be sensitive, was to be explored.

From the American side of the "big picture," XVIII Airborne Corps, whose major elements were the 82d and 101st (detached) Airborne Divisions, was coming into action—the former into the vicinity of Werbomont, west of the Salm River and eight miles west of Stavelot, generally northwest of Vielsalm; the latter, relieved from XVIII Corps control, going to its epic defense of Bastogne. To the east of the 82d's area, CCB, 3d Armored Division, was attempting to seal the gap north of La Gleize, and east of that again the 30th Infantry Division was linking up with the right flank of the Büllingen shoulder defenders, where the 1st Infantry Division was arriving.

These things, of course, were unknown at Division headquarters at

Vielsalm as 20 December dawned in gloom. Gone were the rosy dreams of armored counterattacks which would restore the situation; gone the high hopes that the 422d and 423d Infantry Regiments and their attached units could cut their way out. Grim, dreary silence had replaced the sporadic radio communication with them, silence relieved once during the day when the Division Artillery radio net picked up a message from D Battery, 634th AAA Battalion, up there in the hills with them, indicating that the 590th Field Artillery was still in action, near Radscheid, but surrounded. Then the curtain dropped. One assumes that that message was sent the previous day.[1] For the rest, the Germans appeared to be everywhere.

One thing certain—the 106th Division major elements still in action consisted of the 424th Infantry, the just attached 112th Infantry of the 28th Division, CCB of the 7th Armored, and CCB of the 9th Armored. Of Division Artillery only one battalion, the 591st, was accounted for, in support of the 424th Infantry. The 589th and the 592d had momentarily disappeared from the picture, and Gen. McMahon had sent Col. Craig hotfoot to find the 592d as well as the missing elements of the Division Artillery's Headquarters Battery. The "kidnapped" 589th, it developed, was at a place called Baraque de Fraiture. We will go into its adventures later. Craig found his missing people and got them back that day. His story is worth the telling.

West of the Salm and South of Namur

Craig had chased his erring children all afternoon and evening of the 19th. Information en route indicated they had passed through La Roche—twenty-three miles to the west, and were moving toward Marche.

At Marche, where he arrived in pitch darkness, Craig found one man trying to do a job—Lt.Col. Harvey R. Fraser, commanding an engineer battalion. He had been catching infiltrating Krauts all day, had organized roadblocks and intelligence patrols and was, as Craig says, "in general making things just as difficult for the German Army as any battalion could possibly do."

From Fraser, Craig learned that probably his missing battalion was on the way to Dinant, while the headquarters party, with Lt.Col. Fayram, was going toward Namur, twenty-eight miles away.

Here Craig found the latter, rounded them up and started them back, in two trucks of the 423d Infantry which Fayram had commandeered in his flight.

An all-night drive brought them back to the vicinity of Marche again,

where Craig halted them and resumed his search for the 592d, which
he found at Rosée, fifteen miles west of Dinant. The battalion started
back *pronto;* one doubts not that Craig's words were acid.

In Marche Craig tarried only long enough now to draw small-arms
ammunition and hand grenades from the efficient Fraser for his headquarters detachment, then moved to La Roche, where 88mm shells
interdicted further progress. They turned north to Hotton, seemingly
losing the 592d Field Artillery again, to find the hard riding 3d
Armored Division arriving, dirty, bearded and heavy-eyed after two
sleepless days of rush.

Tough, dependable and most welcome were these reinforcements in
a topsy-turvy world. And here, almost at the same moment, the 592d
came helling in after a roundabout run to avoid that La Roche pocket.
Craig says they were moving faster than he's ever seen an artillery outfit
roll. Together with the armored troops the reunited artillerymen now
pushed for Erizée, where the 3d Armored was concentrating. From
there on the artillerymen were on their own. Local rumor had it that
the road was held by the enemy, but fortunately that proved to be un-
true, for between Manhay and Bra elements of the 82d Airborne were
moving in.

At Bra the word was again that Krauts and Krauts only were to the
east. There was but one thing to do—chance it. So the 592d rolled—
through Lierneux—and at last, a half-mile from Vielsalm, a 106th
Division sentinel challenged. They were back. It was 7:30 P.M. The
592d went to positions near Commanster, to reinforce the 591st.

"Curiouser and Curiouser"

The ubiquitous Slayden, sent by Gen. Jones to the VIII Corps command post at Neufchateau that morning, came back with real news.
Maj.Gen. Troy H. Middleton, commanding the corps, had informed
him on this, Slayden's "biggest day," as he set it down in his diary,
VIII Corps was going under Third Army control. The 106th Infantry
Division would come under XVIII Airborne Corps, which was the
first inkling either to Jones or Hasbrouck of the shift. XVIII Corps,
it seemed, would comprise the 106th, the 7th Armored, 3d Armored,
82d Airborne and the 30th Infantry Divisions, with responsibility
for the line Houffalize–Malmedy.

More amazing, since Jones was senior to Hasbrouck (as was Hoge
at that time), Slayden, who had had to run the gantlet of enemy fire as
he rode through Samrée, reported that the 106th Division had been
attached to the 7th Armored!

Slayden volunteered, he says, to go to Werbomont, where XVIII Corps was setting up its command post, and get details of this plan of which the commanders of the 106th and 7th Armored knew nothing. To add to the confusion, Middleton had told Slayden that he wanted the 168th Engineer Battalion and CCB, 9th Armored, to be returned to VIII Corps.

Slayden went, to find that Ridgway's XVIII Corps in its plan for the defense of the line Stavelot–Vielsalm–Houffalize had not contemplated employment of the 106th Division and its attached units. Corps said that they wished the release neither of CCB, 9th Armored Division, nor of the 168th Engineers, and would clear those matters with First Army; also the odd situation with respect to Jones and Hasbrouck.

In the meantime the immediate front was flaring. The 7th Armored was standing to the north—to CCA had come Division orders to hold "at all costs"; it was imperative that CCA command the road from Recht to Poteau and thus keep the Vielsalm–Sart-lez-St.Vith road open. CCR was building up its protection between Poteau and Vielsalm.

In front of St. Vith along the 106th Division sector CCB, 7th Armored, maintained the Hunnange–Prümerberg–Breitfeld line. CCB 9th Armored, which was receiving a certain amount of punishment, was informed there would be no further withdrawal.

Several attacks were made on the 424th Infantry sector but were repulsed. The 112th Infantry succeeded in its forward movement in re-establishing itself on the Beiler ridge.

Division Artillery headquarters, oriented by its efficient communications net as well as by Col. Craig's report, was able at 5:45 P.M. to give Gen. Jones the approximate locations of the 82d Airborne and 3d Armored Divisions. It had also picked up the fact that Bastogne was now in a state of siege, with Brig.Gen. "Tony" McAuliffe's 101st Airborne Division and its attached units being attacked by strong hostile elements from the north and east.

So it was with no surpirse that a delayed call for help was received from VIII Corps later in the evening, relayed through the 7th Armored Division—not that the 106th could do much about it:

"There is a large attack," read the message, received at 8:46 P.M. though transmitted as of 10:15 A.M., "on Bastogne, from the direction of Houffalize. It has reached a point six kilometers east of Bastogne. Can you send something small to attack the enemy in the rear? The 112th Infantry has a battalion near Gouvy. If it is not engaged, ask the Commanding General to have it advance in direction of Bastogne and hit the enemy in the rear."

Word was passed to the 112th Infantry and G Company moved out. One company—all that could be spared.

There is some excuse for this; news, as we have seen, passes slowly back. Large units are dependent upon their subordinate units for information. The divisions of VIII Corps were, to put it mildly, in a state of flux; their reports to Corps sketchy. And, naturally, Army was dependent upon Corps for its information under normal conditions.

However, this was far from a normal situation, and there is room for speculation on the efforts and operations of liaison officers in higher elements, and on the evaluation made there of such information as they did gather.

A few moments later, 8:55 P.M. to be exact,[2] both divisions received a letter of instructions from VIII Corps, dated 19 December, and particularly illuminating because it indicates that neither First Army nor Corps had at that time fully realized the gravity of the situation.

Army had ordered Corps to stabilize the line from Recht to St. Vith and thence down south to the east of the Houffalize–Bastogne highway, tying in with the 4th Infantry Division near Echternach. "Enemy pockets in rear of that line will be isolated and destroyed where found," it stated. "There will be no withdrawal. Units whose front lines are now west of the line to be stabilized will regain lost ground." This order Gen. Middleton was repeating.

And now to Hasbrouck at 10:30 P.M. came a First Army radio[3] confirming the word Slayden had brought:

"Ridgway[4] with armor and infantry is moving from west to gain contact with you. When communication is established you come under command of Ridgway. You retain under your command following units: 106 Inf Div, RCT 112 and CCB 9 AD. All of above units presently attached. Ridgway has CP in vic of Werbomont. He holds Malmedy, Stavelot and Trois Ponts."

This message was timed 12:30 P.M. that day.

THE ST. VITH FRONT

Clarke's CCB, 7th Armored Division, in the midst of which our engineers were encadred, spent the day of 20 December attempting to improve their thin-held positions, an arc of approximately one mile.

Although the enemy artillery fire kept up, no thrusts were noted, it appears.

As darkness came down a detachment of engineers drawn from the 106th Division units began laying a series of hasty minefields along all possible avenues of approach through the Prümerberg woods, except at the road junction of the main St. Vith–Schönberg highway and the woods road to Schlierbach. Use of mines at this junction had been forbidden to permit the use of the roads for our counterattack—if and when. Four of CCB's medium tanks were emplaced to reinforce this point and cover the road approaches.

On the front of Hoge's CCB, 9th Armored Division, the enemy infiltration to the high ground at Neidingen became apparent before dawn. Attacks by their patrols were reported back to Division at 6:45 A.M. However, by 10:30 A.M. the situation had quieted and Hoge's patrols were probing both flanks and front.

The enemy came back again in the afternoon south of Neidingen against the 27th Armored Infantry. Supported by one light tank, he moved incautiously into the open where he was caught by time fire laid down by the 16th Armored Field Artillery Battalion, and thrown back with heavy casualties. By 6:30 P.M. that portion of the front was quiet.

The gap between the 424th Infantry and CCB, 9th Armored, however, still remained, a running sore which the 62d *Volksgrenadiers* were determined to keep open.

THE SOUTHERN FLANK

Reid's 424th Infantry was also hit by the enemy pushing up from Maspelt west along the Gruflange (Grufflingen) road toward Crossroads 515 in the Bois de Thommen, and spilling to the northwest of Bracht toward Alster, while hot artillery fire came down on Gruflange and the battery positions of the 591st Field Artillery Battalion.

About 5:00 o'clock in the afternoon the threat became serious; five tanks rolled in to support the infiltration and the left flank of the 424th was thrown into disorder.

Reid pulled one company from his 1st Battalion to defend the Alster hill mass, with his left flank refused. The attack, apparently a reconnaissance in force, was driven off after a sharp action in which the 591st Field Artillery Battalion's fire took a good part.

The regimental commander had high hopes that when the 112th Infantry came into position at Leithum he could pull his 2d Battalion back into reserve for a breather, but this was not to be.

After nightfall the 591st Field Artillery displaced from its heavily shelled positions and dropped trails at Braunlauf, a mile to the northwest.

In the 112th Infantry on 20 December Col. Nelson assigned the 2d Battalion to attack Beiler. Debouching from the wooded area west of Malscheid, the battalion, supported by the 229th Field Artillery, crossed the Bastogne–St. Vith highway at 9:00 A.M., took Beiler and the high ground around it and dug in. The 1st and 3d Battalions followed, extending the regimental sector to Leithum. Active patrols to the west covered Huldange, and a firm link was made with the 424th Infantry to the north.

As night came on the 112th Infantry was now between the Bastogne–St. Vith highway and the Our, facing mainly south, buttressing the right flank of the Division against hostile attack coming north. Company G had moved south toward Bastogne, in compliance with Division orders. It never got there. Blocked by heavy Kraut forces, the company fell back and later joined Task Force Jones, 7th Armored Division.

NOTES TO CHAPTER 8

[1] The message might have come from the perimeter defense in the motor park (See page 148, *supra.*)

[2] As noted in G-3 journal, 7th Armored Division.

[3] Annex 2 of 7th Armored Division after-action report.

[4] Maj.Gen. M. B. Ridgway, commanding XVIII Airborne Corps.

Chapter 9: The Sixth Day

The combined forces of the 106th, 7th Armored and CCB, 9th Armored Divisions, on the morning of 21 December were engaged in a salient some eleven miles long by ten miles deep east of the Salm River. Behind that line they now knew that the 82d Airborne and 3d Armored Divisions were gathering. Up north the situation was sadly vague. To the south, the enemy was romping high, wide and handsome through a fifteen-mile gap from the old 112th Infantry positions all the way to Bastogne.

It was all too evident that the full weight of a coordinated enemy attack could not be successfully resisted in this position. Insofar as the 106th was concerned, its 424th Infantry was certainly not more than fifty percent efficient, as its commander had already reported. It had been fighting now without respite for five days; its personnel were suffering from insufficient rest, from cold, from lack of normal supply and from shortages of equipment.

The 81st Engineers had been whittled down to about a war-strength company. The 591st Field Artillery Battalion, supporting the 424th, was in similar situation to the infantry. The 589th Field Artillery— well, we'll come to that three-gun battalion and its amazing adventures later; at present it was not with the Division. The 592d Field Artillery Battalion, back in action in general support of both 424th Infantry and CCB, 9th Armored, was only in fair shape.

The normal attached units, the 634th AAA Battalion and the 820th TD Battalion, had lost considerable part of the personnel and matériel, the latter having but three of its thirty-two pieces left; the 168th Engineer Battalion was down to about company strength.

So far as the general situation was concerned, Hasbrouck's 7th Armored Division was taking care of its defensive front in fine shape. However, CCA's elements were necessarily far-spread and its elements so hotly engaged that no serious additional aggressive action could be expected from it. CCB, in close defense of St. Vith, had already taken quite a bit of punishment, with probably the highest losses to date in the entire Division. CCR, defending the roadnet in shorter arc around Vielsalm, was to all intents and purposes facing three ways this side of the Salm River—north, east and south.

Hoge's CCB, 9th Armored Division, on the right flank of the St. Vith defense, was shaking down into a good fighting force, but it, too, had most of its elements engaged.

The 112th Infantry and the 229th Field Artillery Battalion, cut off from their normal supply channels, badly pushed around—like the 106th units—in the first forty-eight hours of battle, could not be considered as one hundred percent efficient; the regiment even in the beginning of the action contained a large proportion of replacements, following its losses in the action at Schmidt the previous month.

The 14th Cavalry Group, reorganized into a provisional squadron, was taking the field again, attached to the 7th Armored. And the hard-battling 275th Armored Field Artillery Battalion, supporting the St. Vith defenses, had now come under attachment to the 7th Armored also.

That's all there was of fighting troops east of the Salm River, that day.

As for supply and evacuation, ammunition and ration trains were wandering from Namur to Liège, scraping the bottom of the barrel here and there to keep the troops in action. It must be remembered that in the first few days of the rush dumps had been moved to keep them out of enemy hands. And the situation was further complicated in the case of the 106th by the fact that a proportion of its transportation—how much we will never know—had been sucked into the initial westbound panic-stricken evacuation.

Occasionally these searchers for supply came into unexpected battle. For instance, First Sgt. Charles N. Robasse, Jr., and Pfc. Loren R. Meyers of Division's Headquarters Company, tooling a truckload of ammunition back from the west, ran into Hotton on 21 December just as a Kraut attack broke into the village.

They joined the defenders (apparently a detachment of the 3d Armored Division), and took part in the ensuing fire fight. Robasse, assuming command of a squad, stormed a building under heavy fire; he was severely wounded in the leg.

The 331st Medical Battalion, which had lost one of its companies in the Schnee Eifel, was hard put both for its supply and its evacuation. The medical dump at La Roche was used for supply, and a clearing station established there, until the enemy push northward cut the road at Samrée. Evacuation then was to Liège. The task of the medicos was complicated by the fact that evacuation of both 7th Armored and CCB, 9th Armored, wounded also had to be handled.

BUMBLE BEES IN THE FOG

No account of the doings around St. Vith would be complete without mention of the artillery liaison planes, the little flying coffee mills which contain the eyes of the field artillery. We remember that when the

Kraut tide came down the Schönberg road on 17 December it was two of the flying artillerymen who assisted in putting decisive fire on their spearheads.

This was done as the orders to abandon the 106th Division artillery airstrip were being carried out. Like a covey of birds seeking shelter the little planes piloted by field artillerymen went scurrying out for safer places.

Most of the little ships finally settled down at Beho for the night after several passes at alternate fields. The next day they executed several missions although the official report was "ceiling zero." Lieutenants Lauman, pilot, and Neese, observer, reconnoitering the St. Vith road to give a picture of the traffic jam, received a hail of small-arms fire as they swept east of the city.

Other ships carried out some missions in spotting for the 591st, while the majority of the planes rendezvoused at Chérain with some Corps liaison ships. This field got too hot, and they left for Bastogne. There were more ships than pilots, and it was here that Lt. Cassibry, 589th Field Artillery observer, with but fifty-two hours flying time in an L-2, took an unfamiliar L-4 out and got it safely to Bastogne, through weather you could bite into and chew.

The ground crews had moved to Marche and it was not until afternoon of 21 December that the little flying artillery group got together at Vielsalm after a series of hit-or-miss flights.

On the German side of the picture the Sixth SS Panzer Army had now slowly gotten its II Panzer Corps—the 9th and 2d SS Panzer Divisions in column in that order—squeezed out through Büllingen Forest. They were fringing the northern side of the salient. LXVI Corps of Manteuffel's Fifth Panzer Army, consisting of the 18th and 62d *Volksgrenadiers* and the *Führer* Escort Brigade (panzers), were about to swallow St. Vith in coordinated attack, the 18th and armor directly against the face, the 62d with more armor on the southern arc of the bulge.

Below that and through the big gap the 116th Panzer and 340th *Volksgrenadiers* had burst past Houffalize and pushed northwest to La Roche on the Ourthe River. Racing alongside and to the south was the 2d Panzer Division, going like a knife through butter. Manteuffel was really stealing the ball from Dietrich.

Of these southern doings all that the St. Vith salient defenders knew was that German armor was at La Roche, had cut the road at Samrée and was coming up the Houffalize–Huy road; there was serious fighting at the Baraque de Fraiture crossroads. And this was seven miles *west* of Vielsalm.

If the enemy kept on at this pace the St. Vith salient would soon become a beleaguered island. Plans had already been made for a last-ditch stand, an all-around defense. "A sort of Custer's last stand," is the way Gen. Hasbrouck sums it up.

Hasbrouck, of course, took command in accordance with the First Army order. Gen. Jones was sent for by Gen. Ridgway, commanding XVIII Corps, but before he could go another change came in. Ridgway, by radio, told Hasbrouck to inform Jones his presence at Corps was unnecessary. The 106th was relieved from attachment to the 7th Armored as of 11:45 A.M.; both divisions were to cooperate in carrying out Corps orders.[1]

And Hoge, at CCB, 9th Armored, who had queried how come—doubtless in some amazement—when he received a 7th Armored periodic report showing his command as attached to that outfit was now told in effect to forget it.

All this on the lighter side, for the enemy artillery preparation and minor thrusts since dawn left no doubt that this would be a big day.

The shelling was particularly severe on the front of CCB, 7th Armored, along the Prümerberg line. CCB, 9th Armored, received several attacks but repulsed them. The 424th and 112th Infantry fronts received but minor probings.

But at St. Vith the dam broke that afternoon. Infantry and tanks in continuous assault attacked through the Prümerberg position, cracked it by 11:00 o'clock at night, and the tide rolled into St. Vith. CCB, 7th Armored, split, reorganized as it fell back to a position with its left in the Bois d'Emmels a thousand yards northeast of Sart-lez-St.Vith its right at the Bannvenn crossroads, just southeast of the Auf der Leig hill.

The defense of the St. Vith salient was entering its second phase. Five days behind schedule, the Kraut had St. Vith itself, might use the roads to the north. It was, as he found out, too late.

Let's see what happened.

THE END OF ST. VITH

All through the Prümerberg woods that morning of 21 December Kraut patrols probed the positions of the St. Vith defense force. The forest boiled, simmered, boiled again. Nothing hard, just continual friction, incessant firing at gray figures flitting through the splintered trees and snow-patched open spots.

From north to south the defense force as now emplaced differed little from its original line-up. The organized positions ran generally north and south from a point at the corner of the woods five hundred yards north of the Schönberg road, thence through the woods to the Schlierbach road, jogged west for two hundred yards, then carried on a thousand yards more, ending in a slight curve on the southern tip of the Volmers Berg near Galhauser Kreuz.

On the north flank was Company C, 23d Armored Infantry, then in succession Companies A and B, 38th Armored Infantry, with the Schönberg road the boundary between them. Troop B, 87th Reconnaissance Squadron, held a small stretch next south, with Company A, 81st Engineers, on the jog by the Schlierbach road. Then the 168th Engineers (Companies A and B), continued the line for another six hundred yards, with Company A, 23d Armored Infantry, on the right flank.

In reserve was Headquarters and Service Company, 81st Engineers—what was left of it, approximately a platoon in strength—and a provisional platoon made up of the remnants of the 423d Infantry who had dribbled in—Long's and McKinley's groups.

At 3:00 P.M. an intensive barrage opened up, 88s, Screaming Meemies, other artillery and mortars; the Kraut was throwing everything but the kitchen sink. To make matters worse for the defenders, after an hour or so word came from the 275th Field Artillery Battalion that it was running out of ammunition; its howitzers had been blazing counter battery incessantly.

About dusk, 5:30 P.M., the hostile fire died down. The defenders took stock as they waited for the assault they felt would follow. They had been hard hit. Troop B, 87th Reconnaissance Squadron, had some 30 men left out of its original strength of 125; it had lost forty men in the earlier action. Company A, 38th Armored Infantry, already cut down eighty percent of its strength, was so reduced now that the Provisional Platoon, 423d Infantry, was attached to it. One tree-burst at the company command post killed the company commander, the commanding officer of the supporting tank unit and two casualties who had just been carried in.

The Headquarters and Service Company platoon, 81st Engineers, the remaining reserve, was now moved behind B Company, 38th Armored Infantry. Lt.Col. Fuller went back to CCB's command post to ask for future dispositions. It was evident by this time that a strong assault would be stopped only with the greatest difficulty. Riggs assumed command while Fuller was away.

The blow came at 10:00 P.M. Tanks and infantry rolled down the

Schönberg road, which, as we remember, was unmined. The Kraut armor and infantry came in through the night in smooth team play. A tank would throw a flare, whereupon the enemy infantry accompanying it opened rapid small-arms fire. As the flare died down the Krauts hit the ground and the tank opened up with everything it had. This maneuver was repeated in short bounds. Our mortar half-tracks were spotted by these flares with great success.

Just ahead of the tank group, consisting of four Tigers and two Mark IVs, an enemy infantry rush burst through behind B Company, 38th Armored Infantry, and the Headquarters and Service Company platoon, 81st Engineers, was committed against it.

The tanks themselves ground up to the road junction, where our four medium tanks opened up on them. More flares went up in back of the American armor—fired either by infiltrating infantry or the Kraut tanks—silhouetting the Shermans. Two American tanks were promptly knocked out. Two more took their place, coming from the south where they had been supporting the engineers, but after a third American tank was rubbed out the remaining three fell back into St. Vith.

The Kraut tanks began firing point-blank into the four houses at the road junction, in one of which was the task force command post. All communication was out to the rear. Riggs ordered his headquarters personnel to report back to St. Vith with the situation, and he went forward to B Company, 38th Armored Infantry.

The road to St. Vith was open. The enemy tanks moved on, and behind them came a solid column of German troops. Riggs discovered also that on the south CCB, 9th Armored Division, had withdrawn an hour previously[2] taking with them all but a platoon of Company A, 23d Armored Infantry. Now, at long last, German troops were also moving into St. Vith up the Winterspelt road.

All that remained now of the Prümerberg position was the southern part, between the Schönberg and Winterspelt roads, consisting of B Troop, 87th Reconnaissance Squadron; Company A, 81st Engineers; B and C Companies, 168th Engineers; and the platoon of the 23d Armored Infantry—a confused group of small detachments.

The artillery forward observer's radio was still working up at B Company and Riggs reported to CCB, 7th Armored. He was instructed to attack St. Vith, the order coming back through artillery channel at 2:30 A.M., 22 December. Riggs picked a rendezvous point on the Volmers Berg and issued orders to all to rally there. But by 5:00 A.M. only seventy-five men and two officers had gathered at Riggs' disposition.

Dawn was coming shortly. An attack under those conditions would, Riggs considered, be fruitless. He split his survivors into small groups, oriented them as best he could, instructed them to infiltrate back to our lines. They broke up into the night, with the wet flakes of a heavy snowstorm stinging their tired eyes.

Practically all these men, including Riggs, were captured by Kraut mopping-up detachments within the next forty-eight hours. Of the portion of the force which had become separated from the remaining elements at Prümerberg eight officers and men of Company A and thirty-three officers and men from Headquarters and Service Company were all of the 81st Engineers who finally got back to Vielsalm.

The Kraut had pulled out his plum, five days after he had first inserted his thumb. Unfortunately for him, those five days of precious delay had staled the pie, soured the fruit.

Before dawn of 21 December the Neidingen enemy hit the left of Hoge's CCB, 9th Armored Division, again, but was driven back by 8:45 A.M. He was building up his strength in the Reiners Berg area, however, and artillery was moving in. Forward observers of the 592d Field Artillery Battalion reported a six-gun battery firing from just south of Lommersweiler, and supporting Corps Artillery fire was put on it.

Infantry supported by two tanks charged into Crossroads 515 from Maspelt and were driven off. Another infantry attack through the Reiners Berg woods was beaten back.

By 5:00 o'clock in the afternoon Hoge's line was still unchanged. Further infantry concentrations were noted by the artillery observers late in the evening, however, north of Lommersweiler.

The heavy action to the north in front of St. Vith dinned in the ears of CCB, 9th Armored, during the night as the outfit clung to its positions and watched and waited.

Pressure on the 424th Infantry was apparently nil during the day, nor was there any change along the front of the 112th Infantry where the principal excitement was a futile effort to investigate a report that five hundred American prisoners were being held, loosely guarded, at Troisvierges.

And so 21 December ran out.

NOTES TO CHAPTER 9

[1] Annex 2, 7th Armored Division after-action report.

[2] The author has found no confirmation of this early withdrawal.

Chapter 10: A Fortified Goose Egg

On the enemy side on 22 December, 9th SS Panzer Division was pushing in to the southwest in the corridor north of the St. Vith salient. Vielsalm must be secured, for the American defenses to the northwest were solidifying.

The *Führer* Escort Brigade and 18th *Volksgrenadiers* would redouble their efforts to further dissipate the splintered eastern nose of the salient, while southward the 62d *Volksgrenadiers* would drive in the direction of Salmchâteau. The 116th Panzer, already well northwest of Houffalize, would exploit down the Ourthe valley while 2d Panzer went deeper toward Dinant and the Meuse.

Sepp Dietrich, commanding Sixth SS Panzer Army, set up his command post at Meyerode, as we know, to spur his people on, while Von Model himself came in also—which doubtless added nothing soothing to the former's already exasperated nerves. The pressure was on.

American last-ditch plans for defending the St. Vith salient were predicated on the holding of the Vielsalm–Salmchâteau bridgehead over the Salm River, behind which the 82d Airborne Division was now forming.

The 7th Armored Division's sector would run north of the St. Vith–Vielsalm road in front of Poteau, in an arc covering Sart-lez-St.Vith (Rodt) and down to Neubrück. The 106th Division would hold the remaining portion, with CCB, 9th Armored Division, stretching to the Auf dem Gericht road junction nine hundred yards southeast of Braunlauf, the 424th Infantry extending the line to Beho, and the 112th Infantry carrying on from there to Bovigny, thence north to make contact with the 82d Airborne near Vielsalm.

Our St. Vith peninsula, its nose blunted by the smack that crashed through St. Vith itself, was now assuming an oval shape, extending eastward some seven miles from its larger western end, four miles along the Salm River between Vielsalm and Salmchâteau, and approximately six miles in deepest north-south width. Roughly, it was some twenty-two miles in circumference.

This was what people called, in those days of stress, the "Fortified Goose Egg." Into it, it was evident as the minutes ticked into 22 December, the 106th and armored divisions must close their ranks.

So, at 2:40 A.M., General Jones alerted Hoge, of CCB, 9th Armored Division, for a withdrawal, with instructions to coordinate with Clarke's CCB, 7th Armored, on his left. Warning orders also went to the 424th and 112th Infantry Regiments,[1] canceling a projected move of the latter to consolidate along the Our Berg hill mass of Burg-Reuland.

It was not until after 9:00 A.M. that the withdrawal orders were finally issued and all three elements began their move to the rear, again that most-hated maneuver, a daylight withdrawal. For once the weather cooperated, for a driving snowstorm lent merciful cover. It was the first occasion since their arrival in the Ardennes that the 106th Division had reason to bless the weather.

By this time the influence of General Montgomery, who had been placed in control of the First Army and given responsibility for everything north of the line Givet–Prüm, began to be felt. Monty decided that the troops in the St. Vith salient must be withdrawn behind the 82d Airborne Division.[2]

The decision when to withdraw was left by XVIII Corps to the commander of troops in the salient. Just who that was during the morning of 22 December is a question for a guardhouse lawyer to decide. For Ridgway, the Corps commander, in a letter dated 6:35 A.M. that morning, and addressed jointly to the commanding generals, 7th Armored and 106th Infantry Division,[3] wrote:

"1. The following msg. sent you at 0100 is repeated for your information: 'Confirming phone message to you, decision is yours. Will approve whatever you[4] decide. Inform Jones he is to conform.

" '2. In addition to his force, Major General A. W. Jones will command 7th AD effective receipt of this message'."

Hasbrouck would make the decision, Jones would conform, but— Jones would command Hasbrouck. As puzzling double-talk, it would be hard to beat this fifty-odd-word message.

Hasbrouck advised that should a withdrawal take place it could be either through the Vielsalm bridgehead or across the front of the 82d Airborne. Corps, approving, remarked in its radio answer: "Plans should contemplate maximum use of corridor including two bridges rather than west across the front of 82d but both are available. Inform me of plans. Expedite movement of trains. Destroy all gasoline where necessary to prevent capture."

That night Fate decided who would command. Ridgway came to Hasbrouck's command post of the 7th Armored Division at Vielsalm. Here was called Jones, and his second-in-command, Perrin.

Ridgway told them that the troops in the pocket were to be withdrawn; they had fourteen hours to accomplish the task.

General Jones was detailed as Ridgway's assistant in command of

XVIII Corps, which left Hasbrouck as immediate commander in the salient. Hoge, next senior, was delegated from his CCB, 9th Armored, as deputy commander, 7th Armored, and Jones named Perrin as temporary commander of the 106th.

Then Jones' overworked heart gave way. He collapsed, had to be hospitalized. Ridgway attached the 106th and all its attached units to the 7th Armored, appointed Perrin to command the 106th. On his departure Hasbrouck and Perrin sat down to their task of planning the withdrawal.

There were two bridges over the Salm—one at Vielsalm, one at Salmchâteau. To them three roads led: the St.Vith–Poteau highway and the Commanster–Neuville road funneling into Vielsalm and over the first bridge, the Maldange–Beho–Rogery–Cierreux road into Salmchâteau. Over this network must be passed some 22,000 men and their matériel, the while maintaining a firm delaying action. Any breach in the defensive crust could bring about a debacle.

Says Perrin: "Leavenworth never contemplated such a problem." As a classmate of his at Leavenworth, this author demurs. We had a few even more wacky, but casualties down there were personal and mental. In this case a false move meant death and disaster.

We return to the Fortified Goose Egg and its fortunes that day.

Combat Command A, 7th Armored Division found itself speedily embroiled in the increased pressure upon the salient. Not only did the enemy make a determined effort to stab through at Poteau, but he had also rolled down from Ober Emmels northwest of St. Vith and through St. Vith up to Sart-lez-St.Vith, where sixteen tanks attempted to enter the town.

The units of CCB had fallen back to the west, reorganizing on the line Sart-lez-St.Vith–Auf der Leig hill mass.

Combat Command B, 9th Armored Division, found the heat turned on in the northern part of its sector, about 10:00 A.M., with enemy infantry pushing down toward Galhausen, and down the highway from St. Vith toward Neubrück, while it was beginning its retirement. The 3d Battalion, 424th Infantry, was sideslipped to attachment to CCB, 9th Armored, in the morning, acting as armored infantry.

The driving snow cut down visibility, slowed up the hostile probings, enabling a retirement by bounds until the combat command, by nightfall, found itself established generally in front of Braunlauf, maintaining contact on the north with CCB, 7th Armored, and on the southwest with the 424th Infantry.

The 424th, less its 3d Battalion, fell back in the snow to a perimeter defense around Commanster after its proposed link with the 112th to the south had been canceled.

Lieutenant Robert Logan, S-3 of the 2d Battalion, had gone to Beiler that morning to the 112th to arrange the details of the move by which the 112th Infantry would take over the Our-Berg–Oudler sector, relieving his battalion. He returned from Colonel Nelson's command post to find the orders canceled; the 424th would pull back toward Commanster.

The 2d Battalion established itself with G Company west of Braunlauf, practically astride the railway cut, while F Company deployed on active patrol mission in the Langes Venn area, maintaining close contact with both F on its left and E Company, which had established a perimeter defense around the village of Audrange.

To the eastward of these elements was a unit of CCB, 9th Armored —a company of medium tanks beyond Maldange; while a screening shield of light tanks was north of the village. This latter was part of Task Force Jones, 7th Armored, of which more later.

Nelson's 112th Infantry, after its orders to the Our-Berg had been changed, found itself able to move without incident from the Beiler–Leithum ridge to its long defense line from Beho to Bovigny and northward. Its supporting 229th Field Artillery took positions near Bech, a thousand yards southeast of Salmchâteau.

And now we come to Task Force Jones (commanded by Lt.Col. Robert B. Jones), which Hasbrouck had organized for the screening of the southern flank. It consisted of the 814th Tank Destroyer Battalion (less two companies), 17th Tank Battalion (less one company), 440th Field Artillery Battalion, part of the newly organized Provisional 14th Cavalry Reconnaissance Squadron made up of the old 18th and 32d Squadrons of the 14th Group (predominantly 32d Squadron), and G Company, 112th Infantry, which had marched away two days previously to attack (God save the mark!) the panzers then crashing through Houffalize.

Task Force Jones' mission was the organization of a defensive screen around the southern mouth of the Bovigny–Salmchâteau corridor.

The cavalry elements of Task Force Jones consisted of two sub-task forces—TF Lindsey and TF Martin. Capt. Franklin P. Lindsey, Jr., originally commanding B Troop, 32d Squadron, had B Troop, with two platoons each of E (assault gun) Troop and F (light tank) Company screening the Beho–Gruflange road and northerly up to Crombach, where General Clarke of CCB, 7th Armored, now had his command post.

Captain Charles Martin, originally commanding C Troop, 32d Squadron, had the new C Troop with three assault guns of old E Troop, 18th Squadron, and a full light-tank company commanded by Capt. Horace N. Blair, originally of F Company, 32d Squadron. His force was screening through Chérain, Gouvy and Deiffelt, and in constant contact with enemy thrusts probing tentatively from the south.

In this fashion the curtain rises on the last act of the St. Vith salient drama.

NOTES TO CHAPTER 10

[1] No records of these in G-3 journal, but both regiments note receipt of the orders.

[2] Letter, General Hasbrouck to the author, 26 September 1946.

[3] Annex 2, 7th Armored Division after-action report.

[4] According to context, "you" is Hasbrouck.

Chapter 11: The End of the Salient

✦✦

A retirement under cover of darkness is a ticklish affair. It must be planned; the elements getting out must move on a specific timetable; those remaining must be steady, calm, unruffled. Above all, the enemy must, if possible, be deceived. Daylight retirement by troops already engaged is another affair. In the first place one does not retire unless by force of circumstances; *ergo,* the enemy has superiority. He is pressing, harassing, perhaps definitely assaulting. To put it bluntly, in a retirement, one gets out the heavy stuff first, "to let a man run who can run," as one famous instructor at Leavenworth used to remark. Then the remaining troops divide themselves into two categories, those who can march out more or less unhampered, and those who form the last crust—the men on the actual fighting line, now reduced in number to a minimum, who must, at a given moment, get out and stand not on the order of their going. Any dislocation of the timetable, any interruption in the movement can, and frequently does, produce panic. The retirement changes to a rout. That's just too bad.

So, through the night of 22-23 December the orders sped through the Fortified Goose Egg, hampered by the confusion attendant in such circumstances. The heaviest stuff got out first.

The 592d Field Artillery Battalion, which the previous day had fallen back from Commanster to new positions four thousand yards to the west, just east of Neuville, and was now attached to Corps Artillery, moved out just before midnight, dropped trails without incident in the vicinity of Chene-al-Pierre, ten miles west of Vielsalm, where it was to support the 82d Airborne Division.

Craig, the Division Artillery Executive, was in Vielsalm 22 December. He had come in with the S-4 for ammunition for the 591st at Commanster, ammunition needed immediately if the battalion were to keep up its fire, and lacking which, the retirement on the southeastern side of the Goose Egg position might have been turned into a rout. He had obtained nine precious truck-loads only to have them held up by the error of a Division staff officer.

Craig stormed into Division headquarters to release his ammunition, and there found the first news of the proposed withdrawal from the salient. The artillery, scheduled to move within a short time, must be notified. Gen. McMahon had gone to Commanster to install an artillery fire direction center. Craig encoded a rush message by means of his slidex[1] and sent it off. To his, and their, horror, the Commanster party, consisting of the artillery commander, his S-2, S-3, communications

177

and survey officers and his aide, had each forgotten to take a slidex with them!

To talk in plain English on the phone under those conditions would have been suicidal; the Krauts were continually tapping the lines. So Craig thought fast, used double talk.

"We're going to do what the Blues did in the third operation down at Tennessee," said Craig, remembering the retirement problem of the maneuvers. No one remembered what that was.

"Well, remember what the Reds did in the fourth operation? We're going to do that." Still no gleam of comprehension at the other end. And by that time Gen. McMahon had become impatient. His officers were busy, he exploded to Craig on the wire. This was no time to ask riddles.

It was Craig's turn to see red—the minutes were ticking off. Still thinking in terms of Tennessee maneuvers, he remembered a simple transposition code of his youth, which Division Artillery had used down there at a time when the use of private codes and ciphers in emergency was officially urged.

"I'm going to write this in Tennessee cipher," said Craig, "and you'd better find somebody who remembers it!"

He did and they got the message. Not a soul remembered the code until the aide, who had gone to sleep, was dragged out. He remembered. And that's how the 106th Division Artillery got the word.

The 591st Field Artillery, which had also moved by bounds the previous day to the vicinity of Commanster—C Battery covering from Braunlauf until the rest of the battalion got in—pulled out at 11:30 A.M., crossed at Vielsalm where the ebb tide was now flowing fast and closed near Chene-al-Pierre, south of Werbomont, by 4:00 P.M. One howitzer which overturned on the road had to be destroyed. Here the battalion had a few hours of breathing spell.

H-hour for the withdrawal of the troops was 6:00 A.M.; for the crust remaining to protect the movement, 4:00 P.M. Task Force Jones on the south was to hold the Bovigny–Beho line at all costs, the 112th Infantry, less 3d Battalion, the line Bovigny–Burtonville. This schedule was followed, with some variations.

Up on the north, CCA of 7th Armored broke away after repulsing morning attacks in the Poteau area. It moved over the center road, its artillery going first. Its left-flank elements retired through a roadblock near Petit-Thier held by Task Force Navaho (Company C, 33d Armored Engineer Battalion, a platoon of Battery B, 814th Tank Destroyer Battalion, and other odds and ends of CCR) on the St. Vith highway. Task Force Navaho then rolled. The movement was smooth, well spaced. As the last vehicles closed in behind CCR, Troop A, 14th Provisional Cavalry, near Ville-du-Bors, held the final momentary screen. There was a bit of delay as the bridge over the railway at Ville-du-Bors didn't go up when the demolition plunger was pressed. The engineers repaired the line, however, and the bridge blew just as the pursuing enemy came in sight.

CCB, 7th Armored, was hard pressed in its exit. The enemy had infiltrated down the railway line during the night, was swirling about Crombach at dawn. A close-in defense of the town broke up after an hour or more and retirement began to the southwest.

Through some fault of communication CCB, 9th Armored Division, did not receive the final word to pull out that morning until 6:05 A.M., five minutes after the prescribed time.[2] There was but one thing to do and Hoge did it. He opened his radio net and issued his own order in the clear to all his units simultaneously.

It was touch-and-go. The enemy was already surging through Gruflange as the command initiated its move, aiming for the Beho–Bovigny road. Overhead the skies were clearing and American aircraft were beginning to buzz, a welcome assistance to the withdrawal.

Hoge, using the 3d Battalion, 424th Infantry, in cooperation with his 14th Tank Battalion, launched an attack toward Gruflange to disengage his force. One medium tank company operated with each rifle company as the battalion advanced toward the Kreuz-Berg height at Gruflange, I and K Companies abreast, with L Company in reserve.

Company K finally attacked almost due north, and with its tank support worked its way almost up to Crombach. Here, however, enemy pressure coming down to the west of them toward Braunlauf threatened to cut the task force off.

The battalion fell back, with K Company and the tanks in a hot delaying action, swept by 88 and machine-gun fire all the way to Maldange.

In the meantime, in accordance with orders, the rest of the 424th Infantry was getting out with CCB, 7th, and CCB, 9th Armored, as they began rolling toward Beho. The infantrymen clustered on the armored vehicles like groups of flies. And so the long column rolled to Salmchâteau.

Behind them were the screening elements of Task Force Jones, fighting a stiff delaying action, withdrawing by bounds in small groups.

The 112th Infantry on the morning of 23 December had two battalions festooned from Burtonville down to Beho, a good five-mile screening line. The 229th Field Artillery was in support, having displaced to high ground west of the river, near Salmchâteau. The 2d Battalion on the north, with E and F Companies in line and G in reserve, was responsible down to the Commanster–Neuvillle–Vielsalm road. The 1st Battalion, with B and A Companies in line and C in reserve, held the southern sector. The 3d Battalion had moved during the night to the line Vielsalm–Salmchâteau, west of the Salm River, and was attached to the 82d Airborne Division, where it would act as the stormdoor for the Goose Egg exit. Col. Nelson had been given positive orders that the covering force would remain in position until ordered out by the commanding general, 7th Armored Division.

"I'll never again take any such orders without a violent protest," comments Nelson.[3] One can see his reasons as the story develops.

By noon it appeared to the 112th that all elements but the covering force were out. By that time the 1st Battalion began to be engaged with an enemy tank and infantry attack as the Krauts pushed westward after the 424th Infantry and CCB, 9th Armored. Four self-propelled TD guns of Company A, 811th Battalion, loaned to Nelson by Hoge of CCB, 9th Armored Division, were of tremendous help, their M36 90mm guns bringing the enemy Tiger tanks to a standstill.[4]

As the attack on his 1st Battalion waxed in fury, Nelson had kept sending half-hourly reports by radio to the 7th Armored, reiterating his belief that everyone else had gotten away behind his crust. At 3:30 P.M. his message from the regimental command post at the road junction five hundred yards east of Cierreux on the Bovigny–Salmchâteau road was unanswered; communication was lost.

By this time, on the south the situation was growing more serious every minute. The 1st Battalion was being pushed back; enemy tanks had plunged through Rogery, and the elements of the 112th, with some of the 7th Armored Division's TDs and Task Force Martin of Task Force Jones, were in a close-in fight. Be it noted that Task Force Jones' instructions were to break contact at 3:30 P.M., in contrast to the orders which Col. Nelson received.

At 4:30 P.M., with no word yet from Hasbrouck and a tank action raging not two hundred yards from his CP, Nelson ordered immediate withdrawal.[5] The 2d Battalion succeeded in disengaging and withdrawing via Vielsalm according to plan. The 1st Battalion and regimental headquarters found themselves in a different spot.

As the 112th Infantry began moving into the Bovigny–Salmchâteau highway it hit smack into a clogged road. From Cierreux northward vehicles were jammed all the way to Vielsalm. Elements of Task Force

Jones and of the other outfits which had started through the southern route were blocked by an enemy thrust which had gotten into Salm-château itself. And now Nelson's men and vehicles were pressing into the dense-packed causeway.

Up in Salmchâteau two American light tanks were burning; enemy SP antitank guns were shooting down the road. Other enemy artillery bursts began to fall near the railway crossing just north of the Cierreux road junction.

Colonel Nelson managed to work his way forward through the jam and got a light-tank company[6] partly disengaged from the road jam, but there was no forcing a way north.[7] Night had fallen by now on a situation which was rapidly becoming panicky as here and there vehicles began to flame under the spray of 88s.

A side road toward Provedroux offered possibilities. Nelson got the tanks into it as spearhead, while deploying elements of his 1st Battalion engaged infiltrating enemy in that village. At long last the 112th Infantry vehicular column began to pour westward through this by-pass, in clear moon-light.

Several thousand yards southwest of Vielsalm the column moved across country, over a frozen swamp through which the tanks managed to scramble. They, in turn, lent a hand in towing the wheeled infantry vehicles across, finally to reach safety within the 82d Airborne Division's lines. Only eighteen vehicles out of the several hundred in the 112th were lost.[8]

Here it was that Lt.Col. John C. Fairchild's 229th Field Artillery Battalion did a remarkable bit of fire support, dropping a curtain between Salmchâteau and the escape road on the north, as well as to the southeast. The 112th's column moved between these two hosing sprays of 105mm howitzer shell bursts. A battalion of the 82d Airborne's artillery assisted in this fire.

"It was rather nerve-wracking," says Fairchild, "as we were, in effect, shooting at our own troops. So far as we could determine, none of our rounds landed among them, though we were shooting all around them. But it seemed to do the trick."[9]

Back on the highway to Vielsalm, below the railway crossing, the last portion of the crust just froze as wrecked vehicles ahead of them definitely barred exit. Men dismounted, milled aimlessly for a few moments, then began to break for the woods. The tail element, Lt. Richard C. Herren's platoon of C Troop, 14th Cavalry Squadron, destroyed their cars and joined in the rush for cover. Most of the refugees made it safely inside the lines of the 82d Airborne.

Spectacular was the dash for safety of the 440th Armored Field Artillery Battalion, supporting Task Force Jones in withdrawal. Displacing to the rear by successive bounds during the morning, the artillerymen, about to make their last dash via Salmchâteau, found themselves cut off. Limbered up, the outfit charged north, on the east side of the river, with their vehicular machine guns blazing in a running fight at ranges as close as fifty yards. A direct hit destroyed one of the self-propelled howitzers, but the rest of the battalion made it all the way to Vielsalm and there crossed the river.

Up at Vielsalm, Hasbrouck and Perrin, in the 7th Armored Division CP where they were checking their people through, were told that Kraut tanks were in the town (Vielsalm is on the east side of the river). As they left the building, the last ones to go, a tank rounded the corner and blazed at the remaining vehicles, a half-track and two jeeps in front of headquarters. The first shell hit the half-track. They piled into the jeeps and moved away from there. The St. Vith salient was no more; the Fortified Goose Egg a thing of the past. And the 106th Infantry Division had completed its first red week of battle.

Perrin, after shepherding the last of his flock over the Vielsalm bridge, left for his command post at Faweux, and the 106th people moved to assembly areas generally north of Werbomont; all but the 589th Field Artillery Battalion.

For, except in spirit and a handful of survivors, there was no longer a 589th Field Artillery Battalion.

PARKER'S CROSSROADS

The main highway between Bastogne and Liège is an important road. On it one may travel south to Basle, in Switzerland; north all the way to Amsterdam, Holland. It is crossed by the Laroche–Vielsalm highway, a road of secondary importance, connecting with Sedan to the southwest, linking the border roads to the northeast.

Baraque de Fraiture was the name of the height where the crossroads hamlet stood, a huddle of typical Belgian peasant homes with its one and only adornment a four-square, concrete road-marker. In winter, Baraque de Fraiture was a dreary, snow-sifted patch in the middle of one of the Ardennes marsh areas, surrounded by pine forests, and lying eight miles in air-line west and slightly south of Vielsalm.

I say "was" for, although the roads still cross where the shell-scotched ruins yawn, the place is and always will be known to the 106th Infantry Division as "Parker's Crossroads." Let's call it that.

To Parker's Crossroads came, about 3:00 P.M., 19 December, the firing elements of the 389th Field Artillery Battalion, three 105mm howitzers, some machine guns, trucks and nearly a hundred officers and men.

We last noted the 589th when its remnants rolled from the Poteau area on the morning of 18 December, to Bovigny, after its ordeal by fire in the Schnee Eifel and the subsequent running of the gantlet at Schönberg. Incidentally, in that last strafing all fire-control equipment had been lost.

At Bovigny that afternoon the battalion had been commandeered—there is no other word for it—by Col. Herbert W. Kruger, commanding the 174th Field Artillery Group of VIII Corps Artillery, who was moving his outfits out of danger. Kruger, reminiscent of the city editor who sent his reporter back to the man who had thrown him downstairs, with the message, "Tell him he can't intimidate me," simply informed the acting battalion commander that—"VOCG VIII Corps"—he desired the 589th to protect the passage of the 174th, and to go into battery at Courtil. Enemy tanks, it seems, were supposed to be at Chérain.

Major Arthur C. Parker, III, in command, had obeyed the orders. No tanks appeared. Kruger sent the outfit to Bovigny again that night, to provide close-in defense for the 174th. In the morning of 19 December, the 589th was moved back to Courtil, still in its protecting role. Parker in the meantime stripped away all but the actual firing sections and minimum of men necessary to operate the skeletonized outfit, sending the others to the rear areas back of Vielsalm.

Later that day the three-piece battalion was moved to Salmchâteau and thence sent southwest to Baraque de Fraiture to establish a roadblock. Again, it seemed, the 589th was to protect the 174th Group. Enemy tanks had been reported in Samrée.

Parker emplaced his three howitzers, organized a perimeter of defense, and bivouacked. The enemy did not materialize. Thus far the 589th had drawn no food since its kidnapping by the 174th Group, except for some emergency rations; gas and small arms ammunition were low. Trucks were sent to Vielsalm and contact made with Division, which ordered the battalion back to refit.

Before movement began, however, the enemy to the south was reported once more and this time Gen. McMahon ordered Major Parker to hold the roadblock at the crossroads to protect Division supply lines from attack from west or south. Here they were joined by the survivors of Service Battery which had gotten out from the Schnee Eifel. There were now in the battered outfit 110 officers and men.

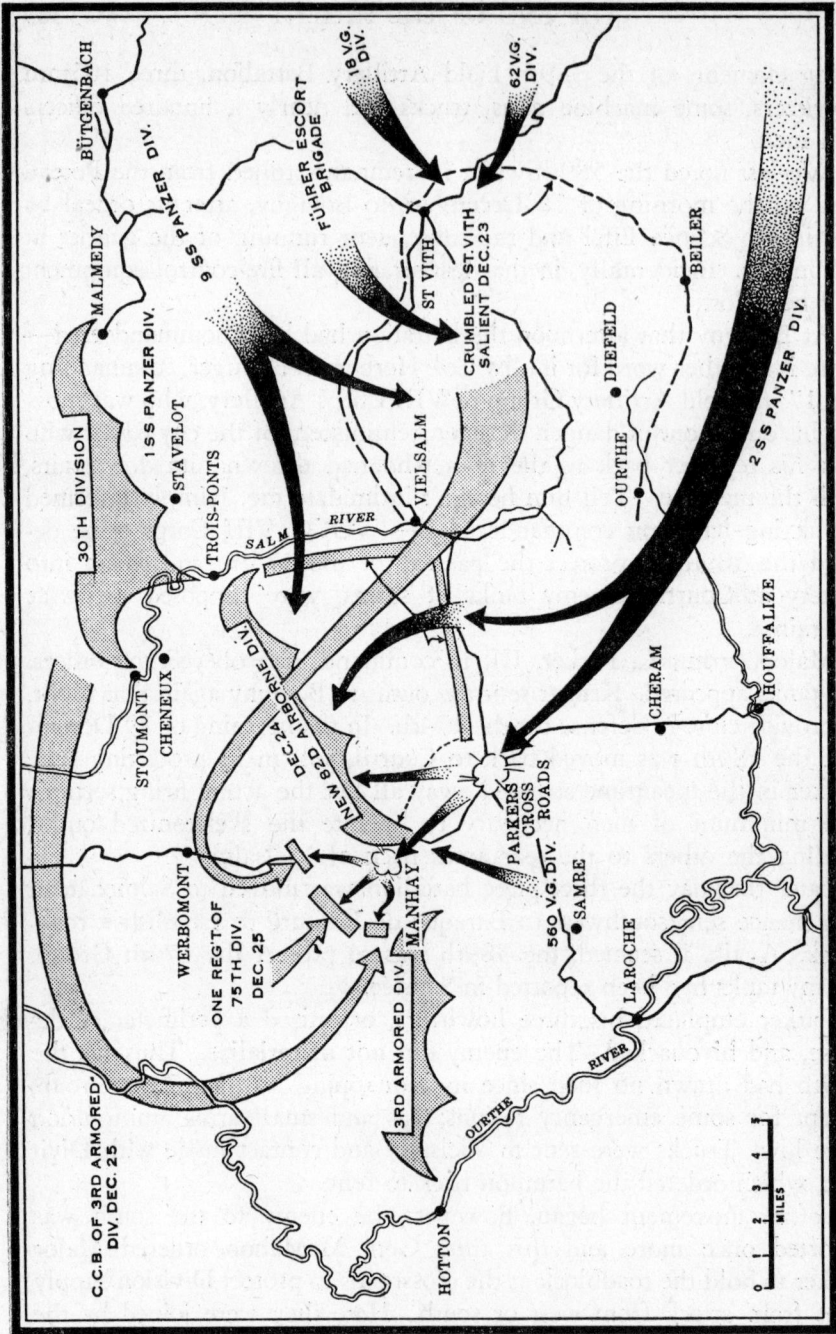

Map 6: Parker's Crossroads. The Big Picture.

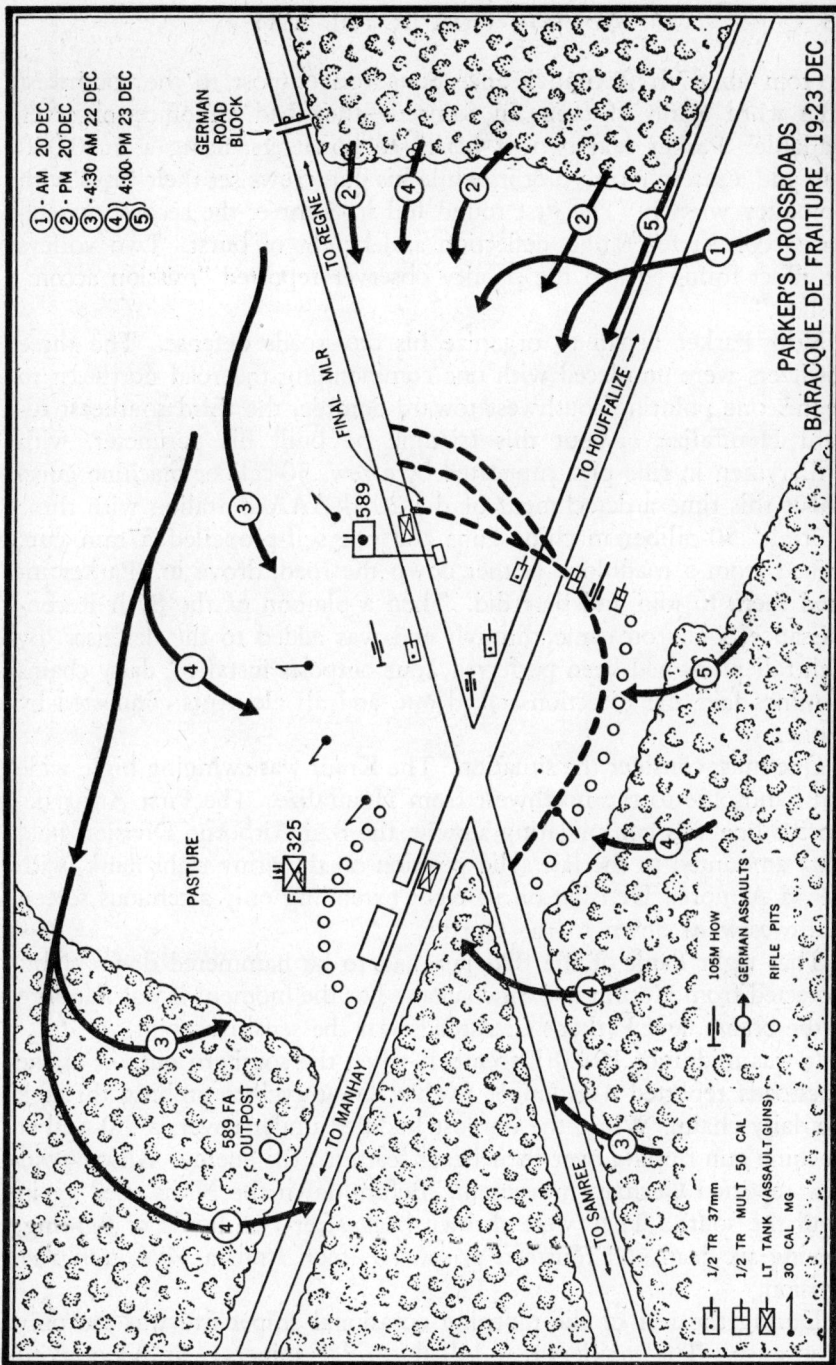

Map 7: *Last stand of the 589th Field Artillery Battalion.*

From an 87th Reconnaissance Squadron outpost to the southwest came word again of tanks in Samrée—they had an officer-observer available. Parker laid two of his three howitzers, using a 1:50,000 map and a safety pin to plot it, while his gun crews set their fuzes with a monkey wrench. The first round fell in Samrée, the second was reported correct for range, deflection and height of burst. Two volleys for effect followed and the cavalry observer reported "mission accomplished."

Now Parker began to organize his crossroads defense. The three howitzers were emplaced with one commanding the road northeast to Regné, one pointing southwest toward Samrée, the third southeast toward Houffalize. About this triangle he built his perimeter, with artillerymen in rifle pits, supported by a few .30-caliber machine guns. About this time a detachment of the 203d AAA Battalion with three multiple .50-caliber machine guns and one self-propelled 37mm gun, pushed from a roadblock farther down the road, drove in. Parker invited them to join and they did. Then a platoon of the 87th Reconnaissance Squadron came through and was added to the defense. By nightfall plans had been perfected, four outposts installed, daisy chains of mines laid, fire direction staked out, and all elements connected by phone.

One must consider the situation. The Kraut was swinging high, wide and handsome to the northwest from Houffalize. The First Army defensive line was consolidating slowly; the 82d Airborne Division held what amounted to the last solid position on the army right flank, with the 3d Armored Division on its right extending only a tenuous screen southwestward down to the Ourthe.

That right flank of the 82d just had to be hammered down tight; protected from Hotton to Salmchâteau. For the moment it was flapping in the breeze, and Parker's Crossroads was the sensitive point.

It was midnight 19-20 December, when the southern outpost at the crossroads reported a group of twelve Kraut cyclists probing through the daisy chain. While the outpost huddled under cover, a .50-caliber machine gun ripping over their heads scattered the enemy. All outposts now reported German movement. Before dawn the Nazis tried again from the south. They were thrown back after two hours of fighting, leaving six dead and fourteen prisoners—men from a *Volksgrenadier* division.

During the rest of the morning occasional sniper fire was the only annoyance. The artillerymen killed several snipers. At noon word came from Division that the 589th was to retire to Bra for reorganization, leaving the 87th Squadron's platoon to defend the crossroads. Parker, however, felt that he should not get out until the cavalrymen had received reinforcements, so he stayed.

At 3:30 P.M. the Germans attacked again, this time from the east, under cover of fog. They were repulsed after two platoons of 3d Armored Division medium tanks came in. These latter, however, were acting under orders of Task Force Jones and not available for Parker's further use. During the night an officer from Battery A, 54th Armored Field Artillery Battalion, supporting the tanks, came in and coordination of fire was arranged.

Came also the good news that infantry of the 82d Airborne Division would come in next day to relieve the artillerymen, and a squad from the 504th Parachute Infantry arrived across country to patrol for and lead them in. They told of Germans digging in to the east, inside the woods.

That wasn't so good. Reconnaissance towards Regné, on the Salmchâteau–Vielsalm road, proved that the Krauts had erected a roadblock completely cutting the crossroads force from direct contact; wrecked American vehicles had been piled deep, and the barrier was covered by infantry and machine guns in the woods. Parker's Crossroads was now an island in the German flood, its only communication with the remainder of First Army the Liège highway to Manhay. This road remained unblocked for the rest of the engagement, though it was swept by Kraut fire, both small-arms and artillery, and running that gantlet was dangerous business.

Expecting another attack, since sounds of vehicles had been heard all night, Parker before dawn 21 December fired a preparation of artillery and machine guns to simulate a counterattack. The enemy didn't attack, but, as the defenders later found out, the infantry platoon leading the relief heard the firing and deployed more than a mile to the north at the village of Fraiture, thus delaying their arrival until just after noon. In the meantime, the 3d Armored Division tanks moved out on another mission, leaving two 105mm assault guns to the defenders.

The relieving infantry were briefed, moved out to take over the perimeter. As they passed outside the defense lines a German mortar barrage came down, compelling their retirement. The 589th men went back to the outposts until the infantry could reorganize. By this time night had fallen.

One gets a picture of stark, continuous battle inside the confines of that beleaguered garrison; of sweeps of mortar fire, small-arms and machine guns searching out the positions, while 88s kept up an almost incessant pounding. Through it all Parker was everywhere, observing at the outposts, moving from place to place along the perimeter as one attack succeeded another. Wounded by a mortar shell on the afternoon of 21 December, while adjusting fire, Parker refused to be evacuated until he lost consciousness. Major Elliott Goldstein succeeded in command.

Harassing enemy fire continued all that day and night. Under cover of this fire and the darkness, the Krauts infiltrated to the edge of the woods running along the east-west road. They attacked simultaneously from southeast, south and north at 4:30 A.M., 22 December, to be driven off again. This time two prisoners from an officer patrol disclosed that the 2d SS Panzer Division of II Panzer Corps was coming from the south.

An uproar of firing outside the perimeter during that night was explained next day; the Germans had supplemented their artillery harassment by four American 3-inch TD guns, firing from the north. These guns had been captured from a platoon of the 643d TD Battalion which had moved up early in the evening outside the defense laager and had been bagged.

Our own assault guns that morning cleared the woods of Krauts to the north, with direct fire, knocking out two mortar crews and a rocket gun.

It was 10:00 o'clock on the morning of 23 December that F Company, 325th Glider Infantry, Capt. Woodruff commanding, hit and fought its way into the crossroads defense lines.

Captain Arthur C. Brown, of B Battery, commanding the three-piece battery, took personal charge of one of the howitzers during attacks, while Lt. Thomas J. Wright, who, it will be remembered, led the forty-five Service Battery people who had cut their way out from the Schönberg road 17 December, handled another. Sgt. Barney M. Alford was in charge of the third piece after Capt. George Huxel, battalion S-3, was wounded.

Alford, with Sgt. Johnnie B. Jordan, manned a multiple .50-caliber machine gun when its personnel had been knocked out, fought the gun until a Kraut shell disabled it.

The medics, all enlisted men, displayed great gallantry and resourcefulness through the action, assisting the wounded. T/4 Melvin R. Pollow improvised bandages and utilized Kraut medical kits which he scrounged under fire.

And T/5 Robert E. Vorpagel braved hostile fire to go out and help a wounded Kraut whose right arm had been shattered; amputating it on the spot, he saved the man's life. It was Vorpagel, too, who on 22 December, loaded twelve seriously wounded men on a truck, with the assistance of the driver, and ran the Kraut fire to the north to get his wounded safely back to Vielsalm. When he got in the truck was found to be studded with mortar-shell fragments and rifle bullet holes.

Even with the reinforcement of the infantry company it was apparent that morning of 23 December that a coordinated enemy attack could not be withstood. So Goldstein, taking with him as exhibits two Kraut prisoners, an SS captain and a sergeant, jeeped it over the Manhay road during a lull to contact there Col. Richardson, commanding a 3d Armored Division combat command.

Hard-pressed as the 3d Armored was—a part of the division was practically cut off over towards Marcourt—Richardson agreed to send in one company each of tanks and infantry to counterattack.[10] He sent a major back with Goldstein, on reconnaissance.

As they approached the crossroads all hell broke loose. Dismounting, they worked their way through the woods to the northeast corner to find the position being overrun.[11]

Tanks and infantry of the 2d SS Panzer Division smashed the line at 4:00 P.M. Sergeants Alford and Jordan got the first two tanks by direct fire from their howitzer, the former having to run back to get additional shells after the first vehicle had been destroyed. They missed a third tank with their last round as it swung its nose toward them; then they fell back, covering one another with their carbines as the Kraut infantrymen began to rush through their position.

The defense began to disintegrate. To Capt. Huxel at the CP, who, although wounded, had refused to be evacuated and was now commanding, Capt. Brown and Lt. Wright reported that the remnants of the 325th Glider Infantry were withdrawing. They decided to shoot their way out in three groups.

Wright led one detachment toward Manhay but they were driven back and captured. Brown got another group away but was himself captured.

Huxel and his group held on in the CP until the roof collapsed. Out of the adjoining barn three frightened cows dashed bellowing and Huxel and his detachment made their own rush in the confusion.

They dodged into a drainage ditch, where our medic, Pollow, stopped to give first aid to two wounded men. Then, dragging their wounded with them, they made the woods to the north and got to Fraiture village and the 325th Infantry lines.

Of the infantrymen themselves, Capt. Woodruff and some forty men got safely back. Some of the other artillerymen, seeking shelter in the damaged CP, hugged the cellar, until the house was surrounded by German infantrymen with burp guns. The building began to burn and this last group was forced out, several being shot, the remainder surrendering.

And that's the story of Parker's Crossroads and the three-piece 589th Field Artillery Battalion; the end of the trail for the three howitzers of Battery A which Eric Wood had gotten out of the Schnee Eifel. It is a story for American artillerymen to cherish along with the saga of O'Brien's guns at Buena Vista.

One cannot help wondering what would otherwise have happened to the thin-spread 82d Airborne Division's right flank as the 2d SS Panzer moved in for the kill.

NOTES TO CHAPTER 11

[1] Mechanical coding and decoding instrument.

[2] General Hoge to the author, 19 December 1946.

[3] Col. G. M. Nelson, 112th Infantry, in a letter to the author, 23 January 1947.

[4] *Ibid.*

[5] *Ibid.*

[6] Evidently Blair's F Company, 18th Provisional Squadron.

[7] Nelson, *op. cit.*

[8] *Ibid.*

[9] Letter to the author, 22 February 1947.

[10] Letter, Major Elliott Goldstein to the author, 19 February 1947.

[11] *Ibid.* Goldstein was unable to get back to his outfit; he joined up with the 54th Armored Field Artillery, 3d Armored Division, that night, got back to Division next day. The counter-attack never materialized; General Gavin, commanding 82d Airborne Division, in his report notes that he found Manhay unoccupied that evening save for one MP.

Chapter 12: Totting Up the Score

✦✦✦

It was the fortune of war that the 106th Division had to learn its first battle lesson the hard way. One can draw a certain analogy between its fight and those of our troops in the beginning of the North Africa Campaign. In both cases it was as if a football team which had never yet played a game were run in against a veteran squad at the height of its season.

It was worse luck that the Division occupied positions not of its own choosing, positions in a rigid defense line originally laid out by the enemy for battle to the west and not, as the fight was fought, to the east. And positions so far-flung, twenty-two miles in all, that only a skillful delaying action in depth, not a last-ditch defense in place, could have cushioned a coordinated enemy attack.

As Lt.Gen. Courtney Hodges, commanding the First Army, later told Brig.Gen. Perrin:

"No troops in the world, disposed as your division had to be, could have withstood that impact of the German attack, which had its greatest weight in your sector. Please tell these men for me what a grand job they did. By the delay they effected, they definitely upset Von Rundstedt's timetable."

While on this question of the original defense dispositions, which the Division and its attached cavalry group, it will be remembered, took over "man for man and gun for gun" from the 2d Infantry Division, one can find much room for criticism.

The cavalry was emplaced dismounted, instead of being truly mobile in traditional cavalry role. Many of the artillery positions violated all normal technique in that access to them was from the front, instead of the rear. In addition, except for the 591st Field Artillery, which had one battery staggered well to the rear, the artillery dispositions did not further a defense in depth.

One cannot help wondering why, when the First Army advance halted after taking the Siegfried positions in the Schnee Eifel, the enemy defense installations were not destroyed, to prevent possible recapture and use by him. This, for instance, was what XIX Corps did when it halted north of Aachen. (There, of course, the similarity ends, for the XIX Corps had an offensive mission.). The point is that one utilizes terrain to further one's ends. And the Siegfried Line in the

191

Schnee Eifel certainly furthered no defensive against an assault from the east.

Let's look at the map.[1] There were in the 106th Infantry Division's area, two essential points to be held in any defense scheme, the Schönberg pass of the Our Valley and the Heckhalenfeld hill mass west of the Schnee Eifel nose. Not only were they the bottlenecks to any westbound offensive, but they also furthered our own later offensive movements eastward. A mobile, elastic defense based on those two points, supplemented by very active patrolling and screening in the Losheim Gap and along the Schnee Eifel, was indicated. This does not appear to have been VIII Corps' solution of the problem.

Instead, what amounted to a cordon defense was instituted; a cordon defense, part of which consisted of a salient into enemy-held territory. When, therefore, the 14th Cavalry Group caved in on the north, the Schnee Eifel positions were finished, as always happens in a cordon defense when any part of the line is punctured.

These things are noted, not in excuse, but in justice to the men who fought and died. No one will say that there were not mistakes in leadership; errors and omissions fostered by an overwhelming surprise and the buck fever of an initial kick-off. No one will dispute the fact that there was panic in the area—including Corps troops. The condition of the Schönberg–St. Vith road on 16 and 17 December, crowded with American traffic westward, tells its own story.

The point to be made is this: The German felt, and laid his plans accordingly, that St. Vith must be captured within the first twenty-four hours. He failed to do it. For better or for worse, credit for the initial derailment of the German plan to capture St. Vith goes to the 106th Infantry Division. The 422d and 423d Regiments, the 590th Field Artillery and their attached units contributed mightily to that initial result.

It was not until late afternoon of 17 December, thirty-six hours after the assault started, that the Kraut came down the Schönberg road, knocking at the door. There, in front of St. Vith, Riggs' engineers held him until the 7th Armored Division arrived.

From that time on, of course, the field belonged to Hasbrouck's 7th Armored. Its magnificent stand, in which the remnants of the 106th took their part, like CCB, 9th Armored Division, and the 112th RCT, maintained the integrity of the St. Vith salient, denied the enemy the use of the vital road junction for five days.

Interesting is the enemy's recapitulation of the causes ascribed to the failure of his offensive. Field Marshal Wilhelm Keitel and Col.Gen.

Alfred Jodl, in a signed answer to a questionnaire on the subject from the Historical Section of the ETO, sum them up on 20 July, 1945, as follows in order of importance:

(1) Soft roads making impossible rapid advance of armored units.

(2) *Tougher resistance than expected* (italics mine, R.E.D.) of, in themselves, weak U. S. troops, especially at St. Vith.

(3) Inadequate training of their own command and personnel.

(4) Shortage of transportation, especially tracked prime movers.

(5) Allied superiority in the air, particularly on 24 December.

(6) Uniform and promptly applied Allied operational counter-measures.

These two German leaders qualified their praise of American troops by remarking that in their opinion the forces occupying the Schnee Eifel could have held out longer.

From the record, one must reiterate the conclusion that had one single commander, forceful and experienced, been in charge of the outfits surrounded in the Schnee Eifel, to fight them as a coordinated force and with complete liberty of action, they might have been used more effectively. As it was, the power of six battalions of infantry and one battalion of field artillery, with TD and AAA attachments, was frittered away in what turned out to be a series of uncoordinated piece-meal attacks.

Its first seven days of fighting had cost the 106th two infantry regiments and two field artillery battalions, two-thirds of its infantry strength and half of its gunners. All these except the lone 589th Field Artillery at Parker's Crossroads, had been lost in the Schnee Eifel. The remaining strength of the Division had been sorely tried in the long week of continual struggle.

On the first day the 106th had met elements of five Kraut combat teams—116th Panzer, 18th and 62d *Volksgrenadier* Divisions, Führer Escort and 150th Panzer Brigades. Later it clashed also with the 1st and 2d SS Panzer Divisions. Its men had fought in snow and ice and rain and fog, fought in some instances without hope of relief, with just the dogged consciousness of snarling give-and-take, kill-or-be-killed. They had fought with the enemy in front and rear and on the flanks, an enemy who sometimes appeared treacherously clothed in our own uni-forms. Now, for the moment, they were out of that hell. It was a battered, disgruntled, groggy aggregation which finally found billets and bivouacs up in the vicinity of Werbomont during the night of

23 December. For some there was shelter, warm fires. But for the 424th Infantry, dead on its collective feet, there was only the wind-swept, snow-covered wooded area around Houssonloge, north of the Werbomont crossroads.

No wonder that Reid, the regimental commander, to this day sets his jaw in bitterness when he talks about it.

What did they do? They did what might be expected—they chopped down trees and lit fires to bring some warmth into their frozen bones. Damn the enemy! Damn the blackout! After all, there's a limit to what flesh and blood can stand. And Reid approved.

Corps raised hell, he admits. But his men kept warm that night, and no one was the worse because of the twinkling red blobs of flame around which cold, exhausted men relaxed. It was good they did, for on Christmas Eve they were alerted to fight again.

NOTE TO CHAPTER 12

1 Page 10, *supra.* See also Chapter 3.

Chapter 13: The Second Round

Christmas Eve dawned clear and cold. Bright sun poured down on aching bones, and skyward-peering eyes saw great flocks of American planes, specks of silver sheen in the air, eastbound to hit the Kraut. It was good to be alive that Sunday morning, and the 106th Division reacted.

The Division's fighting troops were split up, now. The 592d Field Artillery was attached to Corps, the 591st Field Artillery to the 7th Armored. CCB, 9th Armored, with the 112th Infantry, which was now attached to it, had also gone to Corps control.

Hasbrouck called for more infantry to work with his 7th Armored Division, and the 424th was earmarked for attachment to him.

Before dawn the regiment was alerted in its bivouac area. Perrin, at XVIII Corps headquarters, where he had recommended the attachment of the 424th, was ordered to Hasbrouck as Assistant Division Commander of the 7th Armored to coordinate this reinforcement, in addition to his duties as commander of the 106th. Col. Baker, Division chief of staff, took over the active supervision of the remaining elements of the Division.

Ridgway had published a proclamation to the XVIII Corps that day in which he said:

"In my opinion this is the last dying gasp of the German Army. He is putting everthing he has into this fight. We are going to smash that final drive here today in this Corps zone. This command is the command that will smash the German offensive spirit for this war. Impress every man in your division with that spirit. We are going to lick the Germans here today."

It was, in fact, the day which would mark the high tide of the great offensive. The 2d Panzer Division of Manteuffel's Fifth Panzer Army would get its spearheads as far as Celles and Conneux, within sight of the Meuse. The 9th Panzer, from OKW reserve, was near Marche, 116th Panzer approaching Hotton. Sepp Dietrich's 2d SS Panzer Division, having overrun Parker's Crossroads, was pounding northward between Grandmenil and Lierneux, still hoping to find and turn an American right flank.

But "Lightning Joe" Collins' VII Corps was now spreading down to cover the XVIII Corps right flank and Dinant, with the British 30th Corps echeloned behind it.

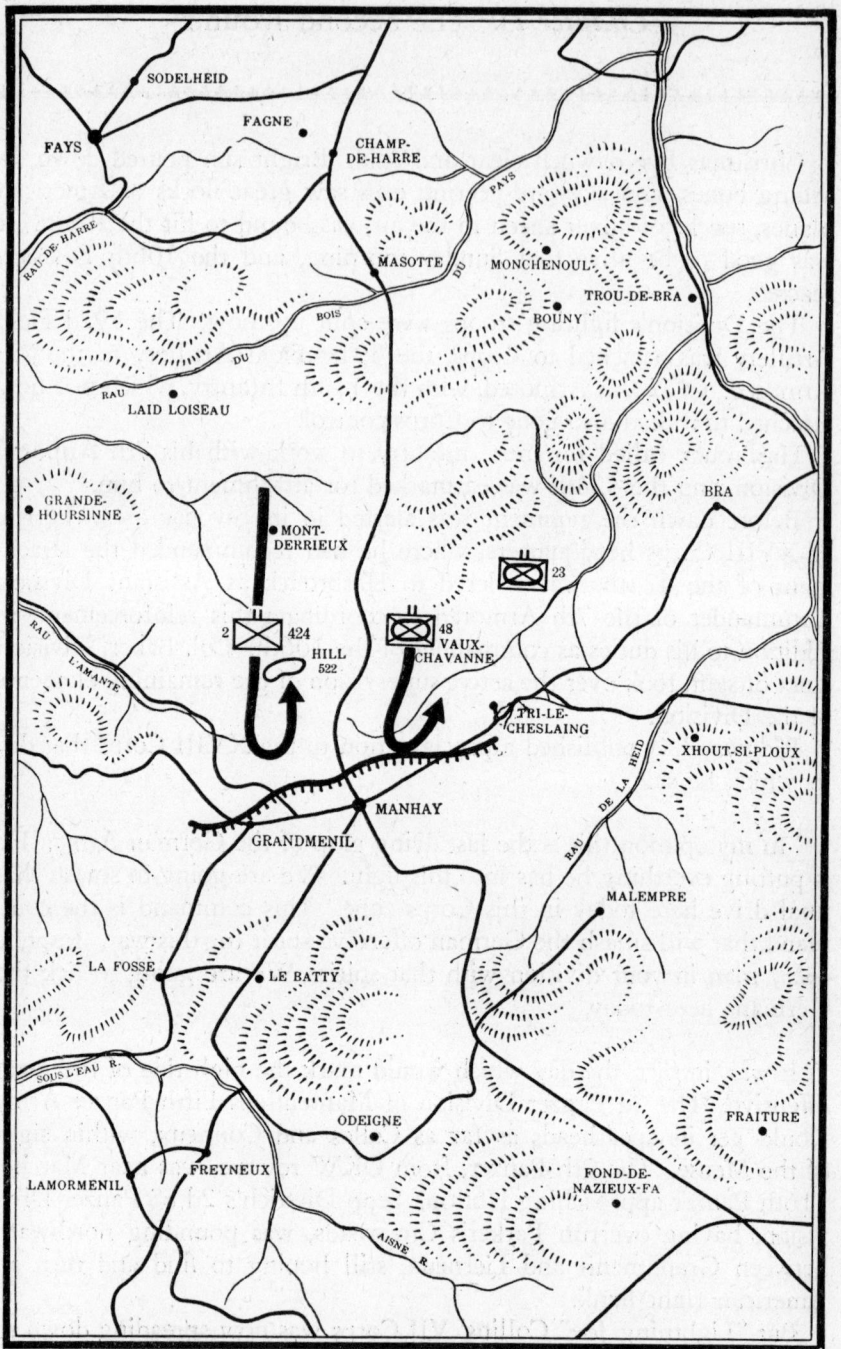

Map 8: *The first fight at Manhay, 25 December 1944.*

The 7th Armored had the task of sealing the gap between XVIII and VII Corps, from Grandmenil to Malempré, facing the 2d SS Panzer and 560th *Volksgrenadiers*. And this fight would mark the comeback of the men of the 106th. Manhay was the keypoint. On the right of the 7th the 3d Armored was having troubles of its own, while on the left the 82d Airborne was standing against heavy thrusts.

Colonel Reid of the 424th Infantry, called upon on Christmas Day for a battalion to work with CCA, 7th Armored, immediately chose Lt.Col Leonard Umanoff's 2d Battalion, which had come out of the previous fighting in better shape than the others.

Hurried into trucks provided by the 7th Armored, the 2d Battalion, 424th, moved out to Harre, whence it was later rushed to Chene-al-Pierre.

The situation was critical locally. CCA, 7th Armored, had been in Manhay, but was about to withdraw to the line Grandmenil–Vaux–Chavanne on the night of 24 December when it had been hit by a severe attack and pushed back to Chene-al-Pierre. Now it was going to try to retake Manhay.

The attack drove down the highway, the Werbomont–Houffalize road—Route Nationale 15—with the 48th and 23d Armored Infantry Battalion and tanks on the left of the road, Umanoff's battalion on the right.

The battalion attacked in column of companies, with Capt. Wiley Cassidy's E Company in the lead, followed by F Company. H (heavy weapons) Company supported the attack, with G Company in reserve.

It was a nasty business. From cellars turned into pillboxes in both Manhay and Grandmenil the Krauts were throwing a knee-high crossfire of machine guns. The attack got to within fifty yards of Manhay, could go no farther. As darkness fell the battalion was ordered to withdraw to the high ground on Hill 522, two thousand yards north of Grandmenil. A concentration of 88s further cut up the battalion as it fell back.

Umanoff's outfit was badly mauled. "Thirty-five per cent casualties," is the estimate of Lt. Robert Logan, battalion S-3. "What had been the strongest battalion in the regiment was now cut to ribbons. We had to ask for help to evacuate our wounded and Jerry picked off the aid men when they went out."

Staff Sergeant John F. Goidosik, handling E Company's mortar section, put his fire on one of the Kraut machine-gun positions holding up the company. A burst of mortar and artillery fire wounded every man in his section. Goidosik, picking up the mortar and several rounds

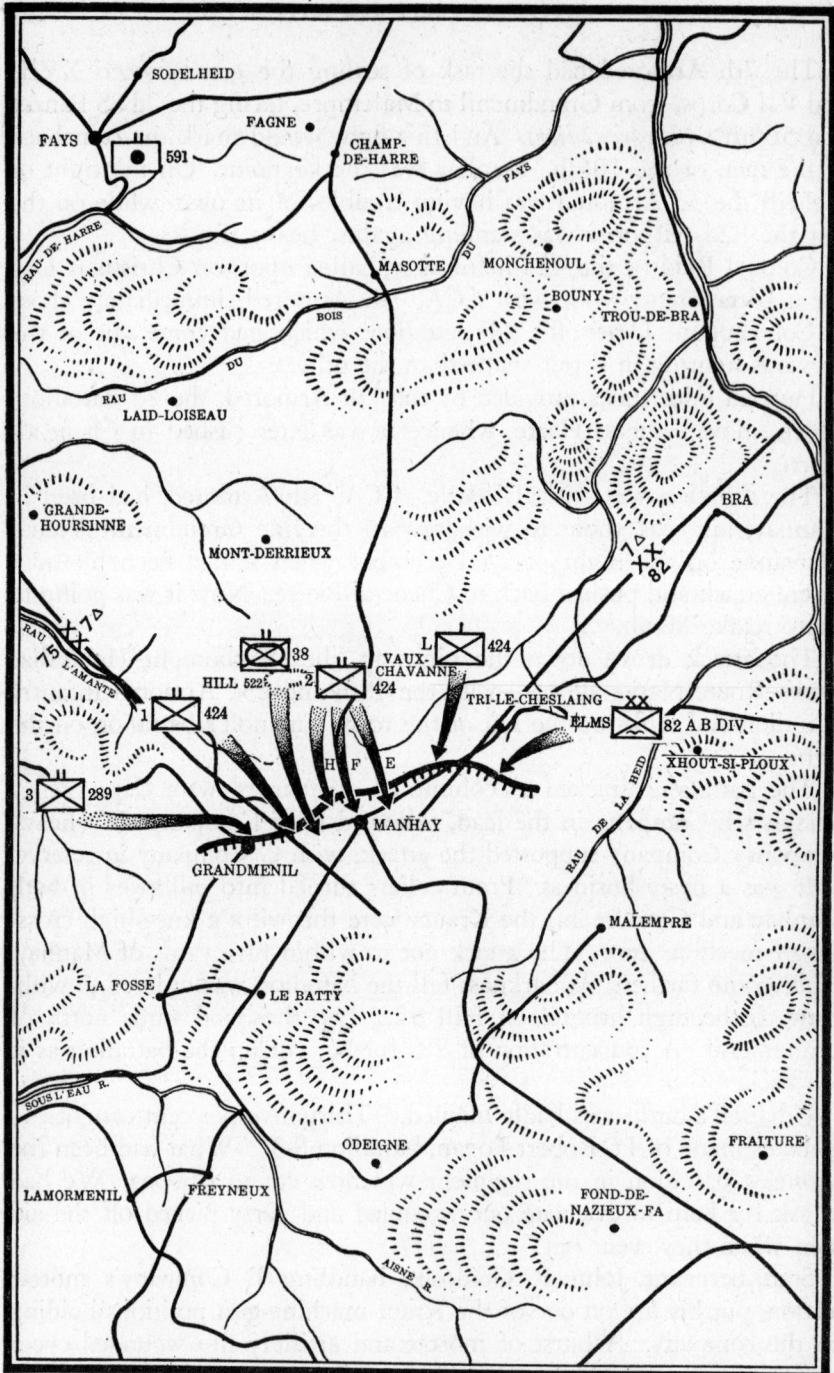

Map 9:   *The second fight at Manhay, 26 December 1944.*

staggered seventy yards out in front of the line, set it up and knocked out the troublesome machine-gun post. E Company then went on.

While E Company was held up Lt. Thomas L. Lawrence led his platoon of F Company in a flanking movement to the left and ran into a concentration of machine-gun and tank fire. Lawrence, encouraging his men, saw a Kraut tank move at the platoon for a wooded patch.

He grabbed a grenade launcher and opened fire on the tank, killing a German standing in its open hatch, and the machine sheered off.

But both E and F Companies were finally ordered to fall back. Lawrence remained behind, directing the evacuation of casualties. Then he worked his way into the outskirts of Manhay, which was being plastered by the 591st Field Artillery, and brought back word that the enemy was pulling out.

The 2d Battalion reverted to regimental control that night, and the 3d Battalion (less L Company) replaced it with CCA, while the rest of the regiment was attached to CCB, 7th Armored.

Manhay, reoccupied during the night, was struck before dawn by Kraut armor reentering the village. While CCA and a battalion of the 82d Airborne Division's infantry pressed in again from the east on the morning of 26 December to get it back, the 289th Infantry Regiment of the 75th Division, which now came up on the right between 7th Armored and 3d Armored, began to exert pressure west of Grandmenil.

Combat Command B, 7th Armored, with the 424th Infantry (less 3d Battalion), moved down to seal the line Grandmenil–Manhay. G Company was attached to the 38th Armored Infantry.

These elements of the 424th with CCB were committed astride the Houffalize road, with L Company on the left of the highway, the 2d Battalion on the right, then the 38th Infantry, and finally the 1st Battalion, 424th. Troop A, 14th Cavalry Squadron (Provisional), was also in this fight, with the 38th Infantry.

The attack jumped off at 9:15 A.M. from the slopes of Hill 522, supported by the fire of the 591st Field Artillery from positions near Fays. The 592d Field Artillery also contributed a heavy wallop, putting down two TOTs on Manhay. Observers entering the village later reported 350 Krauts and 80 vehicles destroyed by artillery fire.

The depleted 2d Battalion had its companies in line, with H—which went in this time as a rifle unit—on the right, then F and E Companies. E Company, fringing the highway in the open ground just north of the east-west secondary road which runs from the northern exit of Grandmenil across to the Houffalize road, was pinned down by a hostile concentration of artillery fire. The infantrymen took cover in a ditch, suffering heavy casualties.

Down the road, in utter disregard for the Kraut, came Chaplain Edward T. Boyle in his jeep. The chaplain halted by the ditch, piled out, began to give first aid and then, picking up a seriously wounded man, staggered with him to his car and drove back.

If the padre could take that fire, E Company could. It surged from the ditch and stormed the road, fighting its way into the outskirts of Manhay.

The 2d Battalion, its objective gained, linked with L Company on its left, which in turn linked with 82d Airborne troops who had now entered Manhay.

On the right the 38th Armored Infantry, its right flank on the Mormont–Grandmenil road, closed its portion of the zone. The 1st Battalion, 424th, west of this road, drove southeast to the outskirts of Grandmenil, linking with the 3d Battalion, 289th Infantry.

Mission accomplished.

It was an eight-hour fight to gain an approximate mile and a half. But at long last it was a real offensive fight for a battered regiment which to this time had only known a succession of thumpings.

The gap was sealed; the Kraut was walled in on the northern flank of his penetration.

In these positions the 424th Infantry remained until its relief 30 December by a regiment of the 75th Infantry Division.

In the 424th, the 2d Battalion had taken the most serious pounding; it came out of the second Manhay fight with an effective strength of 435. E Company had 70 men, F 90, G 80, H 90, and Headquarters Company 105.

The Division totted up its losses: 415 killed in action, 1,254 wounded, and 6,821 missing. This out of a strength of 14,024 on 16 December.

Now, in the vicinity of Anthisnes, Belgium, where the Division constituted XVIII Corps reserve, the battle-scarred survivors, 5,534 strong, started reorganization and reequipment. The 422d and 423d Infantry regiments, the 589th and 590th Field Artillery Battalions and the 106th Reconnaissance Troop were written off by First Army. The survivors of the 589th were distributed among the 591st, 592d and 229th Field Artillery Battalions; this was a hard blow, for twelve new howitzers had been drawn, and Gen. McMahon had hoped that the outfit would rise from the ashes of Parker's Crossroads. But this was not to be until much later. Authorized strength of the abbreviated Division would be 6,569.

The 591st and 592d Field Artillery did not for the moment revert to Division control. Whoever heard of artillery outfits being relieved? They went on, the former supporting the 7th Armored, the latter XVIII Corps, as part of the 211th Group.

Replacements came in slowly, as did equipment. The division shook down. What there was left of it was now a combat outfit seared but tempered in the crucible of war.

Interesting are some of the figures in the report of Lt.Col. Meyer K. Belzer, Division surgeon, for the period. The medics handled in all more than 7,500 patients—it will be remembered that on the 331st Medical Battalion came the brunt of the evacuation load of the entire St. Vith salient fighting. Through the divisional clearing station came 1,781 cases, of whom 1,288 belonged to the Division itself.

Of these, 396 were battle casualties, and 118 others were combat exhaustion cases. These latter, according to Major Martin M. Fischbein, Division psychiatrist, presented a ratio "abnormally low for troops exposed for the first time to enemy fire."

The surgeons put stress on the fact that "not one malingerer" was noted among the patients passing through the clearing station.

There were 529 cases of trench foot, a figure far above the normal ratio.

These medical figures, of course, take no account of the casualties in the organizations lost in the Schnee Eifel.

Of the battle casualties, 228 were caused by shell fragments, 85 by gunshot wounds and 83 by mines, grenades and other weapons. The surgeons noted a high incidence of chest wounds, due either to tree-bursts or because, they say, the men did not hit the ground fast enough.

Small-arms fire caused sixty percent of the casualties among fifty-eight Kraut prisoners of war who came through the clearing station.

Chapter 14: Turn of the Tide

↟↟↟

By New Year's Day the enemy's offensive bolt was shot. On the south of the Bulge, Bastogne had been relieved and the U. S. Third Army was punching northward. On the north the U. S. First Army, at last stabilized on a front generally from Marche to Büllingen, was preparing its counterblow.

Within the salient the Kraut was frantically—and, as usual, efficiently—digging in. By 3 January, when First Army began its attack, there were indications that the battered enemy armor was preparing to get out, under the protection of its *Volksgrenadiers* and artillery, who would stand to the end.

By 9 January, with VII Corps on the right making the main effort and XVIII Corps assisting, our riposte had pushed down to the general line Laroche–Salmchâteau; thence the front line ran north to Stavelot and east to the Büllingen shoulder.

During all this time the 106th Infantry Division, in XVIII Corps reserve and billetted in the vicinity of Anthisnes, was licking its wounds, receiving replacements, and generally shaking down after its ordeal. Except, of course, for the artillery.

The 591st and 592d Field Artillery Battalions remained in action. The former, from positions at Veucy-le-Marteau until 3 January, when it displaced forward to Basse-Bodeaux, was supporting the 82d Airborne Division. During this time the battalion fired 4,997 rounds in 749 different missions, no small contribution.

Nor were the 81st Engineers idle. They were clearing enemy minefields, laying protective mines of our own; repairing, constructing, and also, just in case, preparing for demolition the bridges over the Amblève and Salm. In particular, bridges which would be used for the coming assault had to be taken care of. In addition to all this and to their normal chores of constructing water points and road repairing, there was snow removal; their bulldozers were continually on the go, bucking the snow blocking all roads.

The 592d Field Artillery Battalion, now attached to the 211th Group, XVIII Corps Artillery, was keeping its 155mm howitzers hot with a daily average of six hundred rounds in general support, from positions near Rahier, displacing forward 7 January to Fosse.

But the Golden Lions were now to come back into action. XVIII Corps was pushing on a right-angled front, with the 82d Airborne Division facing east along the Salm River while the 30th Infantry

Division was facing south above the Amblève, from Trois Ponts where the rivers converged, through Stavelot to Waimes. Inside this Nazi salient which must be reduced, the Germans were cannily ensconced, their main line of resistance on the high ground along the line Coquaimont–Les-Neuf-Parcs–Henumont–Butay–Lodomez. And in front were minefields and outposts, cleverly covered by fire.

Corps' plan was to punch this salient smack on its nose, driving it in and overrunning the main line of resistance. The 106th, replacing part of the 30th Division, which would shift to the left for a narrower front, would deliver the sock.

Then, as both 106th and 30th pressed southward, the 75th Infantry Division, attacking through 82d Airborne and across the Salm River, would drive directly east on signal from Corps, toward St. Vith, pinching out the 106th and linking with the 30th.

Reid's 424th Infantry, assembled in the vicinity of Baugnée, was at first ordered to relieve the 117th Infantry of the 30th Division in preparation for the assault. But on 7 January Corps changed its mind. That night the 424th, with C Company, 81st Engineer Battalion, and C Company, 331st Medical Battalion attached, moved to Moulin-du-Ruy to relieve the 112th Regimental Combat Team, at present part of the 30th Division.

The transfer was effected by morning of 9 January, after considerable delay caused by the abominable condition of the snow-covered roads. Our old friends of Nelson's 112th and their supporting 229th Field Artillery Battalion were shifted over to replace the 117th Combat Team. But it was high time that they got a breathing spell, so they in turn were relieved by a new partner in the 106th—the 517th Combat Team, consisting of the 517th Parachute Infantry (less 2d Battalion), 460th Parachute Field Artillery Battalion and 596th Parachute Engineer Company. Also Company A, 643d TD Battalion, and C Company, 740th Tank Battalion, were attached to the 106th, which Brig.Gen. Perrin would now lead into battle.

The Golden Lions regarded their new combat team with interest. The 517th was a businesslike outfit, with ninety-four days of previous combat under its belt when it first arrived in the Ardennes. A lone wolf element of the First Allied Airborne Army, part of no division, it had been attached to XVIII Corps since 1 December at Soissons. Alerted with the rest of the airborne outfits in SHAEF reserve on 18 December, it reached the front 21 December to fight in turn with the 30th Infantry, 7th Armored and 82d Airborne Divisions. Its 2d Battalion was still attached to the 7th Armored.

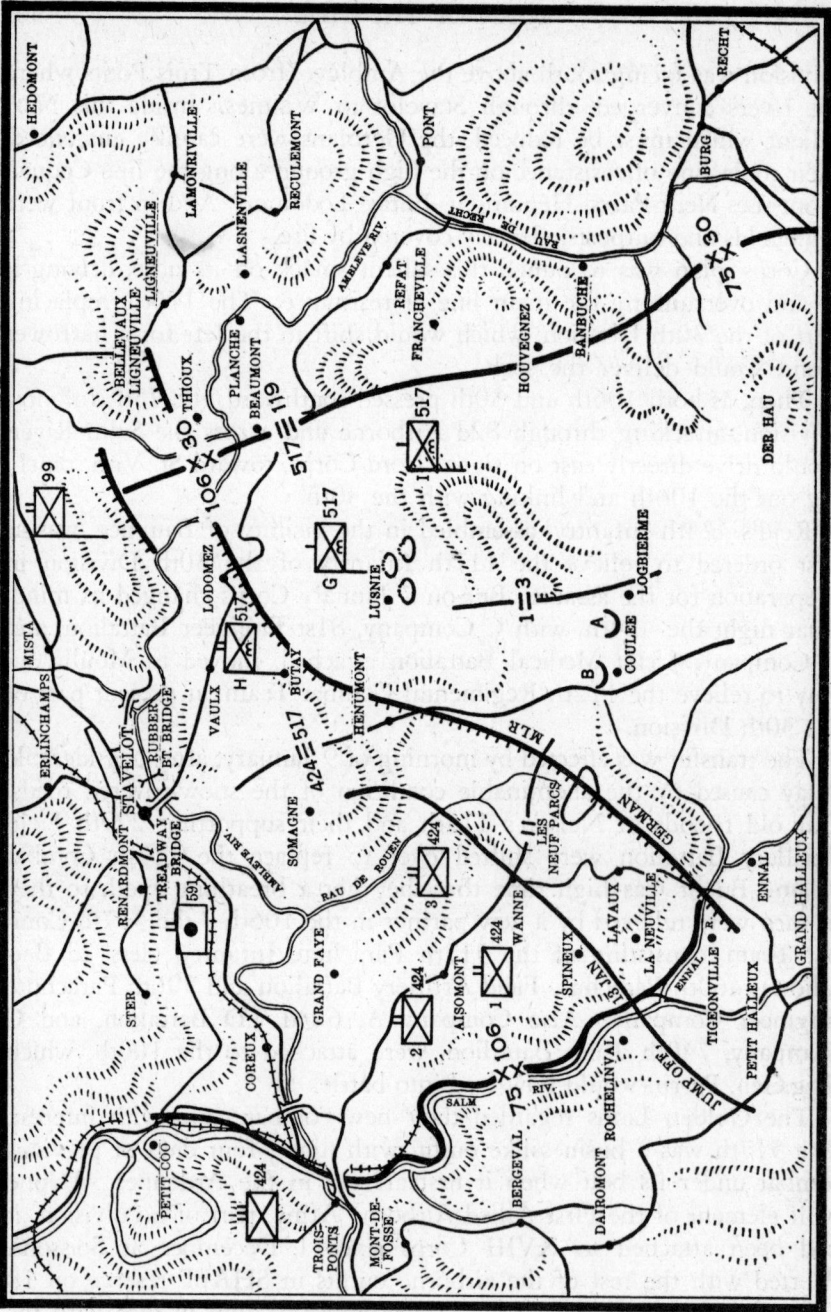

Map 10: First offensive: Attack across the Amblève, 13 January 1945.

On 12 January the 591st Field Artillery Battalion, relieved from the 82d, which it had supported in successive moves to Odrimont and Arbrefontaine, thence to Moustier and Roanne, took its rightful place as part of the 424th Combat Team, displacing to the vicinities of Ster–Parfondruy on the north bank of the Amblève. The 460th Field Artillery went into position three kilometers north of Stavelot to support the 517th, while additional supporting fires were arranged with the XVIII Corps artillery.

That night, near Stavelot, the 596th Engineers threw a rubber-boat footbridge previously constructed by C Company, 81st Engineers, across the Amblève, and a platoon of B Company, 517th Infantry, dashed over to establish a bridgehead. The stage was set.

The 106th went into action before dawn, 13 January, combat teams abreast, 424th on the right, 517th on the left. At 4:30 A.M. the 3d Battalion, 517th, started across. G Company[1] went over the original footbridge, while Company A, 81st Engineers, began construction of a treadway bridge beside it. By 7:45 A.M. the entire battalion was across and G Company had seized Lusnié, northeast of Henumont, and approximately two miles south of the Amblève. The 460th Field Artillery pushed up to the river's edge, just east of Stavelot, in support.

In this area a great belt of wooded country reaches from the river down to Poteau on the Vielsalm–St. Vith road. In its center rises Hill 572, known as Hautes Fanges.

Company I, pushing on to the left, pressed through this dense wooded thicket, bordered by ice-stiffened swamps, to seize and hold the hill mass, while H Company, after getting on its objective at Butay, though driven back at first by a heavy concentration of artillery, mortar and machine-gun fire, finally reestablished itself there.

The end of the day thus found the 517th settled in three spots, echeloned forward to the east, and flanking the Kraut positions from Henumont to Coulée, a definite threat.

The 424th Infantry on the right had stiffer going, as well it might, since it was driving squarely against the enemy positions. The regiment jumped off from the line Spineux–Wanne–Somagne, 1st and 3d Battalions in line from right to left, plunging east by south. The 2d Battalion at Aisomont was in reserve. Fresh snow flurries during the night of 12-13 January assisted in impeding ground movement over the already snow-packed, slippery ground.

Colonel Reid had considered putting his command post in Aisomont, but that morning when he picked the one sheltered room remaining in the shell-torn hamlet, his medical officer protested violently.

"Of course you can take it, Colonel," stormed the medico. "You're in command. But if you do—and its the only sheltered spot I've been able to find—you're condemning wounded men to death from exposure. I won't be responsible!"

Reid grinned.

"OK, Major," he responded. "You take it for your dressing station."

So the wounded would get their shelter—and a busy place it was to be—while the regimental command post went instead into a wind-swept corner of rubble on a road bend a mile east of Trois Ponts.

The regiment went into action with a strength of 2,360 men and 124 officers, and it would come out with 2,115 and 112 respectively; twelve officers and 245 men battle casualties, including the regimental commander, a battalion commander and four company commanders.

The 1st Battalion, with Companies A and B abreast in assault, from right to left, was to drive on Coulée, while the 3d Battalion, assaulting with K and I Companies from right to left, would strike at Henumont, was then to turn south on Coulée. Antitank and Cannon Companies would be in general support.

With the 591st Field Artillery in continuous support—the battalion fired 1,198 rounds that day and lost several officers and men of its forward observer parties with the infantry—the 1st Battalion moved out at 8:00 A.M. and by midday had smashed its way into Lavaux. It squared away eastward then for Coulée.

Clearing the rear of Lavaux, an enemy counterattack rocked Company A back on its haunches for a moment. Lt.Col. Welch, the battalion commander, and his S-2, Lt. Huddleston, up with the advance, rallied the command and Company A, on the run, pushed through the snowy woods to capture or kill all the Krauts.

Just southwest of Les Neuf Parcs the ground rises and the wandering Wanne–Coulée road tips over a bare knob well named Faix du Diable —the Devil's Load. The battalion reached this ridge, right in the enemy main line of resistance, then pressed in the dusk on down the slopes towards Coulée on the far side of the Ponceau ravine.

And the enemy fire came down. Artillery cross fire, from the high ground across the ravine and from the Coquaimont ridge directly south on their flank, hit both companies cruelly. The assaulting elements wavered, halted. Lt. Robert G. McKay, leading Company A, was killed. B Company, passing through A, was also hard hit, and its commander, Lt. Herman Slutzky, wounded.

Enemy light tanks and SPs opened up. Welch and his staff, up front, were caught in the shell bursts raking B Company. Welch and his S-3, Capt. Ross L. Edwards, were wounded. Young Huddleston, the S-2, had both feet taken off by a light tank shell.

The wounded battalion commander found that a first-aid man was apparently ignoring Huddleston, lying among four other wounded soldiers, although it was quite evident that he was the most seriously injured. He asked the soldier why he wasn't taking care of the lieutenant.

"I tried, but he won't let me!"

Welch asked Huddleston why.

"No, no!" responded Huddleston. "Not until all the soldiers are taken care of. I feel fine. How is the battle coming? Don't you think you had better go see how the boys are making out?"[2]

The storm was too great to be breasted. Lt. Herbert A. Pihl, 591st Field Artillery liaison officer with the battalion, rallied one of the infantry platoons thrown into momentary confusion and straightened it out. But the battalion just could not move ahead. Slowly it retired on the Les Neuf Parcs ridge and dug in, as Lt.Col. Orville M. Hewitt assumed command.

The medics got the gallant Huddleston out later that night, still conscious, but he died as they were carrying him through the woods.

The 3d Battalion, on the left of all this, also ran into stiff resistance as it advanced from the woods around Harenne. K Company, its right flank element, moving into the Rouen ravine, astride the Wanne–Bouen road, was hit by both small-arms and machine-gun fire, while rocket bursts scotched Wanne itself.

The lead platoon was pinned down by the initial bursts from concealed positions. Lt. Maxwell M. Brown, platoon commander, rose and walked forward, drawing more fire and uncovering an enemy machine-gun position, until he fell, mortally wounded. Pfc. George S. Vasquez crawled out toward the gun, then, leaping to his feet, charged with rifle blazing, wounded two of the gunners, captured three more and the gun. The platoon moved on.

Another Kraut machine gun began to chatter. Pfc. Ray W. Wandell rushed across the snow to lob a hand grenade into the position and capture the gun and three gunners. But K Company, though it reached the edge of the woods, could go no farther, and dug in.

Company I, on the left, debouching from the woods east of Wanneranval, got to the outskirts of Henumont before it, too, was stopped by intense concentrations of artillery, machine-gun and small-arms fire. Lt. Raymond S. Kautz, commanding, with his center platoon as a base of fire, sent the other two around for a double envelopment.

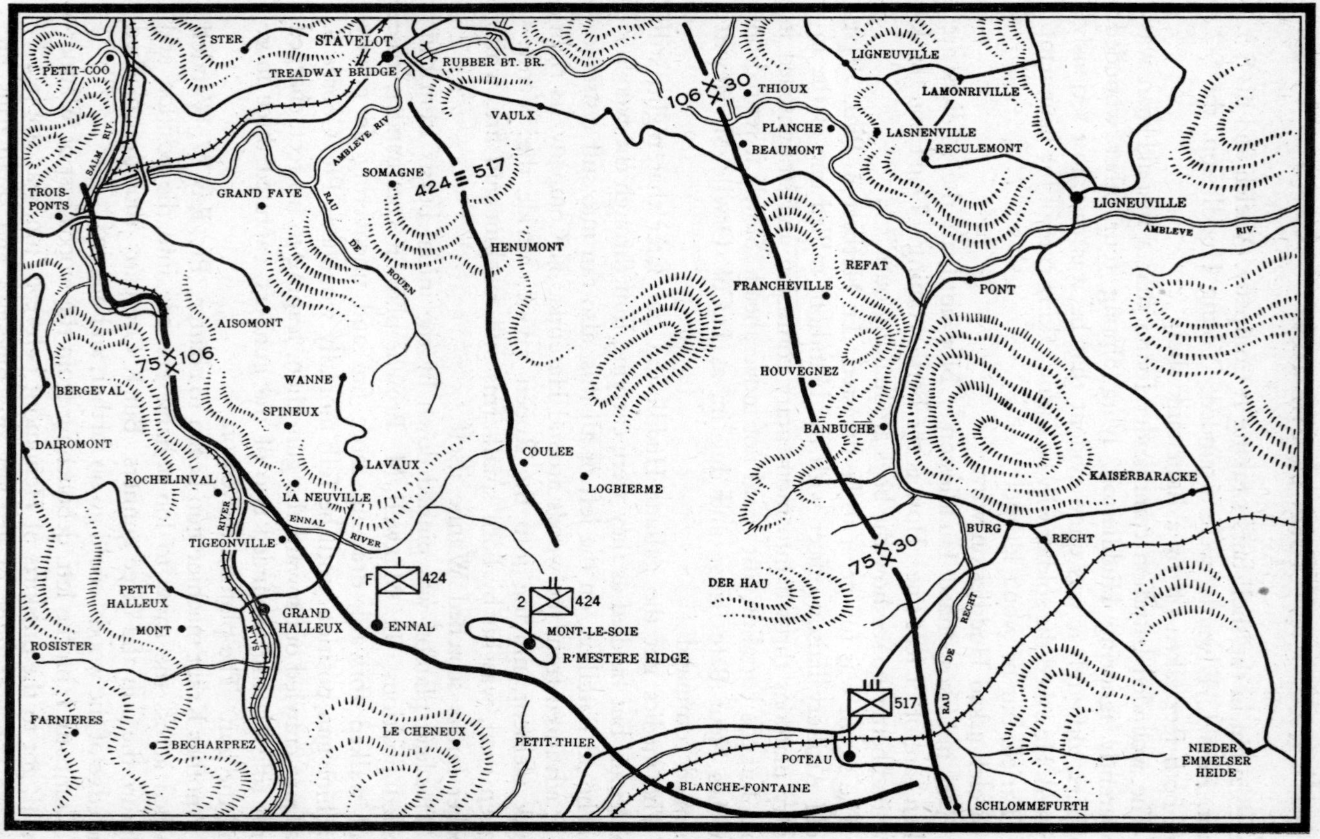

Map 11: *The fight for the ridge, 14-15 January 1945.*

Both were caught by cleverly laid cross fires and halted. Kautz charged frontally at the head of the base platoon over a snow-swept field, and smashed the initial resistance, only to be killed at the last minute, as was Lt. Robert Engstrom, Weapons Platoon leader, beside him. Tech.Sgt. Harold R. Johnson assumed command of the company and fought on until he had been wounded four times.

Company L, in reserve, was ordered to continue the attack into the village, with a platoon of C Company, 740th Tank Battalion. But mechanical failures stalled the tanks and the assault was called off. The 3d Battalion dug in for the night one thousand yards west of Henumont.

It was quite evident that the Kraut was not giving up his main line of resistance that day. Col. Reid called for artillery fire and all that night Division and Corps artillery threw everything but the kitchen sink into the bunkers and strongpoints around Henumont while the 2d Battalion was moved at nightfall to the Les Neuf Parcs woods, passing through the hard hit 1st Battalion, which became regimental reserve.

Division ordered the attack to be resumed the next morning. The 517th Infantry would assault Henumont from the east to relieve the pressure, while the 424th advanced southward across the Coquaimont ridge.

Accordingly, at 11:00 A.M., 14 January, the 1st Battalion, 517th Infantry, moving from reserve, attacked Henumont from the Lusnié woods to find the village deserted. The Kraut had decamped in the night. The battalion pressed rapidly southward, through Coulée to Logbierme, halting on its portion of the prearranged Division objective, an east-west line through Coquaimont to La Neuville.

The 3d Battalion, 517th Infantry, on the Division left, threw up a roadblock at Lodomez, while it extended and consolidated its forward position to contact the 30th Infantry Division on the east by patrol, at 2:30 P.M.

In the 424th Infantry zone, the 3d Battalion, on the left, moved forward as soon as the Henumont ulcer on its eastern flank was reported cleared, which was about 2:00 P.M. It reached its portion of the objective by nightfall, halting and digging in.

It was during this advance that Lt. Dale R. Carver, of 3d Battalion headquarters, discovered that the one passable road back to the rear areas and over which all battalion supply and evacuation would move, had been heavily mined around and about a culvert bridge near Les Neuf Parcs. Carver called for a volunteer to help him, and Pfc. Elmer L. LaFleur stepped out.

Working in water, mud and slush, at times actually ducking into the icy stream under the bridge as continued enemy interdiction fire fell about them, Carver and LaFleur unearthed twenty-seven mines by feeling for them with their bare hands, succeeded in removing them and neutralized them.

The 2d Battalion, with Company A attached, slicing to the southeast from the Lavaux–Les Neuf Parcs line, met heavy opposition in the form of fire from the high ground east of Ennal as it assaulted the Coquaimont ridge on its portion of the objective.

Company G found itself pinned down, but First Sgt. Wallace G. Rifleman did something about that. We remember Rifleman as one of the stout hearts who cut their way back from the Schnee Eifel when Puett's 2d Battalion, 423d Infantry, were told they were on their own at the time of surrender.

Rifleman now rushed forward into the open, throwing lead, and G Company followed, to win the objective.

Colonel Reid, with his 2d Battalion, late that night received word from Division of a proposed new attack. Corps felt that the assault of the 75th Infantry Division to pinch out the base of the salient could not be successfully launched until Ennal and the hill mass to its east, heavily fortified by numerous bunkers, were reduced. The 106th would assist in this, so the 424th would take Ennal.

The 2d Battalion attacked at daylight, 15 January. Company F on the right drove straight for the village, while E and G Companies pushed on up the eastern hill mass. Both the regimental and division commanders were with F Company as Lt. Edward F. Marcinkowski deployed his company for the assault.

In the snow-covered rubble of Ennal, as was later learned, was one Kraut company of infantry. Two other infantry companies and some engineers were on the eastern hill.

Company F crossed the Ennal ravine. Marcinkowski sent two patrols in turn into the edge of the village, but both were thrown back while the rest of the company began to take a heavy pounding. Lt. Benkman, leading the first patrol, was wounded; Staff Sgt. Lenahan, succeeding him, was killed, as were two other men. Lt. Lawrence, leading the second patrol, was wounded slightly, but remained with the company.

Each house in the village, it seemed, was loopholed for defense and every loophole was spitting accurate fire. Company F, baffled momentarily, was split into two platoons on Gen. Perrin's order. One platoon, led by Marcinkowski, assaulted from the east, while the other, under Lawrence, hit the place from the west.

Perrin and Reid advanced with Marcinkowski. Reid fell, wounded in both legs by small-arms fire, and was evacuated. Perrin, carrying on as his doughboys plunged into the village, fought with them from house to house. Marcinkowski himself was wounded. But F Company wouldn't let its Division Commander down, even if—and they smile when they say it—he lost his pistol as he scrambled and stumbled with them over rafters and rubbish, hunting out the Krauts.

Company F took Ennal.

Companies E and G stormed the bunkers on the R'emestère ridge, and held, though they did not complete their mopping up that day.

And the 517th Infantry swept through the Bois de Reuland to the outskirts of Poteau.

The flank of the 75th Infantry Division was clear for its drive as it slashed directly east that day to link with the 30th Division. General Ridgway, commanding XVIII Corps, congratulated the 424th Infantry for its Ennal attack which, he stated, "removed a thorn in our side."

The weather was clear that day and as the Kraut pulled out, leaving his defensive screen to fight to the end, the gunners of the 591st Field Artillery had what they describe as a "field day," picking off vehicles and matériel attempting to scrabble out of the salient. It also fired a number of missions in support of the 75th Division. The 592d Field Artillery, through all the action, had taken its share of Corps artillery missions.

Next day, as the 1st Battalion, 424th, remained in the Henumont area, and the 2d Battalion went about its mopping-up job, the 3d Battalion was attached to the 517th Infantry as regimental reserve. It was not called on, however.

Our 81st Engineers were still busy as the proverbial beavers along the river. They had tried to complete a captured German bridge east of Stavelot, but due to lack of prefabricated sections, had to abandon the job. Now, on 16 January, C Company commenced erection of a forty-ton timber bridge fifty yards downstream, which also replaced their initial treadway span. This bridge, by the way, was so solidly constructed, the story goes, that First Army engineers later chided our battalion for its precociousness. Anyway, First Army people thought well enough of it to place on the structure a sign reading "By Courtesy of First Army Engineers," a quip not too well taken by the 81st Engineer Battalion.

On the 17th the 2d Battalion, 424th, found there was still a kick left in the dying Kraut. A platoon of E Company, screening the woods towards Mont de Soie, was rocked back on its heels by a sudden burst of burp-gun and small-arms fire from a die-hard group. Company E attacked in force and that was that.

Next day the 75th Division's drive had passed by all along the length of the 106th Division's sector. The Golden Lions, pinched out, reverted to Corps reserve. The 517th Parachute Infantry Combat Team passed on to control of the 30th Division and the 106th once more licked its wounds—this time with a certain pride. It could give, it had found, as well as take.

The supporting 591st Field Artillery had displaced forward with the attack, B Battery to Aisomont 16 January, Batteries C and A to Lavaux and Spineux two days later. The mediums, our 592d Field Artillery, came rolling into the vicinity of Petit Halleux, Battery B on 17 January, Batteries A and C next day, from their previous positions near Fosse.

Notes To Chapter 14

[1] Thus the 517th Infantry's after-action report; apparently G and H Companies had been brought from the 2d Battalion to be attached to the 3d Battalion.

[2] Lieutenant Colonel Welch, relating the incident, adds, "The U. S. Army never had a braver soldier, nor one who thought more of fellow soldiers than Jerry Huddleston did."

Chapter 15: Into the Losheim Gap

++

Once more the Division took a breather, as it moved into the Trois-Ponts–Stavelot area for rest and reorganization. Even the artillery, for the 591st Field Artillery got a chance to overhaul its matériel. The 592d, however, continued on fire missions as part of Corps Artillery, displacing from Petit Halleux to Petit Thiers, moving slowly over icy roads. Several times the battalion got a taste of German shelling, too, as the enemy raked the area with interdiction fire.

But on 20 January the 424th Combat Team was alerted. The regiment, commanded for two days now by newly joined Col. John R. Jeter, together with the 591st Field Artillery, would hit the line again, this time attached to the 7th Armored Division. Meanwhile the 517th Parachute Infantry Combat Team had been reattached to the 106th, but this was purely for administrative purposes, and on 23 January the paratroopers finally parted company with the 106th, going to the 82d Airborne and then to the 7th Armored.

The fortune of war assigned the 424th to a zone north of St. Vith roughly corresponding to the defensive sector originally assigned the 14th Cavalry Group in December—that bitter time which seemed so long ago—a three-mile front extending south from Ebertange, west of and roughly paralleling the St. Vith–Büllingen highway, in front of Amblève, Meyerode and Medell.

So the 424th Infantry moved out at daybreak, 23 January, and by 9:00 P.M. that night had taken over from the 508th Parachute Infantry. Attached to the regiment were the 40th Tank Battalion (less B Company), B Company, 643d TD Battalion, and a platoon of Company A, 81st Engineers.

The 591st Field Artillery Battalion, which would be in direct support, had early that morning moved up to the vicinity of Ondrival and Thirimont, only to find itself some eight thousand yards behind the lines. So a hurried displacement was made, despite the snow-covered roads, to positions on the north edge of the Wolfsbusch near Monteneau. Forward observer parties were already in position with the infantry.

Before we go into the details of the attack, let's look at the big picture. First Army had hit the line again on 22 January, driving the Kraut out of places with familiar names. On the south the VII Corps, pushing its divisions into Beho and Gouvy, battering in the last stubborn defensive action of 9th SS Panzer Division, had been pinched out by the offensive action of U. S. Third Army on the south and XVIII Corps on the north.

XVIII Corps had rammed the 75th Infantry Division into Commanster; the 30th Infantry Division was in Ober and Nieder Emmels, and the 7th Armored, driving south, was closing in on St. Vith, through Wallerode and Hünningen. V Corps on the north was swelling out of the "hot" Büllingen corner. Nazi armor was rolling eastward in frantic effort to escape, while our air forces were taking vicious toll of his columns winding through the hills in the now clear, cold weather. The salient was melting fast.

By 23 January the 7th Armored had crunched through into St. Vith, rolling back on the way a small but violent Kraut counterattack ripping out of Wallerode. The 30th Division had reached Neundorf to be pinched out by the 7th above it, and the 75th below it, which latter had itself reached Braunlauf and Maldingen.

Now the 424th would become the left flank unit of the 7th Armored in a southeasterly push, with the battle-scarred 16th Infantry Regiment of the 1st Infantry Division—right flank unit of V Corps—on its left, and its former partner, the 517th Parachute Infantry, on its right.

All day of 24 January was spent in careful preparation. That afternoon the attack order was issued. The regiment, with 2d and 3d Battalions in assault, from right to left, and 1st Battalion in reserve at Ebertange, would cross and secure the Büllingen–St. Vith highway. Pressing east, the 2d Battalion would capture Medell, then seize and clear the wooded slopes of the Deperts Berg, a thousand yards to the southeast. The 3d Battalion, by-passing Amblève, now an enemy strongpoint, would seize the bare slopes of the Adesberg, then drive southeast into Meyerode, organizing a strongpoint on the eastern slopes of the Adesberg when the final objective was secured.

Company A, 40th Tank Battalion, would be attached to the 2d Battalion, 424th, C Company to the 3d Battalion. Small detachments of engineers and of Antitank Company were distributed to both.

On the north the 1st Infantry Division on the right flank of V Corps would take up the assault one day later, in its turn by-passing the Amblève position which would then be captured from the rear.

That night, 24 January, some time after midnight, as the assault elements of the 424th assembled, a strange call came in over the 2d Battalion OP wire.

"This is Beer," said a voice in correct English. "We're between you and the Germans."

And while the observation post people were scratching their heads—there were some rather crazy code names floating about but no one had heard of an outfit slugged "Beer"—the call came in again.

"This is Beer. We're verifying positions. Just where is your observation post? Coordinates, please?"

The OP operator stalled and battalion called back to Division. No, no one there knew of any outfit with code name of Beer. Said they were in front, did he? Well, well! So Battalion rang up the 591st Field Artillery. A quick concentration seared the area between the Auf der Hardt ridge and Medell. Beer didn't call again.

But it was that night that a Kraut mortar shell scored a direct hit on a 591st Field Artillery observation post manned by C Battery people. This was no accident; some unidentified individual had gone up to the carefully camouflaged spot in broad daylight in plain enemy view. Lt. Ronald J. Kaulitz, who had stuck with Division Artillery's Headquarters Battery during the strafing at Poteau; Staff Sgt. Ray H. Blackwell and Pfc. Homer W. Mullen were killed; T/5 William L. Monroe, the remaining occupant of the post, was wounded.

The 424th jumped off at 7:15 A.M., 25 January, while the artillery —Division and Corps—brought down a heavy concentration of HE and smoke on Amblève to neutralize it. The 1st Battalion also kept up a long-range fire on the town.

The 3d Battalion on the left, with I and L Companies abreast from north to south and Company K in reserve, had its assault elements across the highway, the initial phase line, by 9:00 A.M. and moving up the bare snowy slopes of the Adesberg—Hill 560. A concentration of fire from the 591st Field Artillery then smothered the hilltop and the shell-raked church on the skyline. By 10:40 A.M. the assault conpanies were on the objective.

It wasn't quite as easy as that sounds. On the way up, heavy fire threatened the left flank of I Company. Sgt. Richard L. Schmit, a machine-gun squad leader, set up on an exposed knob and himself wriggled into a fire-swept zone to lay his weapon. When the gunner and assistant gunner were wounded, Schmit, unaided, worked the gun, although wounded himself, until the riflemen he was supporting got on the crest.

And out in one of the fields from which fire was coming squatted two suspicious looking haystacks, snowy mounds. Sgt. Alvin P. Swanson took a four-man patrol to look them over. While his patrol covered him with small-arms fire, the sergeant crawled through the snow to bag eight Krauts with three machine guns snuggled in the straw.

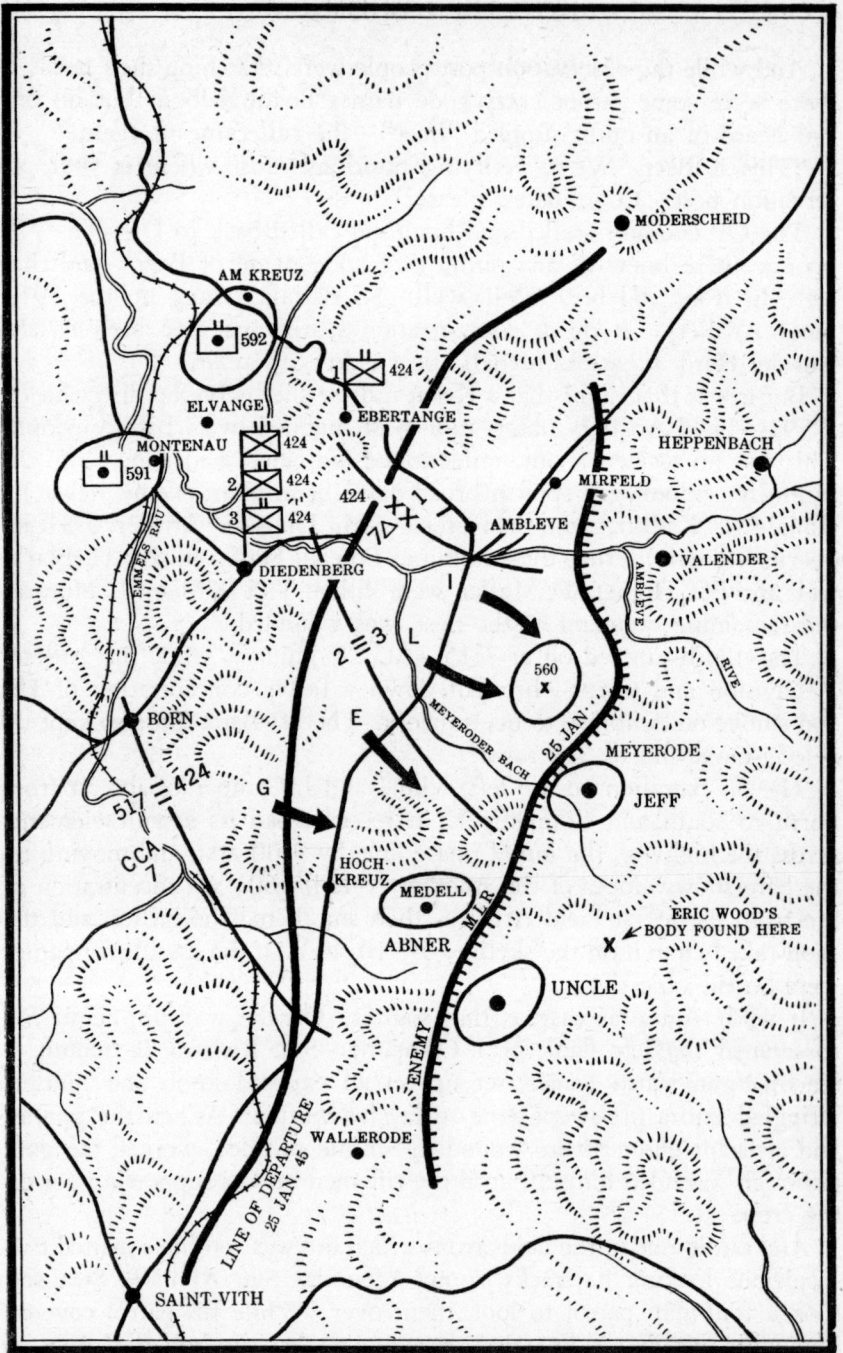

Map 12: *Into the Losheim Gap, 25 January 1945.*

Private First Class Edward J. Cole, another machine gunner supporting I Company's advance, several times wounded as he played his fire, refused to abandon his piece until the Adesberg was taken. Cole had done some cool shooting only a few days previous in the attack on Henumont.

While these things were going on K Company had moved from reserve to establish a roadblock on the highway south of Amblève. Upon the capture of the Adesberg, Company A moved in from Ebertange to relieve it, and K followed its battalion. Companies I and L resumed their advance, pushing combat patrols toward Meyerode and its bare protecting Hill 546 just north of the village. The enemy was found to be there in strength, so regiment ordered a halt for the night and consolidation of the objectives already attained.

The 2d Battalion on the right half of the regimental zone advanced that morning with E and G Companies in assault from north to south, and F Company in reserve. Company E, encountering no resistance, was well across the highway by 9:00 P.M. and halted, waiting for G to close up. But G Company had run into trouble.

As the assault waves debouched from the woods west of the highway, they were pinned to the ground by a sudden heavy burst of bazooka and automatic-weapons fire from Hochkreuz, junction of the Medell road and the highway. Lt. Tom Wilson, commanding, was killed, and a few moments later Lt. Aubrey D. Morgan, who took over, was wounded.

Company G just couldn't gain ground across that open slope, so F Company and a tank platoon were committed. A three-hour fight ensued as F Company, covered by the tanks, pushed toward the road junction. An 88 SP gun began slugging into the infantry advance. Staff Sgt. David F. McErlane spotted the gun position, dragged himself in the snow to within a short distance and effectively drove off the gunners with his carbine fire. Then he guided a tank into the position.

The company moved on, but another 88 came into action. Again McErlane crawled out and began to pick off the gunners with his accurate shooting, and again guided the tanks into the position. During this last episode McErlane was wounded several times. The tanks finally cleared the road junction, though one of them was knocked out by bazooka fire in that task.

The 2d Battalion straightened out to resume the advance, F Company absorbing what was left of G. Krauts in Medell itself began to put down more fire. A call for air support brought a flight of fighter-bombers sweeping in at 1:30 P.M. and a direct bomb hit in the center of the village brought results; five tanks went scuttling eastward.

Company E got to within a scant hundred yards of Medell, with F and G Companies alongside it, when direct fire from more 88s slowed them down. On call, the 591st Field Artillery cracked down. Behind its bursts the battalion surged forward into the village, resistance ceasing at 4:40 P.M. Patrols pushed into the Deperts Berg beyond in the gathering dusk now met instant resistance, so the 2d Battalion, too, was halted and consolidated for the night.

Patrols from the 16th Infantry of the 1st Division, on the north flank of the regiment, entered Amblève during the day to find it deserted. Accordingly the 16th pushed on to Mirfeld, a day ahead of the original schedule, relieving the 424th of any anxiety on that flank.

Next morning K and L Companies closed in on Meyerode, with C Company, 40th Tank Battalion. On the objective by 9:00 A.M., they spent the rest of the day mopping up, under desultory enemy fire.

In the 2d Battalion zone, E Company shoved off into the snow-hung firs of the Deperts Berg and gained the ridge by 11:00. It was here that Staff Sgt. Richard J. Maslankowski, leading a heavy-weapons section, when the platoon he was supporting met a burst of automatic-weapons fire, cradled a light machine gun in his arms and moved into the woods spraying it. The gun jammed. Maslankowski cleared the weapon under fire, resumed his one-man assault until he had reached a Kraut machine gun and killed its two-man crew.

Thirty minutes after E Company had won the ridge a minor counter-attack was repulsed without much difficulty, the enemy's last gasp in this particular neighborhood.

The remainder of that day and the next were spent by the 424th in patrolling, extending and consolidating the regimental zone. The 592d Field Artillery had moved forward to Am Kreuz by 27 January, and on 28 January the 325th Infantry of the 82d Airborne Division assaulted through the 424th. Another smashing drive was on.

The regiment moved back to Division control that day. It had done its job, played its part in knocking the Kraut out of some of the same ground he had overrun in December. But probably no one realized at the time the symbolic significance of that last assault. For in the Adesberg, over which the 3d Battalion had poured, was where a last stand had been made by 106th Division people. And, not five hundred yards east of the 2d Battalion's final objective on the Deperts Berg ridge, lay the still body of Eric Wood.[1]

NOTE TO CHAPTER 15

[1] See 150, *supra*, "Powerful . . . and Brave of Spirit."

Chapter 16: Last Lap of Battle

It was 3 February that the 106th was alerted for what would turn out to be its last combat assignment. The 424th Infantry, together with the 591st and 592d Field Artillery Battalions, were to move to Amblève, to be attached to the 99th Infantry Division preparatory to the 106th's taking over as the right flank element of U. S. First Army in its advance towards the Rhine.

First Army was taking the Roer Dams; the final battle west of the Rhine was in the making. Far to the north Canadian First Army was striking southeast into the upper end of the Cologne Plain, while the British Second Army, a skeleton force for the moment, was holding along the Maas in front of Venlo. U. S. Ninth Army was preparing to launch its offensive over the Roer. U. S. First Army would sweep up a little more, then regroup to assist the Ninth and itself to crash to the Rhine. U. S. Third Army, south of an east-west line through Losheim, was continuing its battering crunch through the Eifel.

The German side of the picture was black. Scarred elements of Sixth SS Panzer Army were scuttling eastward to meet the Russians. Left behind were its now weary *Volksgrenadiers,* with what remained of Fifth Panzer Army, in a last-ditch effort to man the Siegfried Line—the Westwall. But the Kraut, no longer fighting with the frenzy marking the assault into the Bulge, like all cornered animals was still dangerous —dangerous as one of the wounded wild boars of the Ardennes, snuffling and snarling in the hills.

V Corps controlled the right flank of First Army and, now a part of it, the 106th was the southernmost unit, making contact with Third Army's 87th Division. Its task was one of aggressive defense, of continuous pressure. But it was not to take the offensive; Corps' orders were explicit: its role was as pivot of maneuver.

The combat-team elements of the Division moved on 5 February, the remainder following. On 7 February Maj.Gen. Donald A. Stroh assumed command, and by 9 February the Division was once more in action as a unit. This time it was in the dreary crags of the Gerolstein Forest, astride the steep banks of the headwaters of the Kyll River.

The position ran in a 7,000-yard arc, bulging to the east, from Neuhof on the north to the vicinity of Losheim on the south. The line followed the high ground on the east bank of the Wilsam River to its confluence with the Kyll, thence southwest over Hill 616, a promontory jutting into the Kyll Valley between that river and a creek which

219

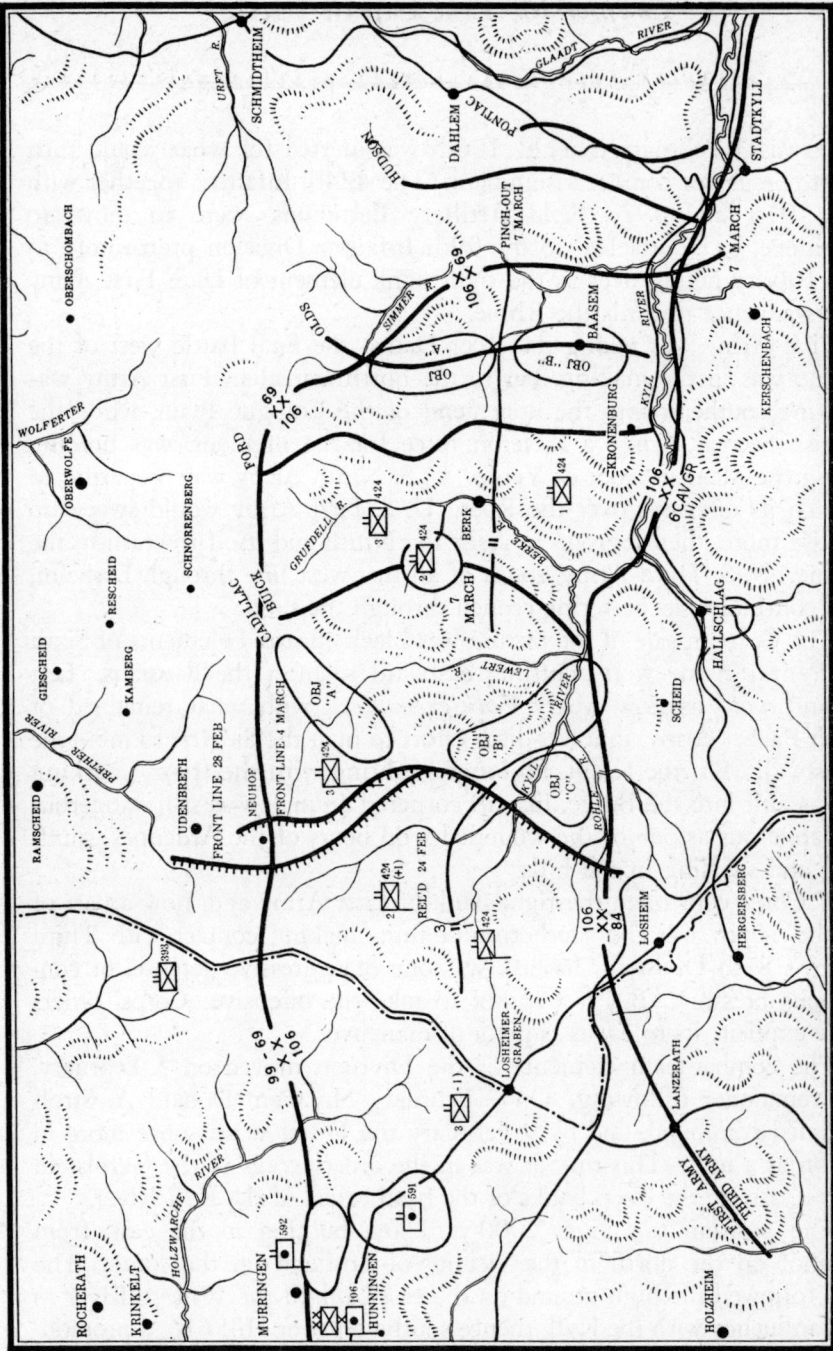

Map 13: Journey's end, 7 March 1945

changes its name three times in three thousand yards—Eulen, Lang and Rohles.

The zone ahead was a jumbled mass of hills and watercourses. Bisecting it progressively eastward were three streams, the Lewart, Grusdell and Simmer, draining from north to south in winding valleys deepening to three hundred feet when they fed into the Kyll.

It was no terrain to be taken frontally, organized as it was and backing against prepared Siegfried Line positions on the ridge east of the Grusdell. Each ridge could be turned from the north flank, but one lone regimental combat team of three infantry battalions could not be expected to do the job against determined resistance.

The 2d Battalion, 424th Infantry, with I Company attached, held the northern sector, including the two hill masses 656 and 655, the latter a definite bulge into enemy territory. The southern sector slanting toward Losheim was held by the 1st Battalion. In reserve, at the deserted hamlet of Losheimergraben (original boundary point on 16 December), where the Schönberg–Scheiden road, of ill-fame to the 106th, crosses the Prüm–Büllingen highway, the 3d Battalion dug in. Losheimergraben, on the dominant plateau of Hill 676, was to be the sheet anchor of the line; no chances were being taken to ensure its holding. And on 12 February Lt.Col. Robert H. Stumpf was put in command of the 424th.

The 591st and 592d Field Artillery Battalions were in positions just east of Hünningen and Mürringen, respectively. Company A, 814th TD Battalion, attached, made up additional fire power for the combat team. The Division command post was at Hünningen.

The forward zone was a mess. In the first place the Kraut had scattered mines and booby traps in enormous quantities, with his usual ingenuity. Secondly, while the dense woods were crisscrossed by trails, these had become masses of mud from rain and thaw. Even jeeps could not negotiate them; the only vehicles which could be used off the main roads were a number of Weasels which had been drawn for Division use. The engineers slaved endlessly, corduroying and laying wire matting on the principal routes.

Active patrolling at once disclosed the enemy to be well dug in in successive delaying positions. The first reconnaissance patrol to penetrate the forest morasses flushed a heavily armed enemy combat patrol. Now a reconnaissance patrol, it must be remembered, has no business standing and fighting; its duty is to get and, above all, bring back information.

So Pfc. Thomas F. Dowgin, of Headquarters Company, 424th Infantry, the lead scout, opened up on the Krauts with his tommy gun while the rest of the patrol decamped across a creek.

Dowgin's spitting submachine gun pinned the Krauts to the ground long enough for his comrades to gain cover; then, as they opened fire, he crawled back, badly wounded.

Next day an enemy demonstration on the front of the 2d Battalion in G Company's zone included two small attacks, which were promptly disposed of by our artillery, mortar and small-arms fire.

So the time passed in desultory bickering; but with each fracas along the front lines the 106th positions were inched a bit farther. It was all very monotonous. Regiment and Division kept making attack plans and sending them up to Corps, to no avail.

On 16 February Company A, 661st TD Battalion, relieved the men of the 814th. And next day another hostile demonstration in front of the 2d Battalion was squelched without trouble. On 24 February the 3d Battalion came up and relieved the 2d, which, leaving E Company behind, went back into the perimeter defense position at Losheimer-graben.

With Washington's Birthday had come news of the great assault across the Roer. Minor assaults to right and left of the 106th were in the making. The 69th Infantry Division, which had replaced the 99th on the left, was slated to attack Ramscheid, the 106th Division Artillery assisting in fire support. The 87th Division on the right, left-flank element of Third Army, was to attack to the east. But the 106th would stay put. It was all rather exasperating.

The 3d Battalion, itching for a fight, sent a platoon from L Company poking into the woods on 25 February to stir up a momentary hornets' nest. The Kraut began putting down fire which halted it. Staff Sgt. Ralph G. Duff took a six-man patrol around the flanks and jumped the Krauts. Duff, badly wounded, nevertheless continued to direct this patrol by hand signal, under heavy fire. And the enemy was pushed back another hundred yards.

On the nose of Hill 586, in front of the 1st Battalion, Jerry had a particularly obnoxious pillbox bunker, commanding the Kyll Valley. Battalion felt it must be removed and finally got permission. Accordingly, on 28 February a rifle platoon of C Company, with some engineers, supported by concentrations of artillery and mortar fire, took it on, swarmed over it and captured nine men, killing four more.

The worst part of the attack was getting through the minefields surrounding the Kraut defense. Here it was that Capt. John Graham, Medical Corps, who accompanied the platoon as a volunteer, gallantly rescued one of his aid men who had gotten himself entangled in a mass of mine trip-wires. Patiently the medical officer unravelled the wires under a continuous rain of machine-gun fire, and got the man free without exploding a mine.

All in all a frustrating month, February, for the 106th, in constant but inconclusive action, with a casualty score of 18 killed, 87 wounded and 21 missing.

Now, however, the Kraut's last bastion was cracking. Extended patrolling which probed deeper each time, statements of prisoners who were coming in in steady trickle, all indicated that. The 87th Division on the right flank was moving east. On the left the 69th Division would jump off as the First Army's main effort to the north went crashing toward the Rhine. At long last the 106th would take the offensive with its solitary combat team.

The 424th moved out 5 March, 3d Battalion on the north, 1st Battalion on the south of Hill 655. By nightfall it had attained the initial ridge line with ease and had established contact with neighboring elements on both flanks.

Next day, 6 March, strong patrols penetrated the ridges all the way to the Simmer. Mines and abominable road conditions were the only obstacles; the Kraut had decamped. Battery A, 591st Field Artillery, got its pieces up to the vicinity of Hill 656, east of Neuhof, with much difficulty by 6:00 P.M. The remainder of the artillery prepared to hike forward.

And 7 March, as the 69th Division lunged forward in a wide southeastern swing down the ridge lines from the north towards Dalheim, 1st and 2d Battalions, 424th Infantry, pushed almost five miles across the hills to make contact with it, the 3d Battalion following fast. The artillery displaced, the 591st dropping trails near Battery A's new position, the 592d moving into the western slopes of the Lewart, about one mile northwest of Frauenkron. But the howitzers would not bark again. The 69th Division's move had pinched out the 106th, making contact with Third Army near Stadtkyll. The Division had lost one man killed, 30 wounded and one missing in that last week.

The 106th Infantry Division's combat role had ended, ended in victory, just seven miles northeast of the original left-flank Schnee Eifel positions of the ill-fated 422d Infantry on 16 December 1944, eighty-one days previous. This day First Army was on the Rhine, this day Hoge's CCB, 9th Armored Division, was gobbling the Remagen bridge. This day was a good day.

Chapter 17: Prisoners by the Million

By 1 April six Allied armies, four of them American, had swept across the Rhine, had advanced more than one hundred miles into Germany beyond it and had completely surrounded the major part of the German armies in the West. Through the month they kept pushing eastward toward their objectives—the line of the Elbe and Mulde Rivers and the Erzgebirge mountain nose of Czechoslovakia.

Some 198,000 prisoners were already in various army cages; more than 300,000 additional, entrapped in the greatest double envelopment in history[1]—the encirclement of the Ruhr by the Ninth and First Armies of Bradley's magnificent 12th Army Group—were surrendering as the days ticked on. Third Army was storming toward the Danube in scythe-like sweeps. Seventh Army in the south was slicing through Bavaria and on to the Austrian Alps.

The fabric of armed Naziism was crumbling to dust. By 7 May came the unconditional surrender and complete collapse.

Vast uncounted hordes of German prisoners were streaming westward all through April—beaten, baffled, demoralized flotsam and jetsam, herded by entirely inadequate escorts of military police from the victorious armies. So far as Communications Zone, responsible for their care, was concerned, the situation was rapidly getting out of hand. For some reason no adequate preparation had been made for this eventuality. This is hard to understand when one realizes that the collapse of the Afrika Korps at Bizerte, concluding the North Africa Campaign, had presented a similar problem on a smaller scale. But there it was—we were not ready to receive our guests.

It was the irony of fate that the 106th Infantry Division, which had lost to the Germans more prisoners of war than any one other division in ETO, should have been hurriedly selected in mid-April to take custody of the entire bag of prisoners of war collected on the field of battle by the U. S. First, Third, Seventh and Ninth Armies. It was an assignment unique, unprecedented and serious.

During a period of eleven weeks the 106th would stand guard over some 920,000 Krauts, would process through its cages more than a million and a quarter individuals of the "Master Race" of all ranks and ages, and of both sexes. The motley crew would include sixty-eight Axis general officers, from the rank of field marshal down; twenty-six hundred women, representing the equivalent of WACs and nurses. The age gamut ran from boys of seven to men of eighty years. Some eighteen nationalities were represented.

The task came as a complete surprise. The Division had moved out of the battle zone on 14 March, traveling by rail and motor to St. Quentin, France, for reorganization, rehabilitation and training, passing from First to Fifteenth Army command. Its mission was to reconstitute and train new units with the same designation as those of its elements "lost" in the Bulge. It would prepare for another operational mission, at the same time becoming tactical reserve for the 66th Infantry Division in the "forgotten war" against the Nazi pockets of Lorient and St. Nazaire. Later it would take over from the 66th.

So the Division had moved again; this time to Rennes, ancient capital of Brittany, closing in the vicinity on 6 April. To it came two new combat-team partners, the 3d and 159th Infantry Regiments and the 401st and 627th Field Artillery Battalions, just arrived at Camp Lucky Strike near Havre from the United States. Here too came individual replacements, to the tune of 6,606 officers and men; 2,227 of them from infantry replacement centers in the States, the remainder drafted from other arms of the service and whipped into infantry during a six-weeks course at ETO reinforcement training centers.

There was a three-ring circus of training and reorganization. In the first place, the 424th Infantry and 591st Field Artillery Battalion, in addition to everything else were on a five-hour alert status to reinforce the 66th Division on call. The newly arrived outfits were fitted into the Division framework. And the elements to be reconstituted were being built up from the replacements, around cadres consisting of the handful of survivors of the original units and selected officers and men from remaining divisional elements.

It wasn't as easy as it sounds on paper. Trained officers and men were short; so were such basic matériel as 105mm howitzers and antitank guns. But all hands drove in with a spirit of make-do. And on 15 April, in solemn ceremony, the 422d and 423d Infantry Regiments, the 589th and 590th Field Artillery Battalions and the 106th Reconnaissance Troop were reborn; receiving their respective colors, standards and guidons.

Two veteran 106th officers commanded the artillery units. Major Arthur C. Parker, III—Parker of Parker's Crossroads—now recovered from his wounds, led the new 589th; Major Carl H. Wohlfeil, smart executive of the 591st, was at the head of the new 590th. And next day big Tom Riggs—Tom Riggs who had stopped the Nazis at the threshold of St. Vith—reported in from his odyssey of imprisonment, escape and fighting in the Russian ranks to take over his old 81st Engineers. Those two days were Golden Lions' days in Rennes.

And the next day the Division was tapped for its new assignment— Germany and the POWs. Leaving the reconstituted units attached to the 66th Division the revamped 106th moved to the Rhine, the 159th Infantry to Remagen, Division Artillery to Mannheim and the re- mainder of the Division to the vicinity of Stromberg. By 25 April all elements had closed in.

During this period the reconstituted units in the west saw some action. The 627th Field Artillery Battalion (Lt.Col. Harris) supported the 66th Division Artillery from positions southwest of Nantes, and the 423d Infantry, with the 590th Field Artillery Battalion in support, clashed with the Krauts in the St. Nazaire pocket, the day before it folded.

Followed hectic conferences with the Provost Marshal of ETO and representatives of AdSec (Advance Section, Communications Zone) serving 12th Army Group and ConAd (Continental Advance Section, Communications Zone) serving 6th Army Group. Even then the real magnitude of the task did not fully reveal itself.

The Division would be responsible for guarding POWs in four general zones along the Rhine—from the Dutch border to Baden. And by 30 April it had taken over five inclosures containing a total of 165,272 prisoners. A big task, the 106th people thought; they hadn't, as it turned out, seen anything yet.

The task was not just "to guard prisoners of war." That was the simplest part of the problem. The task was to administer (including actual construction of inclosures), screen, segregate, transfer, evacuate, process, discharge and transport all over France and Germany more than one million human beings.

Take a large, empty field, bare of shelter or other facilities for human habitation. Start thousands of POWs streaming toward it. Then in- form the 106th Division. This, in a nutshell, it seemed, was the ETO prescription for handling Krauts as the great collapse of the Reich went on.

Most camp sites were completely destitute of shelter. There were no messing facilities, and worst of all, no food. The water supply was either uncompleted or entirely inadequate. One camp, requiring a hundred and fifty thousand gallons of water daily, was being supplied by five-gallon jerricans. Sanitary provisions, except for straddle-trench latrines, did not exist. Most inclosures consisted of but a single barbed- wire fence, and guard towers were conspicuous by their absence.

Medical supplies lacked; medical personnel was spread thin—the

331st Medical Battalion and the unit organic medical detachments. The weather was cold and rainy.

Example is the Remagen inclosure at this period. Originally designed to accommodate a hundred thousand prisoners, twice that number were herded inside the barbed wire the day the 106th took over; ten thousand of them were on sick report. Up at Büderich, just below the Netherlands border, at a new inclosure, truck convoys from at least seven different divisions were jam-packing the access roads bumper to bumper, crowded with Krauts, the day it opened. Seven railway trains crammed with prisoners were shrilling on the river bank for right of way over the only bridge. Some thirty-five thousand of these new arrivals went into the gates of the partly completed inclosure that first afternoon.

Over all this the specter of mass epidemic haunted the dreams of the 106th medicos—when they found time to dream!

To handle the mess General Stroh had one extemporized infantry division—two of his combat teams were newcomers, it must be remembered—without the slightest previous training or experience for the mission. Primarily, one thing stood out; there were just not sufficient men in the 106th to stand guard. So ComZ rushed three new units to Division attachment—the 6950th, 6951st and 6952d Provisional Guard Battalions—consisting each of a thousand officers and men thrown together haphazardly. Also, in the same haphazard manner, came ten thousand individual replacements, which were now attached to the 106th in ratio of a hundred men per company, troop and battery. This tremendous influx of new personnel was in itself a test of leadership which under normal conditions would have been a big job. Here it became a minor problem; there was so much to do now—right now, this instant.

The medical problem was solved by attaching to the Division and its harassed medical personnel a number of field hospitals on 9 May. Units came from the 9th, 12th, 50th, 61st, 62d, 78th and 83d Field Hospitals, together with an assortment of ambulance companies. Finally, a complete ambulance battalion, the 428th, was attached; the usual complement of a field army. Some idea of the magnitude of this part of the task may be gained from divisional medical statistics for May:

Cases treated on sick call	1,143,177
Cases evacuated to hospital units	26,366
Deaths in the inclosures	1,404
Deaths in hospital units	733
Admissions of communicable diseases	5,615

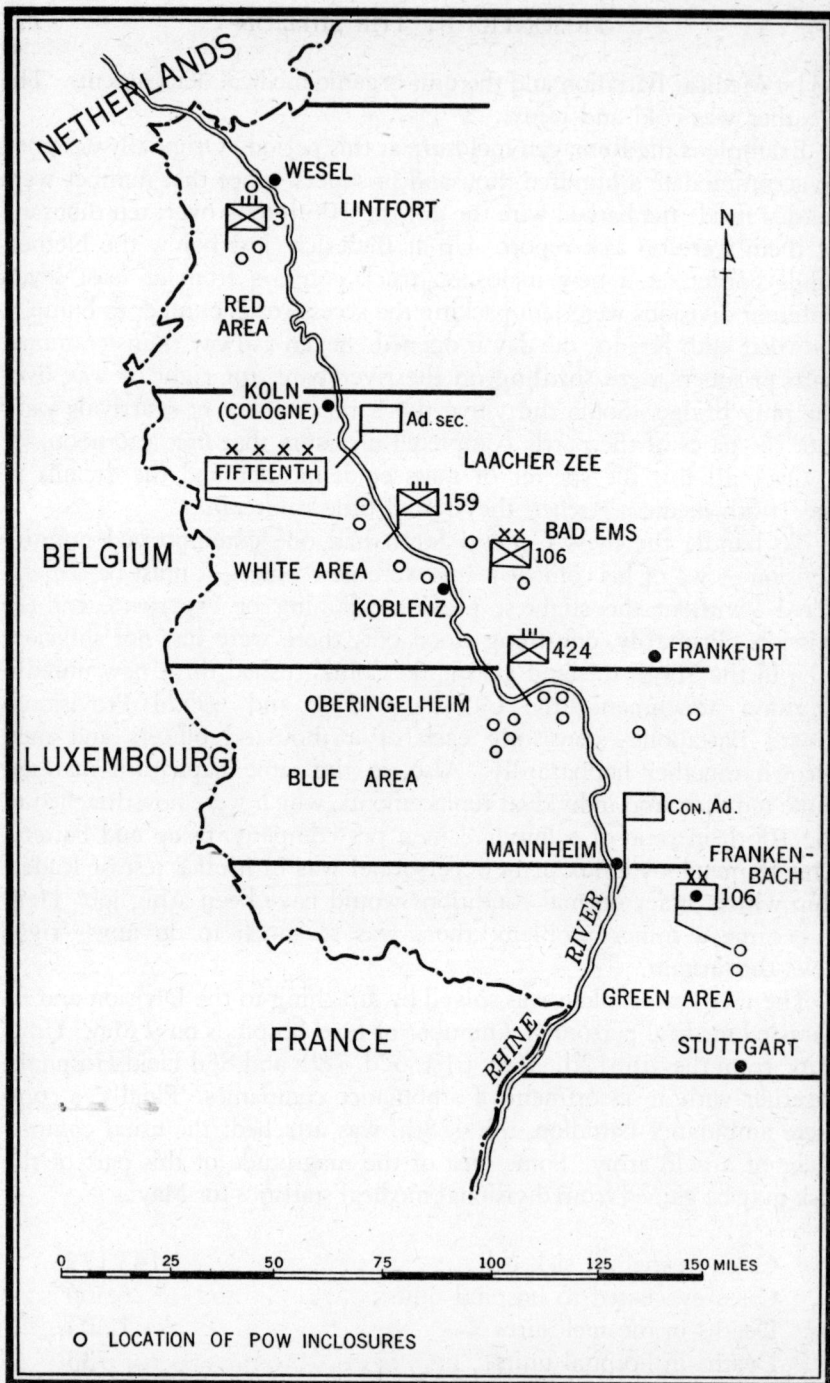

Map 14: *Here came the Nazi debris. The POW area of the 106th Infantry Division.*

This last item breaks down into categories which tell their own tale:

Respiratory	2,034
Gastro-intestinal	2,409
Diphtheria	232
Typhus	11
Typhoid	45
Others	884

The Division command post was at Bad Ems. The strength of the command had swollen to forty thousand. The four areas occupied along the Rhine—known respectively as Red, White, Blue and Green —were as follows from north to south:

Red Area. Command post, Lintfort; Col. Herbert J. Vander Heide, 3d Infantry, commanding
    Camp A-4, Buderich; 1st Battalion, 3d Infantry.
    Camp A-1, Rheinberg; 6950th Provisional Guard Battalion.
    Camp A-9, Wickrathberg; AT and Cannon Companies, 3d Infantry.

White Area. Command post, north end of Laacher Zee; Col. Leon L. Kotzebue, 159th Infantry, commanding.
    Camp A-2, Remagen; 6951st Provisional Guard Battalion.
    Camp A-5, Sinzig; 3d Battalion, 159th Infantry, with Company F and detachments of Cannon and AT Companies attached.
    Camp A-11, Andernach; 2d Battalion, 159th Infantry.
    Camp A-10, Coblenz; 1st Battalion, 159th Infantry.

Blue Area. Command post, Ober Ingelheim; Lt.Col. Robert H. Stumpf, 424th Infantry, commanding.
    Camp A-12, Heidesheim; 2d Battalion, 424th Infantry.
    Camp A-7, Biebelsheim; 1st Battalion and AT Company, 424th Infantry.
    Camp A-6, Winzenheim; 3d Battalion, 424th Infantry.
    Camp A-3, Bad Kreuznach; 6952d Provisional Guard Battalion.
    Camp A-8, Dietersheim; 2d Battalion, 3d Infantry.

Green Area. Command post, Weinheim (later Frankenbach); Brig. Gen. Leo T. McMahon, commanding.
    Camp C-3, Heilbronn ⎱ 106th Division Artillery.
    Camp C-4, Heilbronn ⎰

The 3d Battalion, 3d Infantry, during this period was encamped in the woods five miles southeast of Mainz in reserve. Camp A-16 at Zahlbach, and A-17 at Hechtsheim were also conducted later, for Russians and Czechs, respectively.

Linking this sprawling conglomeration into a communications net along two hundred miles of Rhine banks was another task—far beyond the normal duties of a combat division signal company. The 106th Signal Company constructed, rehabilitated and used more than 1,500 miles of wire communications. Division Artillery planes maintained a shuttle air-courier service, and this was supplemented by ground courier. The system was far from ideal, but it worked. It had to.

By 3 May the Red Area contained 129,000 prisoners, White, 250,000, Blue 160,000. Business was light in Green, which was fed from Seventh Army, and ConAd, in contrast to AdSec, was careful not to overburden. But the POWs continued to come in, day and night, at all hours, without advance notice in the other areas. Guard detachments had to be ready on call to rush to detraining points, take over new drafts and conduct them into camp. The inclosures grew in size and number until the 106th and its attached units were holding down the lids on sixteen camps. By 18 May the influx reached its peak, 917,217 inside the wire. There it steadied while a new phase began—transfer, evacuation and discharge.

In the meantime the Division had the task of screening this heterogeneous mass. This counter-intelligence job was performed by trained interrogation teams from MIS assisted by Divisional personnel. Once the goats, war criminals and other suspects, were separated from the sheep they had, of course, to be permanently segregated to undergo further interrogation. Further breakdowns by sex and by category of rank, nationality and status resulted in at least sixteen separate groups within each inclosure.

The Division lived from hand to mouth, scouring the countryside for captured German material and food supplies for their prisoners, ranging far and wide to find dumps for their own rations and supply. The former task was the biggest. Rations were hard to obtain in sufficient quantity. What was supplied by SOS included many components inedible unless cooked—flour, lard and raw potatoes, for instance. Most prisoners lacked individual cooking equipment. Communal mess gear in the cages didn't exist. The 106th Division scroungers gathered up a large number of 200-gallon boilers, but these were designed to operate on electricity or oil, and precious time was wasted transforming for coal and wood heating. Empty oil drums were used for cooking purposes. In one camp an old locomotive was run in on an improvised track to furnish steam for the cookers.

From the prisoners, of course, came their own mess crews. And local German bakeries were impressed into service, the bread components being furnished them.

Like everyone else in the Division the 81st Engineers had their hands full. Wire inclosures, latrines, guard towers, access roads, kitchen and food storage shelter were among their construction tasks. ComZ supplied some general service engineer units, and the prisoners were sorted out into labor units to do their own interior construction work under supervision.

It was a hair-raising job, the greater part of which should, of course, have been completed before a single prisoner set foot behind wire.

Transportation was at a premium. Divisional transport was kept running; some trucks were procured, but not many. The 339th QM Company was attached on 1 June, and toward the end of the period fifty ten-ton semi-trailers were also furnished by ComZ. The maintenance problem involved was in itself colossal from a combat division's viewpoint.

The docility of the vast horde of prisoners materially aided in carrying out the mission. Few attempts to escape were made, though under the conditions in the early portion of the period such action would have been quite feasible. The guard problem resolved itself into a ratio of one guard per 150 prisoners average. The various inclosures were made self-governing. One of the most efficient German camp commanders, in an inclosure confining nearly a hundred thousand, was a first-class private.

German medical personnel were used extensively in the inclosure hospitals and dispensaries; German clerks prepared necessary papers. In the last stages German finance officers handled the payment of dischargees.

Following the peak of the flood tide, another phase began—transfer, evacuation and discharge. First drafts out in the ebb tide following were for labor in France. These men were packed forty to each 40-and-8 type railway car. Use of American type freight cars was expressly forbidden.[2]

Further transfers to other zones went on and finally came discharge on the grand scale. By the use of German clerical personnel the machinery for this was speeded up to the point of a daily average of nine thousand men, the transportation of whom was another headache. Prisoners residing within a 100-mile zone were delivered by truck to their communities; this was the "Retail Zone." "Wholesale Zone" deliveries, to the areas of other armies, were usually by rail, the Division delivering fully processed individuals to army reception centers, whence local distribution was made.

June and summer weather saw the job nearing completion. Great drafts of POWs were being discharged daily. By 12 June the British took over inclosures and prisoners remaining within them, of the Red area. Gradually camps east of the Rhine were transferred to other army commands. The 3d Infantry on 13 June moved to Wiesbaden, taking over four semi-permanent inclosures in which would be held nondischargeable prisoners. The regiment was relieved from attachment 23 June when Seventh Army took it and the camps over. For a short time Headquarters and Headquarters Battery, 106th Division Artillery, together with the 591st and 592d Field Artillery Battalions were attached to Seventh Army, while the 401st and 627th Field Artillery Battalions left the Division for permanent army assignment.

And on 10 July the 106th Division began to drop the prisoner-of-war business, gladly. At Bad Ems in formal pomp the entire remaining area and its 128,141 POWs were turned over to the French 10th Infantry Division. The attached units were relieved to Communications Zone. The 106th was going away from there.

NOTES TO CHAPTER 17

[1] The World War I Battle of Tannenberg, 26-29 August 1914, heretofore had been held up as the greatest modern example of the classic Cannae maneuver—double envelopment. At Tannenberg in East Prussia, the German Eighth Army, under Von Hindenburg, destroyed the Russian Second Army, under Samsonoff. According to Colonel McEntee's *Military History of the World War,* Russian losses were 92,000 prisoners, 6,739 dead and 350 guns. German losses were 1,750 dead, 6,864 wounded and 4,613 missing.

[2] Because of lack of ventilation, as tragically proven on at least one occasion in the winter of 1944, when a number of German prisoners being transported to the rear in these American freight cars were suffocated.

Chapter 18: Tallyho and Finis

†††

While the Division was in the midst of its cycle of shepherding POWs, other things were being accomplished. The reconstituted units moved up from Brittany by motor following the surrender of the Nazi pockets and closed in at Nachtsheim, ten miles west of Mayen, Germany, by 27 May, to continue their training under Division control. The Assistant Division Commander, Perrin, and G-3 personnel of the Division staff moved in to supervise. The training area was christened Camp Alan W. Jones, in honor of the first Division commander.

The redeployment plan also began to pinch. Transfers in and out began to flow, disrupting both training and the normal routine in the prisoner-guard problem.

All work and no play, we know, has certain dulling effects. It was high time that some recreational facilities be provided, and they were. XXII Corps' recreational center at Eupen, Belgium, was taken over and staffed by the 106th, under the name of "Withee Recreation Center," much to the later astonishment, as we know, of T/5 Edward S. Withee on his return, alive and well, from captivity.[1]

Later, through arrangements with AdSec, the Namur recreation center was also taken over by the Golden Lions. This was christened "Martin Recreation Center," in honor of Lt. Albert Martin.[2]

By the end of June both centers were in successful operation, much to the gratification of the men who were rotated there on furlough.

During this time the 424th Infantry received back its colors lost in the Schnee Eifel. They had been found by a 2d Infantry Division soldier upon a German POW captured in Austria!

On 12 July another move began. The Division would take over the Bruchsal–Karlsruhe Landkreise from control of the 84th Infantry Division, moving into the vicinity of Karlsruhe where the Division command post opened. It was now under command of Seventh Army.

The area, part of the zone originally occupied by the French and later by the 84th Division in slight strength, had never been really combed. The 106th combed it. Operation Tallyho was a VI Corps proposition to check credentials of all civilians, displaced persons, and military personnel, to uncover prohibited articles, such as firearms and ammunition, radio transmitters, vehicles and war matériel, and also any black-market operations.

Initiated in great secrecy, the operation commenced at 4:30 A.M., 21 July, when forty-six roadblocks throughout the Division area were manned and a house-to-house check began which lasted for forty-eight hours. One gathers that it consisted of much sound and fury, without tangible results. At any rate, it resulted in a thorough, if somewhat informal, introduction of the Golden Lions to the good and not-so-good burghers of the area.

After this the Division settled down to occupational duty. The reconstituted units continued their training at another Camp Alan W. Jones, at Oestringen, thirty miles north of Karlsruhe. I&E people turned up with orientation programs. The shake-ups of redeployment went on—life was one continual turmoil. Division Artillery returned to the fold. The 159th Infantry Regiment was detached. Came word of Hiroshima, of Nagasaki, and then VJ-day.

And at long last, 1 September came orders that everyone was looking forward to. The 106th was going home.

There isn't much more. On 10 September, the 422d Infantry leading, the Division started on the last, long trek. Camp Lucky Strike and the numbing wait in the woods for transports. Then—on board ship and home.

The various outfits came back individually. They arrived by different ships and at different ports, between 1 and 2 October, between New York and Hampton Roads.

Division Headquarters, at Camp Shanks, New York, received the formal inactivation order 2 October.

World War II was over for the Golden Lions.

NOTES TO CHAPTER 18

[1] See page 34, *supra*.
[2] See page 111, *supra*.

Appendix I: Operation Greif

The following is a free translation of documents captured by Lt. William V. Shakespeare, 424th Infantry, near Heckhuscheid, 16 December, 1944. The material was rushed by 424th Infantry to 106th Division headquarters at St. Vith. The translation, made there, is furnished by Col. Robert P. Stout, former Division G-2, and published in THE CUB, December, 1946.

SUBJECT: UNDERTAKING "GREIF."
   (1) Higher Headquarters planned to include in the operation Undertaking "Greif."
   (2) Undertaking "Greif" could also include own forces with American equipment, American weapons, American vehicles, American insignias, especially the five-pointed yellow or white star.
   (3) To avoid confusion with enemy troops, the forces employed in Undertaking "Greif" will identify themselves to our own troops:
   a. During the day by taking off their steel helmets.
   b. At night by red or blue light signals with flashlights.
   (4) Forces of Undertaking "Greif" will also indicate the employment by painting white dots on houses, trees, and roads used by them.
   (5) Employment of forces of Undertaking "Greif" is planned along the following roads:
   a. Trois Ponts (5 km SW Stavelot), Basse Bodeaux, Villettes, Bra, la Fourche, Harre, Deux Rys, Roche-a-Frene.
   b. Recht (8.5 km NW St. Vith), Petit Thier, Ville-du-Bors, Vielsalm, Salmchâteau, road crossing at point 444 (0.5 km N. Joubleval), Hebronval, Regné, road crossing at point 538 (2 km SW Malempre), Manhay, road fork at point 430 (E Grandmenil), road crossing at point 200 (1 km N Mormont), Roche-a-Frene.
   c. Roche-a-Frene, Aisne, Juzaine, Bomal, road fork 2 km SW Bomal, Tohogne, Oneux, Amas, Ocquier, Vervox.

REFERENCE: G-3 66 Corps
SUBJECT: UNDERTAKING "GREIF."
The following further identification for our own troops has been decided upon:
Swastika flag, white flares, partial head bandage.
For the General Staff:

SIEBERT, C o S

CP 15 Dec. 1944.

62 Volksgrenadier Division G-3
The above mentioned identifications are to be followed precisely.
For the Division Staff:

TROITZSCH, C o S

CP 15 Dec. 1944.

183 Infantry Regt., S-3
Above order acknowledged and to be followed precisely.
DUVE
Major and Regtl. CO.

Appendix II: Order of Battle

Special Troops:
  106th Division Headquarters Company
  106th Signal Company
  806th Ordnance (LM) Company
  106th Quartermaster Company
  106th Reconnaissance Troop
  106th Military Police Platoon
422d Infantry Regiment
423d Infantry Regiment
424th Infantry Regiment
106th Division Artillery:
  589th Field Artillery Battalion (105mm how.)
  590th Field Artillery Battalion (105mm how.)
  591st Field Artillery Battalion (105mm how.)
  592d Field Artillery Battalion (155mm how.)
81st Engineer Combat Battalion
331st Medical Battalion

Attached Units

14th Cavalry Group	December 7 to 18, 1944
275th Armored FA Battalion	December 10 to 20, 1944
820th Tank Destroyer Battalion	December 8 to 29, 1944
	January 1 to 5, 1945
634th AAA Battalion	December 9 to 25, 1944
	January 11 to 19, 1945
168th Engineer Combat Battalion[1]	December 16 to 26, 1944
802d Tank Destroyer Battalion	December 15 to 16, 1944
Company C, 740th Tank Battalion	January 11 to 19, 1945
112th Regimental Combat Team	December 19 to 23, 1944
(112th Infantry Regiment)	January 11 to 12, 1945
(229th FA Battalion)	
517th Regimental Combat Team	January 12 to 16, 1945
(517th Parachute Infantry, less	January 20 to 23, 1945
2d Battalion)	
(460th Parachute FA Battalion)	
(596th Airborne Engineer Co.)	

---

[1] This unit was placed in direct support of 81st Engineer Battalion, December 11, 1944, by verbal orders, Engineer Officer, VIII Corps. It served directly under command of 81st Engineers in the defense of St. Vith.

Co. A, 661st Tank Destroyer Bn.	February 16 to March 3, 1945
Co. A, 814th Tank Destroyer Bn.	February 9 to 16, 1945
Co. A, 643d Tank Destroyer Bn.	January 11 to 19, 1945
Battery C, 965th FA Bn. (240mm)[2]	December 20 to 23, 1944
CCB, 9th Armored Division	December 17 to 22, 1944
(27th Armored Infantry Bn.)	
(14th Tank Battalion)	
(16th Armored FA Battalion)	
(Troop D, 89th Cav. Rec. Sq.)	
(Co. B, 9th Armored Eng. Bn.)	
(Co. B, 2d Medical Battalion)	
(Co. C, 131st Ord. Maint. Bn.)	
(Battery B, 482d AAA Bn.)	
(Co. A, 811th TD Battalion)	
(Detachment, 489th Ambulance Co.)	
CCB, 7th Armored Division	December 17 to 22, 1944
(31st Tank Battalion)	
(23d Armored Infantry Bn.)	
(38th Armored Infantry Bn., less Company C)	
(Co. B, 33d Armored Eng. Bn.)	
(87th Cav. Rec. Sq., less Troop D)	
(Company A, 814th TD Bn., reinforced)	
440th AAA Battalion	December 16 to 23, 1943[3]
159th Infantry Regiment	March 16 to July 31, 1945
3d Infantry Regiment	March 16 to June 23, 1945
401st Field Artillery Battalion	March 16 to June 23, 1945
627th Field Artillery Battalion	March 16 to June 23, 1945

The following units were attached to the Division beginning April 30, 1945. They were relieved prior to the departure of the Division for the Karlsruhe area, in July.

6950th, 6951st and 6952d Guard Battalions(Provisional); 142d, 301st, 302d, 303d, 304th, 305th, 308th, 311th, 318th, 321st, 323d, 324th, 325th, 326th, 327th, 328th, 330th, 331st, 335th, 336th, 339th, 341st, 346th, 347th, 348th, 349th, 351st, 415th, 427th, 432d, 465th,

[2] The 965th Field Artillery later reinforced Division Artillery fire, January 12 and 13, 1945.

[3] Last date is approximate.

467th, 491st, 556th and 595th MP Guard Escort Companies; 229th MP POW Processiong Platoon.

9th, 12th, 50th, 61st, 62d, 78th and 83d Field Hospitals; 538th, 554th, 558th, 559th, 560th, and 592d Medical Ambulance Companies; Headquarters & Headquarters Detachment, 428th Medical Battalion; Detachment, 92d Medical-Dental Company (Provisional).

339th QM Company.

DETACHMENTS

424th Regimental Combat Team	
To 7th Armored Division	December 24 to 30, 1944
	January 22 to 30, 1945
To 30th Infantry Division	January 9 to 12, 1945
To 99th Infantry Division	February 5 to 8, 1945
3d Battalion, 424th Infantry	
To CCB, 9th Armored Division	December 20 to 23, 1944
591st Field Artillery Battalion	
To 82d Airborne Division	Dec. 28, 1944 to Jan. 8, 1945
592d Field Artillery Battalion	
To XVIII Corps Artillery	Dec. 24, 1944 to Jan. 29, 1945
Reconstituted 422d and 423d Infantry Regiments, 589th and 590th Field Artillery Battalions, 106th Reconnaissance Troop	
To 66th Infantry Division	April 15 to May 15, 1945

Appendix III: Organization and Training

The 106th Infantry Division (less 106th Quartermaster Company and 806th Ordnance Light Maintenance Company) was activated at Fort Jackson, South Carolina, 15 March 1943, and assigned to XII Corps. The 106th Quartermaster Company was activated 15 December 1942 at Camp Forrest, Tennessee, with cadre furnished by the 80th Infantry Division. The 806th Ordnance Company was activated 23 December 1943, at Camp Perry, Ohio. Both these units were thus prepared to take up the "housekeeping" of the Division when it came into being.

In Chapter 2 we have detailed the original commanders of the Division and its artillery. The original General Staff were:

Chief of Staff: Col. William C. Baker, Jr.
A C of S, G-1: Major Max J. Roadruck
A C of S, G-2: Lt. Col. Robert P. Stout
A C of S, G-3: Lt. Col. George L. Descheneaux
A C of S, G-4: Lt. Col. George C. Nielsen

The Special Staff as originally assigned were:

Adjutant General: Lt. Col. Frank I. Agule
Chemical Warfare Officer: Capt. Herbert B. Livesey, Jr.
Engineer Officer: Major William J. Himes
Finance Officer: Major Royer K. Lewis
Headquarters Commandant: Capt. Walter S. Glenney
Inspector General: Lt. Col. Frederick R. Ryan
Judge Advocate: Major Byrne A. Bowman
Ordnance Officer: Major William T. Manahan
Provost Marshal: Major William L. Mowlds
Quartermaster: Lt. Col. Donald C. Foote
Signal Officer: Lt. Col. Donald R. Bodine
Special Service Officer: Capt. Robert B. Davis
Surgeon: Lt. Col. Thair C. Rich
Chaplain: Major John A. Dunn

The officer cadre—from company to regimental commanders, the General Staff and some Special Staff officers—was provided by the 80th Infantry Division. Other officers came from Infantry Replacement Training Centers, from Fort Benning and from OCS. Most of the officers of the cadre attended special and ·refresher courses at the various service schools, in accordance with the established procedure of organization of new divisions, prior to activation.

The enlisted cadre came also from the 80th Infantry Division. Two complete cadre lists had been provided, under the orders of Maj.Gen. Joseph D. Patch, commanding the 80th, each comprising some 1,250 men, with complete statements of qualifications and experience. Until the final decision, when Gen. Patch drew one of the lists "blind" from his desk drawer, no one in the parent organization knew which list would be selected, a good antidote to the quite natural proclivity of organization commanders to sluff off undesirables.

The cadre moved from Camp Forrest to Fort Jackson early in February 1943, all elements closing by 15 February, including a supplemental cadre of fifty specialists from Camp Wheeler, Georgia. Here ensued a frantic period of intense training in administration, motor maintenance, intelligence, clerical, courts-martial, physical, signal communications, supply and medical field service ending 1 March, when five reception units were formed to take care of the coming fillers—the men who would make up the complete division.

The fillers—recruits to you—began arriving on 12 March, and by the prescribed activation date 3,400 men had passed into the reception units. It was during this time that the Division insignia, prepared by the Heraldic Section, OQMG, was officially approved:

A lion's head, gold, on a blue background, representing the Infantry, with a red border indicating Artillery support. It was officially donned 1 May 1943.

The activation ceremony, 15 March, had for its highlight the presentation of the new Division's colors before the massed troops. Master Sgt. Jay G. Bower, veteran of World War I, acting as representative of the parent organization, 80th Infantry Division, handed the colors to 18-year-old Pvt. Francis Albert Younkin, 422d Infantry, while Maj.Gen. William H. Simpson, commanding XII Corps, and the Honorable Olin D. Johnston, Governor of South Carolina, looked on.

Filler replacements came from First, Second, Third, Fourth, Fifth, Sixth and Seventh Service Commands, the Sixth providing the largest number, 4,076 men. Each troop train to arrive was met by one of the two Division bands, Infantry and Field Artillery. The new arrivals were played to a reception center, whence they gravitated to regimental and battalion assignment. The majority of the fillers were in by 25 March, when the Division strength had risen to 12,318 men.

Recruit training started at once, under regimental and battalion control. By 27 March the 424th Infantry had held its first review, and two days later the entire Division started its basic training program. This individual training period ran until 10 July, with emphasis through the fourteen weeks of hectic work on physical condition, tactical training and marksmanship. Obstacle courses—"something that your muscles won't let your mind forget"—as one soldier put it, sopped up the sweat of the Golden Lions throughout April and May. Then began 16-mile hikes to the Leesburg range, where in turn each unit camped and fired its small arms, its machine guns and mortars. The artillery units, when not standing gun drill, were firing 37mm AT guns. Orientation courses were sandwiched in with other special training.

Officer and NCO training included special and general service school courses. One unusual school was established for the education of enlisted men who had not had opportunity to attain minimum educational standards (less than fourth grade), or who were not immediately suited to absorb the regular basic training. Here some 430 men studied twice weekly for twelve weeks. Of these, 123 were illiterates, five did not speak English, and 302 were Grade V men (AGCT Test) requiring special training. The faculty consisted of 10 officers and 33 enlisted men especially picked as instructors.

It was on 19 June that the Division got its first look at itself in a full-strength parade held at Ancrum Ferry Field. At this ceremony the first decorations for valor awarded to 106th men were given out; the Soldier's Medal to Staff Sgt. Richard L. Nierman, of Cumberland, Maryland, and Pvt. Robert K. Maahs of Savannah, Georgia, both 423d Infantry, for jumping into the Wateree River on

11 May, without regard to personal safety, to rescue a comrade who had slipped and fallen into the swift current.

Corps training tests which started 5 July and ended in pouring rain, closed this period of training.

During this period the Golden Lions had had time to organize a divisional boxing tournament whose winners represented the 106th at the Fort Jackson "Tournament of the Champions" on 8 May and walked away with the post crowns. In baseball the Division fought in the local military league that summer, holding on to first place up to the last four games of the series, when they slid back to third place. A Division softball tournament and Division basketball league accounted for other recreation hours, while weekly dances at the Service Club were well relished by the "parlor snakes."

The unit training period kept all hands busy for twelve more weeks, beginning 12 July, with the major part of the time in the field, and ending with regimental tactical exercises. It was during this time (22 July) that Lt.Gen. Lesley J. McNair, CG of Army Ground Forces, visited and inspected the Division, expressing his satisfaction at the conclusion of his stay.

Combat firing proficiency tests ended this phase of training. Each rifle and weapons platoon, rifle company, .30-caliber machine-gun platoon, 81mm mortar platoon, infantry heavy-weapons company and mechanized cavalry platoon ran through its paces, as did the field artillery batteries.

Division schools ground ceaselessly throughout this period; officers' and NCO schools, radio, intelligence, motor mechanics, air-ground, ordnance, small arms and mortars, artillery mechanics, ammunition and ordnance supply classes were all functioning. And, of course, reviews; the most important being a review in honor of Gen. Enrico Gaspar Dutra, Brazilian Minister of War.

In the sports field the 424th Infantry won the Division swimming and volleyball tournaments, and the 422d Infantry glovers won the boxing tournament.

It was in August, too, that the Division was reorganized in accordance with the latest change in TO. Cannon companies were incorporated in infantry regiments, the Special Troops organized into a battalion, and the two existing bands, Division Artillery and 423d Infantry, were amalgamated into the 106th Infantry Division Band.

The combined training period, beginning 3 October 1943 and ending 8 January 1944, consisted of exercises in divisional and regimental combat-team problems. The going was getting tougher as the trainees hardened up and began to feel that they were soldiers. Regimental CT exercises were preceded by command post exercises. It was 1 November when each battalion underwent combat firing tests. Then came the D series of problems in which the Division participated as a combat team, judged by officer-umpires from the 78th Infantry Division.

And now the 106th had its first taste of winter maneuvers, with rain and sleet chilling the men's bones as they worked their way from one problem to another. Three days respite for Christmas was followed by another week of gruelling work, before the troops moved back into cantonments at Fort Jackson to prepare for maneuvers.

The XII Corps cumulative Status of Training Report, published 6 January 1944, disclosed the following ratings: Air-Ground and Field Artillery Battery Tests, *Very Satisfactory;* MTP, Physical Fitness, Platoon Combat Firing, *Satisfactory;* Field Artillery Battalion Tests, *Unsatisfactory.*

Two of the artillery battalions, it seemed, had fallen down in their field tests. But the Division Artillery retook its tests—9-19 January—and the redlegs came out right this time. It was a lesson well learned; they proved that later in the Ardennes.

In individual marksmanship the qualification score read:

M1 rifle	88.6 per cent
'03 rifle	88.1 per cent
Carbine	77.6 per cent
.45 pistol	68.6 per cent
Submachine gun	100.0 per cent

Certain equipment shortages were still to be filled, and substitution of weapons had had to be made during some of the tests, as for instance, ground or train defense type .30 caliber MG in place of the combat vehicle weapon of the same caliber; M1917/M1918 155mm howitzer for M1 155mm howitzer; and scout cars instead of light armored cars.

Changes in commissioned personnel on the Division staff up to this time were as follows:

Lt.Col. Milton S. Glatterer became G-4, relieving Lt.Col. George C. Nielsen; Lt.Col. Meyer S. Belzer became Division Surgeon, relieving Lt.Col. Thair C. Rich; Lt.Col. Jewell K. Watt relieved Lt.Col. Frederick R. Ryan as Inspector General; Major Harry F. Killman became Division Quartermaster, relieving Lt.Col. Donald C. Foote; Major Thomas J. Riggs relieved Major William J. Himes as Division Engineer and CO, 81st Engineer Battalion.

Chaplain (Major) John A. Dunn was relieved by Chaplain (Lt.Col.) Frederick C. Frommagen, who was in turn relieved by Chaplain (Lt.Col.) William D. Veasie. Other changes were Capt. Oscar C. Krieger, relieved by Major John E. Ketterer; Major Buford W. McNeer, relieved by Major Howard R. Clement; Capt. George W. Prichard, Jr., relieved by 1st Lt. LeRoy Strong; Capt. Robert E. Doe, relieved by Major Louis J. Russo; and 1st Lt. Francis M. Marshek, relieved by Capt. Robert S. Lowther.

Let's look at the Division strength now, as it entered its maneuver period, the capstone of its training. Up until September the outfit had been overstrength; then approximately 3,300 men were transferred out. Throughout the year of 1943 it was overstrength in officers. From 703 officers, 2 warrant officers, and 15,995 enlisted, as of March 31, it had shrunk to an enlisted strength of 12,301 by the end of the year; officers rose to 789, and warrant officers to 38.

The age grouping is interesting. As of September 1943, 35.4 per cent of its enlisted personnel were 18-19 years old; 29.8 per cent fell into the 20-22 category and 11.6 per cent were 23-25 years old. Only 0.9 per cent were "old" men—38 years of age or over.

The AGCT groupings of the same date ran as follows:

Grade I:	4.2 per cent	Grade IV:	27.6 per cent
Grade II:	31.2 per cent	Grade V:	3.8 per cent
Grade III:	33.2 per cent		

Linguists in the Division were many. Twenty-five men could speak Italian, twenty-three Polish, thirteen German, eleven Spanish, ten French, seven Greek, four Yiddish. Conversationalists in the Chinese, Dutch and Hungarian languages were two each; and one man each was found who could speak, respectively, Japanese, Yugoslavian, Portuguese, Norwegian, Russian, Hebrew, Slovac, Slavic, Gaelic and Finnish.

On 20 January began the Division's trek by motor from Fort Jackson to the Tennessee maneuver area. The movement was in three serials, commanded, respectively, by Col. Walter C. Phillips, CO 422d Infantry; Col. Charles C. Cavender, CO 423d Infantry; and Col. J. L. Gibney, CO 424th Infantry. Three days were required for the move, all serials following the same route, bivouacking in turn the first night just outside Athens, Georgia, the second night at Fort Oglethorpe, Georgia, and the third in the vicinity of Murfreesboro, Tennessee, the final stop. The distance run was 442 miles.

Fort Oglethorpe was at that time a WAC training center, a fact which caused much discussion and speculation on the part of the Golden Lions. To their intense disgust the men of each serial on arrival found themselves restricted to their bivouac area.

It was springtime in Tennessee when the Division arrived and for a week the men reveled in the sun. Then came the rains, and the sleet and—believe it or not—snow. On 13 February the mercury went down to 13 degrees above zero; on 24 February it was up to 72 degrees. Rain fell for sixteen of February's twenty-nine days (leap year). Mud was everywhere; in bivouac, on the roads, on clothing and blankets. March came and with it seventeen more days of rain. Streams were in flood stage. And through it all the Golden Lions wallowed from maneuver to maneuver in a series of mock engagements of attack and defense. Looking at that time in retrospect, one might feel that Nature was doing her best to acclimate the 106th for its future in the Ardennes.

Air-ground cooperation was the keynote of the exercises, fifth series of maneuvers in Tennessee sponsored by Second Army. The period opened with a map exercise held in one of the maneuver area theaters, followed by a field demonstration illustrating execution of staff plans.

The first maneuver problem, 31 January to 2 February, found the 106th with the Blue force—XII Corps, including the 78th Infantry Division, one tank battalion and two TD battalions supported by Blue Tactical Air Division. The corps mission was to advance north of an east-west line through Murfreesboro, seize the general line Greenwood–Bairds Mill–Gladville, and be prepared for further movement on Hartsville. Opposing was the Red force consisting of the 26th Infantry Division (reinforced), supported by Red Tactical Air Division.

The 106th, advancing in three columns, reached corps objectives by afternoon of the second day and continued turning the enemy flank until the conclusion of the maneuver.

The second exercise, 7 to 9 February, was again an attack problem, with Blue and Red forces approximately the same as in the previous maneuver, with the Blue mission to advance rapidly north, seize the South Branch of the Cumberland River between Lebanon–Beloat Road and Old Lick Branch, destroying all Red forces encountered. Red's was a delaying mission. Again the 106th carried out its part of the problem.

Different was the line-up of the third problem, 14 to 16 February. This time the 106th (less CT 424), the 78th Infantry Division, 17th Airborne Division, and an armored group of three tank battalions made up XII Corps. Blue, concentrated west of Lebanon had a mission to advance east, seize rail facilities at Carthage Junction and destroy Red forces west of Caney Fork.

The Red force opposing consisted of the 26th Infantry Division, CT 424 and a TD group of three battalions, concentrated west of Rome–Alexandria. The initial part of the problem, securing the line Liberty–Hames Gap–Rome as a line of departure for a coordinated attack, was accomplished by noon of the second day. Late that afternoon the attack was launched, the 106th advancing with two regiments abreast, reinforced by the attached armored group. When the operation ended the Division was approaching New Middleton.

The fourth exercise, 21 to 24 February, found the 106th with the 26th Infantry Division and the armored group operating as XII Corps (Blue) with mission to advance from their concentration area north of Lebanon–Gordonsville, break through the Reds (78th Infantry and 17th Airborne Divisions and TDs) between Vine and Cottage Home, capture the high ground in the vicinity of Milton, then advance south to capture Wartrace and prevent Red concentration.

Advance was slow the first day, but by evening of the second day the 106th, reinforced by the 15th Armored Group, had broken through and created a gap in Red positions at Milton. Early next morning a strong Blue attack was launched which by nightfall had secured the first objective, the high ground south of Milton. During the night the Golden Lions continued to press the attack successfully.

The fifth exercise found the 106th Division on the Blue Force, with the XII Corps, the 26th Infantry Division, and an armored group of three tank battalions. Maj.Gen. Willard S. Paul was in command. The Blues were concentrated east of Murfreesboro. Their mission was to advance on Hartsville, driving north of the Cumberland River any Red forces encountered, and establish a bridgehead north of Hartsville.

The Red force, commanded by Maj.Gen. Edwin P. Parker, Jr., and consisting of the 78th Infantry Division, the 17th Airborne Division, and a tank destroyer group of two battalions, was concentrated north of Lebanon–Gordonsville.

During the first day the 106th (which was motorized) moved into an assembly area at Bairds Mills, south of Lebanon. Early the next morning the Division moved out in an attack aimed at seizing the south bank of the Cumberland River. Delayed by blown bridges and mines along Spring Creek, as well as by enemy resistance, the attack moved slowly. Crossings of Spring Creek were effected, however, and by the close of the operation, elements of the 106th had reached the Cumberland River at Hunters Point and northwest of Providence, while elements of the 26th Division reached the Cumberland in the vicinity of Cedar Bluff.

The 106th Division was with the Red force for the sixth exercise (7 to 9 March) together with CT 328 of the 26th Infantry Division and a tank destroyer group of three battalions. Maj.Gen. Alan W. Jones was in command. The Reds were concentrated east of Bellwood–Watertown, and were supported by the Red TAD and Army Service Units. The mission was to occupy, organize, and defend a position within an assigned sector along the general line Rome (inclusive)–Holmes Gap (inclusive) to protect the north flank of the Red Army.

The Blue force was commanded by Maj.Gen. Gilbert R. Cook, and consisted of XII Corps (26th Infantry Division less CT 328, 17th Airborne Division and an armored group of two tank battalions). It was concentrated west of Leesville.

Its mission was to capture the high ground south of Carthage and from there prepare to operate to the southeast.

During the first day the Red covering force withdrew under pressure, but the outpost line remained intact. Throughout the day and evening, barriers including mined and mustardized demolitions were executed by Red engineers, and units on the battle position continued organization of the ground. By 1400 of the second day the 422d Infantry had withdrawn from outpost and was assembled as force reserve near New Middleton: it had suffered thirty-two per cent casualties. At about the same time, an attack against the MLR, two miles north of Commerce, was repulsed by the 424th Infantry, but pressure in this vicinity continued. The Blues launched a coordinated attack at 0900 of the third day aimed at penetrating the Red line near Grant and seizing the corps objectives. About noon, Blue infantry, supported by tanks, attacked in the sector of the 423d Infantry. Red TD units and infantry AT weapons destroyed most of the tanks. The Division reserve counterattacked at 1315 and at termination of the operation Grant was still held by the Red force. In its sector, the 424th Infantry committed its reserve battalion and halted the Blue advance.

The seventh exercise (13 to 17 March), opening in a snow storm which changed to rain and sleet, with frost filming the soft mud, ended in thunder, lightning and continued downpour. It was fit setting for a maneuver which, as it turned out, was in fact a dress rehearsal for the tragedy of the Ardennes.

The 106th Infantry Division, with attached TD group of three battalions, was the Red force, supported as usual by tactical air. Concentrated north of the Cumberland River, east of Gallatin, Maj.Gen. Alan W. Jones' mission was to defend the river line from Lock 4 to Lock 7.

Against the Division were committed the Blue forces—XII Corps, commanded by Maj.Gen. Henry Terrell and consisting of 17th Airborne, 26th and 78th Infantry Divisions and an armored group of two tank battalions. Blue, concentrated mainly northeast of Murfreesboro, had as mission to advance north, force crossings of the Cumberland River between Locks 4 and 7, and capture Westmoreland.

On the first day the Division covering force, consisting of two reinforced rifle companies, assisted by mock demolitions executed by the engineers, inflicted considerable delay south of the river, only to be *cut off in bulk* by late afternoon as the Blues in overwhelming force surrounded it. By nightfall Blue elements were on the southern river bank all along the line.

The next two days were spent in Blue preparations for the river crossing, while the 106th Division Artillery and the Red Tactical Air Division impeded their movements by heavy concentrations and by bombing, strafing and gassing. Division patrols succeeded in crossing the river and obtaining much vital information of the Blue activities.

Early on the fourth day Blue made the river crossing in assault boats, gained a toehold, built up its strength and advanced northward. A succession of 106th Division counterattacks that day was successful in holding the main Blue force south of the Gallatin–Hartsville highway. But the exercise closed with the 106th clinging to a line generally north of this highway, while Blue spearheads penetrated to the vicinity of Rogana on the west.

The maneuver, as most maneuvers must be, had a "canned" solution; that is, the expected happened—an inferior force carried out to the best of its ability a delaying action against overwhelmingly superior forces. It was a lesson, an illustration, so far as the deadly finality of war can be illustrated. Coming events cast their shadows before. The 106th had had its dress rehearsal for battle. But it had it in the open, with full liberty for mobility in action, and no defensive trench-line cordon to induce false confidence.

During the final problem (20 to 23 March), the 106th Division was with the Blue force, joined with XII Corps (26th Infantry Division, 78th Infantry Division less CT 311, and an armored group of two tank battalions). Maj.Gen. Terrell was in command. Concentrated around Westmoreland, the Blues had as their mission to advance south, force crossings of the Cumberland River between Lock 4 and Wilburn Creek, and capture the high ground north of the general line Gladville–Watertown.

The Red Force, commanded by Maj.Gen. William M. Miley, consisting of the 17th Airborne Division, CT 311 of the 78th Division, and a tank destroyer group of three battalions, was concentrated south of the Cumberland River around Lebanon. Its mission was to defend the line of the Cumberland River.

The Blues advanced with three divisions abreast as planned, meeting no resistance and but little delay from demolitions and gas. Leading elements secured the north bank of the river at most points along the entire front by 1020. Strong combat patrols crossed by boat and ferry during the evening of the second day and early morning of the third. The strong river current made boat and ferry crossing extremely difficult, several boats being lost.

All foot elements of the 422d Infantry and the 424th Infantry had crossed the river by 1845 of the third day. The 1st and 3d Battalions of the 424th Infantry met strong resistance four miles south of Hunters Point, and being out of ammunition, were captured; the 2d Battalion withdrew north. The 422d Infantry advanced against light resistance. At midnight the regiment was ordered to withdraw to the area Dixon–Centerville and protect Averitts Ferry. Red units, however, passed in the rear of the 422d Infantry and seized Averitts Ferry. During the early morning of the fourth day, the rest of the Blue force was also withdrawn to positions protecting bridge sites.

And so the 106th Infantry Division concluded its maneuvers. It had participated in a wide variety of problems under particularly trying weather conditions. It was, so far as preparation for combat goes, a trained combat team. At least, that was the theory; but in fact, even in the midst of the maneuvers, there was an ebb and flow of personnel—not too serious, however, for it was in line with what might have occurred in combat.

On February 1st the strength of the Division was 912 officers, 12,556 enlisted men. During the month, 232 enlisted men were assigned to the Division. Of these, the largest number (69) came from the various service commands. The next largest groups were those transferred from Infantry Replacement Training Centers (53) and from Field Artillery Replacement Training Centers.

During the month, 94 enlisted men were transferred out of the Division. The largest number (57) went to the 83d Infantry Division. Fifteen men were transferred to the 94th Signal Battalion at Camp Elkins, West Virginia.

On the first of March, the Division's personnel consisted of 707 officers, 12,950 enlisted men. During March 1,214 new men came into the Division and 871 were transferred out.

Of the men transferred into the Division, the overwhelming majority (1,157) were from Army Specialized Training Program schools. The transfer of these men was in line with the War Department policy, adopted at that time.

Of the 871 enlisted men transferred out of the Division during March, almost seven hundred were sent to the replacement pool at Fort Meade, Maryland. The others were transferred to various service command units and officer candidate schools.

On 27 March 1944, the 106th left the Tennessee area for what would be its final station in the United States, Camp Atterbury, Indiana. Moving in three serials, following a single route, the Division closed in the new area 31 March. Each serial in turn bivouacked at Fort Knox, Kentucky, the first night out, a distance of 129.6 miles, and reached Camp Atterbury the next afternoon, 110.2 miles farther.

Once again the routine of instruction started, running the gamut of basic, individual, unit and combined training. Tactical tests galore were undergone; most of the month of August was devoted to a series of regimental combat team exercises. But now the Division was being systematically bled of its trained men, and training—real intensive combat training—of the replacements coming in, was a heart-breaking, endless job.

Transferred out in April were 3,145 men; in May, 877; during June, 195; July, 136; and in August—stiffest blow of all, for the drain was now sapping the trained strength—2,894. More than 6,100 of these men went to the Fort Meade replacement depot.

Replacements came in, of course; men from ASTP, AAF, AGF replacement depots and volunteers for infantry. Five hundred and fifty of these were from other branches: antiaircraft, coast artillery, post complements, air units, medical, engineer, ordnance, military police, quartermaster and TD units.

Major command changes during this period were Lt.Col. George L. Descheneaux, Jr., from Division General Staff to command the 422d Infantry (Lt.Col. Charlie A. Brock relieved him as G-3), vice Col. Walter C. Phillips and a succession of changes in the 424th Infantry. Col. Jesse L. Gibney, commanding the regiment since its activation, left the Division 6 May, Lt.Col. Orville M. Hewitt becoming acting regimental commander until 19 June, when Col. Paul J. Black assumed command. He left 7 August and Hewitt again assumed command until the arrival of Col. Alexander D. Reid, 24 August. Parenthetically, it would be Hewitt's role to become acting regimental commander again in the Ardennes, when Reid was wounded, but he was once again to be replaced, after holding combat command, by fresh blood from outside the Division. Such is the fortune of war.

So the days went on at Atterbury—hard, driving days of training, with recreation in Indianapolis and Columbus sandwiched between. With such events as the two-day demonstration, 19 to 20 May, for the delectation of the Hoosier State Press Association; another demonstration, on 3 June, for the Under Secretary of War, Robert P. Patterson, and an Infantry Day exercise, 15 June, for more than five thousand visitors. And on 4 July the Division participated in Independence Day parades at Indianapolis and Cleveland simultaneously.

During this period the *Cub,* Division newspaper initiated during the Tennessee maneuvers, came to full flower, while on the sports side the Division baseball team captured the Indiana State championship, and so won its way into the National Semi-Pro Tournament at Wichita, Kansas.

The Division's 1944 boxing championship went to the 423d Infantry, taking four of the individual championships; three others went to the Division Artillery and one each to 422d Infantry and Special Troops.

The Medical Detachment, 424th Infantry, won the Division softball championship, while the volleyball crown went to Company C, 331st Medical Battalion. Staff Sgt. William K. Dwyer, Company K, 422d Infantry, garnered the Camp Atterbury table tennis tournament.

And thus the 106th Infantry Division carried on in the Indiana sun until the autumn came and the leaves were turning and the call for overseas movement came.

For the record, let us review briefly major Division command status as the Golden Lions prepared to go overseas:

Division Commander: Maj.Gen. Alan W. Jones
Assistant Division Commander: Brig.Gen. Herbert T. Perrin
Division Artillery Commander: Brig.Gen. Leo T. McMahon
CO 422d Infantry: Col. George L. Descheneaux
CO 423d Infantry: Col. Charles C. Cavender
CO 424th Infantry: Col. Alexander D. Reid
CO 589th FA Battalion: Lt.Col. T. Paine Kelly, Jr.
CO 590th FA Battalion: Lt.Col. Vaden Lackey
CO 591st FA Battalion: Lt.Col. Philip Hoover
CO 592d FA Battalion: Lt.Col. Richard E. Weber, Jr.
81st Engineer Battalion: Lt.Col. Thomas J. Riggs, Jr.
331st Medical Battalion: Lt.Col. Meyer S. Belzer

Appendix IV: Distinguished Unit Citations

The *81st Engineer Combat Battalion* is cited for outstanding performance of duty in armed conflict with the enemy from 16 to 23 December 1944. On 16 December 1944, line companies of the *81st Engineer Combat Battalion* were deployed on various sectors of the front of the 106th Infantry Division, in support of the three combat teams of the division which were committed in defense in the Schnee Eifel area of the Siegfried Line. In the early morning of 16 December 1944, powerful German forces of tank-supported infantry launched a full scale offensive which eventually surrounded elements of the division and forced other elements to retire slowly as they stubbornly sought to stem the enemy advance. All elements of the *81st Engineer Combat Battalion* were from the start of the ensuing decisive action committed as infantry and successfully fought without rest or relief for 5 days to hold an enemy force of far superior numbers and fire power. When the enemy effected local penetrations in the sectors of the three combat teams, the respective line companies of the *81st Engineer Combat Battalion* stubbornly counterattacked and effected delaying actions in Auw, Bleialf, and Winterspelt, Germany. When forced to withdraw with the 424th Regimental Combat Team, *Company C, 81st Engineer Combat Battalion,* prepared demolitions on bridges and, in one case, blew the bridge as the enemy stood on it. Members of the same company, despite intense artillery fire and standing in icy waters, used winch cables to pull a large number of trucks abandoned by another unit across a stream and returned them to their unit for use in evacuation. *Company B, 81st Engineer Combat Battalion,* fought steadfastly with the 423d Regimental Combat Team, displaying courage and initiative under heavy fire, until completely cut off from other units of the division. On 17 December 1944, when the enemy effected a serious penetration with armor and infantry in the center of the division sector and were advancing rapidly on the division headquarters in the vital road center of St. Vith, Belgium, *Headquarters and Service Company,* and remaining elements of *A Company, 81st Engineer Combat Battalion,* together with other reinforcing engineer troops, were given the mission of stemming the enemy advance. Establishing a defense line astride the road from Schönberg, Belgium, to St. Vith, they effectively halted the enemy column 1 mile east of St. Vith, although they were out-numbered and out-gunned. From 18 December until the early morning of 22 December 1944 with reinforcements of infantry and armor, these units composed a task force which repeatedly threw back vicious attacks of combined infantry and tank forces, constantly counterattacking and regaining previous positions when forced to withdraw temporarily. At all times a high fighting spirit was maintained in the face of withering fire from artillery, mortars, and rocket guns. After the position east of St. Vith had been completely overrun by a powerful force of infantry and tanks on the night of 21-22 December 1944, elements of *Headquarters and Service Company* and *A Company, 81st Engineer Combat Battalion,* formed patrols which harried the enemy's rear and attempted to return to friendly lines until captured 2 days later. The selfless devotion to duty and unyielding fighting spirit displayed by the *81st Engineer Combat Battalion,* in the defense of a vital communications center, effectively impeded the progress of the extensive German counteroffensive in the Ardennes forest. This display of stubborn courage and initiative under fire in its initial commitment to battle reflects great credit on itself and the armed forces of the United States. (General Orders 74, Headquarters 106th Infantry Division, 7 September 1945, as approved by the

Commanding General, United States Army Forces, European Theater, Main.) *{General Orders No. 100, War Department, 7 November 1945.}*

The *634th Antiaircraft Artillery Automatic Weapons Battalion* is cited for outstanding performance of duty against the enemy from 16-21 December 1944. During the violent enemy counteroffensive near St. Vith, Belgium, the battalion was deployed in advance positions which necessarily committed it as a ground fighting unit. Despite this shift from their primary mission, the members of the battalion temporarily held the numerically superior enemy forces throughout 5 days of bitter fighting. *Battery D,* although completely surrounded, gallantly continued the fight and maintained communication with the battalion during the entire period of heavy combat. *Battery B* aggressively fought its way from encirclement and, displaying consummate skill in using its mobile weapons, protected the withdrawal of a field artillery battalion. *Headquarters Battery* and *Batteries A and C* were assigned defensive positions on the north flank of St. Vith and courageously held their ground while the infantry and tank destroyers withdrew through their thin but tenaciously held line of resistance. When the enemy attacked with an overwhelming number of tanks and infantry on the morning of 18 December, the Bofors guns of the battalion made little impression upon their heavy tanks, but the battalion dauntlessly maintained a constant stream of harassing small-arms and machine-gun fire which stopped and completely routed the German infantry. Despite direct, close range tank fire which resulted in heavy casualties and the loss of vitally needed guns, the officers and men of the intrepid *634th Antiaircraft Artillery Automatic Weapons Battalion* held their ground against the surging enemy forces with fearless determination and unbreakable spirit until relieved by friendly armored elements. (General Orders 180, Headquarters Third Army, 18 July 1945, as approved by the Commanding General, United States Army Forces, European Theater, Main.) *{General Orders No. 108, War Department, 23 November 1945.}*

The *112th Infantry Regimental Combat Team,* consisting of the *112th Infantry Regiment* with the *229th Field Artillery Battalion; Company C, 103d Engineer Battalion; Battery C, 447th Antiaircraft Artillery Battalion;* and *Company C, 630th Tank Destroyer Battalion* attached, is cited for extraordinary heroism, efficiency, and achievement in action against the enemy during the Battle of the Ardennes from 16 to 24 December 1944. On 16 December 1944 the *112th Infantry Regimental Combat Team* from Lutz Kampen, Germany, to Leiler, Luxembourg, was holding six and one-half miles of the front line sector assigned to the 28th Infantry Division. During the period 16 to 18 December 1944, despite repeated enemy infantry and tank attacks involving the elements of nine enemy divisions, the *112th Infantry Regimental Combat Team* held its ground. In this period it inflicted estimated casualties on the enemy of 1600, including over 200 prisoners taken and successfully evacuated. All elements of the *112th Infantry Regimental Combat Team* were involved in this action. The *229th Field Artillery Battalion* was engaged in direct fire on the enemy at a range of 150 yards. The *Cannon Company* of the *112th Infantry Regiment* and *Company C, 630th Tank Destroyer Battalion,* by direct fire, succeeded in disabling 18 enemy tanks. *Company C, 103d Engineer Battalion,* together with the *2d Battalion, 112th Infantry Regiment,* repeatedly counterattacked enemy penetrations. The *Head-*

quarters, Headquarters Company, and *Service Company* manned the lines and drove off by fire a number of groups of the enemy which had infiltrated into the rear areas. The kitchens, being overrun on night of 16-17 December 1944, the kitchen personnel fought with rifles to recover the positions. All this was done under withering small-arms and artillery fire from enemy positions throughout the entire front. On the night of 17-18 December 1944 under orders from higher headquarters, the *112th Infantry Regimental Combat Team* was withdrawn to the high ground west of the Our River. This withdrawal was accomplished successfully in spite of strong enemy infiltrations throughout the entire sector. From 18 until 23 December 1944, the *112th Infantry Regimental Combat Team* was continually engaged in rear guard action covering the withdrawal of the right flank of the First American Army. On the night of 23-24 December 1944 the action of *112th Infantry Regimental Combat Team* was especially notable. Being ordered by higher headquarters to act as a covering force for units withdrawing to the American lines it held its position under furious enemy infantry and tank attacks until the *Regimental Headquarters* and *1st Battalion, 112th Infantry,* were surrounded. The *1st Battalion* then fought its way clear to friendly lines bringing with it a number of vehicles and personnel of other units. The gallantry under extremely hazardous and physically trying conditions, the stubborn defense of the sectors assigned them, and the heroic conduct of all personnel of the *112th Infantry Regimental Combat Team,* in 9 days of continuous fighting, exemplify the highest traditions of the armed forces of the United States. *{General Orders No. 63, War Department, 11 July 1947.}*

Combat Command B, 7th Armored Division, composed of the following units: *Headquarters and Headquarters Company; 17th Tank Battalion; 31st Tank Battalion; 23d Armored Infantry Battalion; 38th Armored Infantry Battalion; 87th Cavalry Reconnaissance Squadron Mechanized (less Troop D); 275th Armored Field Artillery Battalion; 434th Armored Field Artillery Battalion; 965th Field Artillery Battalion; 168th Engineer Combat Battalion; 3d Platoon, Company F, 423d Infantry Regiment; Company B, 33d Armored Engineer Battalion;* and *Company A, 814th Tank Destroyer Battalion (SP),* is cited for outstanding performance of duty in action from 17 to 23 December 1944, inclusive, at St. Vith, Belgium. *Combat Command B, 7th Armored Division,* was subjected to repeated tank and infantry attacks, which grew in intensity as the German forces attempted to destroy the stubborn defenses that were denying to them the use of the key communication center at St. Vith. By the second day, the flanks were constantly threatened by enemy forces that had bypassed the St. Vith area and pushed far to the rear in an effort to encircle the command east of the Salm River. The attacking forces were repeatedly thrown back by the gallant troops who rose from their fox holes and fought in fierce hand-to-hand combat to stop the penetrations and inflict heavy losses on the numerically superior foe. As the command continued to deny the important St. Vith highway and railroad center to the Germans, the entire offensive lost its initial impetus and their supply columns became immobilized. By 21 December, the German timetable was so disrupted that the enemy was forced to divert a corps to the capture of St. Vith. Under extreme pressure from overwhelming forces, this command, which for 6 days had held the St. Vith area so gallantly, was ordered to withdraw west of the Salm River. By their epic stand, without prepared defenses and despite heavy casualties,

Combat Command B, 7th Armored Division, inflicted crippling losses and imposed great delay upon the enemy by a masterful and grimly determined defense in keeping with the highest traditions of the Army of the United States. *{General Orders No. 48, Department of the Army, 12 July 1948.}*

Appendix V: Award of Croix de Guerre

With Silver-Gilt Star

DECISION NO. 247

589th Field Artillery Battalion (105 How)

The President of the Provisional Government of the French Republic cites to the Order of the Army:

CITATION

A remarkable battalion whose brilliant conduct was greatly valued during the battles of St. Vith and Manhay on 16 to 23 December 1944. Attacked by an enemy operating in force but filled with the desire to conquer at any cost, it remained in position and, with direct and accurate fire, kept the attackers from access to vital communications south of Manhay. Short of food, water and pharmaceutical products, the **589th Field Artillery Battalion** endured three attacks without flinching, inflicted heavy losses on the enemy and forced him to retire.

PARIS, 15 July 1946
Signed: BIDAULT

General of the Army JUIN
Chief of Staff of National Defense

A NOTE ON THIS BOOK

This book is published by the Infantry Journal Press, one of the publishing activities of the U.S. Infantry Association. It was produced under the editorial supervision of Orville C. Shirey and N. J. Anthony, designed by George P. Petrakis, printed by The French-Bray Printing Company and bound by Moore and Company. The text has been set in 12 pt. Linotype Garamond.

The U.S. Infantry Association also publishes the Infantry Journal, a monthly magazine for the ground combat forces of the United States. The U.S. Infantry Association is a non-profit organization composed of soldiers and civilians interested in all phases of national defense. Its various publications cover all levels of military affairs, from technical books on weapons and tactics, to historical, psychological, political and economic books on the higher aspects of war. Its membership includes all branches of the active, reserve and retired armed services: Army, Navy, Marine Corps, Air Force, National Guard, Coast Guard, Organized Reserve Corps, and civilians. Readers desiring catalogs of its publications, and information on membership, can obtain them from the U.S. Infantry Association, 1115 Seventeenth St., N.W., Washington 6, D. C.

PHOTOGRAPHS

Major General Alan W. Jones

Major General Donald A. Stroh

Brigadier General Herbert T. Perrin

Brigadier General Leo T. McMahon

Colonel William C. Baker, Jr.

Dreary was the road. The 422d RCT convoy nears St. Vith on 8 December 1944. The vehicles are from the 589th FA Battalion.

Entrance to the Schnee Eifel. The 422d RCT's convoy near Schönberg, 8 December 1944.   (Photos by Hayslip)

In the Schnee Eifel. The command post of the 489th FA Battalion near Schlausenbach, 12 December 1944. Private Rudy Hirsch, Headquarters Battery, beside the gun.

A machine-gun position and guard post of the 589th FA Battalion in the Schnee Eifel. Battery B's howitzers were emplaced almost directly in rear.

(Photos by Hayslip)

They stopped three German tanks. The 4th Section, Battery A, 589th FA Battalion.

Packs are dropped when Company K, 424th Infantry, attacks. Private James Donnelly stands guard.

Revenge is sweet. Kraut prisoners bagged by the 106th Division at Medell, Belgium.

Holding the Fortified Goose Egg. A howitzer of the 591st FA Battalion near St. Vith.

The panzers passed this way. Debris near Auw.

Smilin' through the Bulge. Private David S. Emmert, Headquarters Company, 424th Infantry, keeps his chin up near St. Vith.

Outpost in the Ardennes near Medell, Belgium.

Parker's Crossroads, looking northwest.   (Photo by Hayslip)

The Foot of the Rainbow. Looking north at Schönberg, goal of the 422d and 423d Infantry Regiments.

Last stand of the 589th FA Battalion. Parker's Crossroads, looking east.

Looking south from the scene of the 589th FA Battalion's last stand at Parker's Crossroads.　(Photos by Aspinwall)

One man, three cannon: Lieutenant Eric Fisher Wood, Jr.

Manhay, after the battle.

The flooded Our River near Steinebrück. Across these hills the 424th Infantry fought.

Looking south across the Amblève River at Stavelot.

Command post of the 106th Division at St. Vith—afterward.

Recaptured St. Vith.

Last stand at Vielsalm, 23 December 1944. A 7th Armored Division roadblock.

Prüm, Germany, target of 106th Division Artillery.

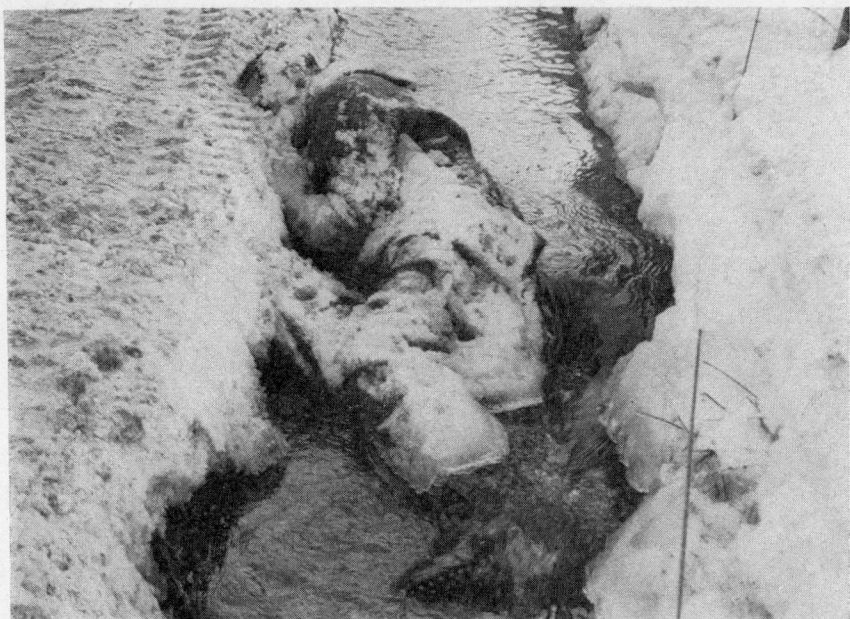

A dead German soldier lies in a ditch near Langlir, Belgium.

American trucks and trailers line the roadway in Büllingen, left there when the Germans made their big push.

The Siegfried Line near

Brandscheid, Germany, west of Prüm.

This Tiger remained at Stavelot. A group of 106th Division men stand beside the wreck in January 1945.

St. Vith—after the battle.

(Photos by Hayslip)

Reconstitution ceremony at Rennes. Colors and guidons of the 422d and 423d Infantry Regiments and 590th FA Battalion fly anew.

The last push. The 424th Infantry advancing near Berk, 5 March 1945.

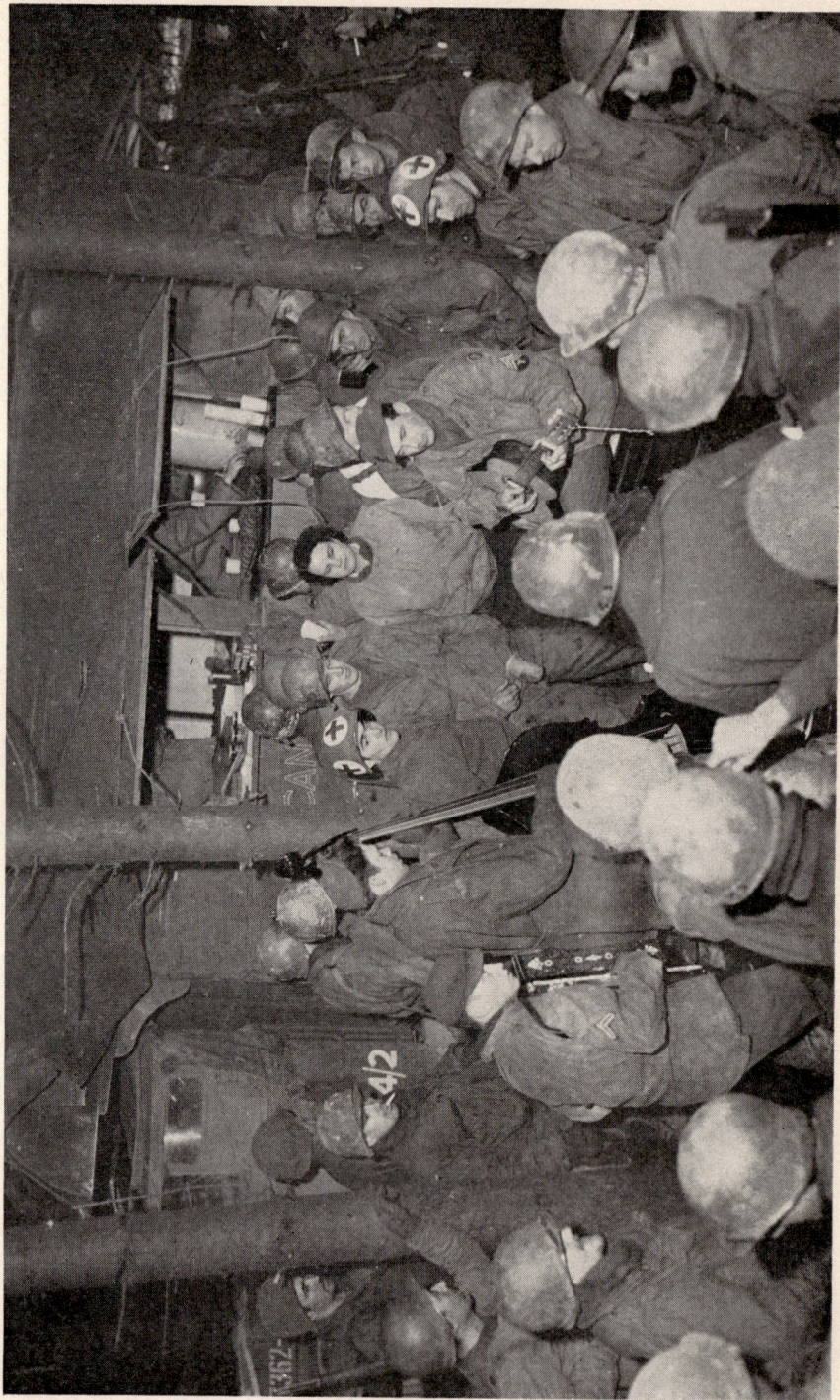

Time out for coffee, doughnuts, and music. Men of the 2d Battalion, 424th Infantry, meet the Red Cross at Losheim.

Troops of the 424th Infantry advancing near Berk, 5 March 1945.

The 106th held them at Bad Ems, Germany, 14 May 1945. Nazi bigwigs in our MP net. In the group are Major General Hermann Leythaeuser, Lieutenant General Theodor Triendl, Major General Ernst von Horstig, Lieutenant General Joseph Russwurm, Major General Gustav Geiger, Major General Otto Amann, and Lieutenant General Rudolf Habenicht.

Honorable discharge. The last and final Army pay, plus mustering-out pay. Sergeant Faulkner, Company B, 422d Infantry, is out of the Army.

WANNE

FOSSE

19

23

82 AB

GORONNE

BURG

17

19/20

9 SS PZ
21

20

GRAND HALLEUX

POTEAU

18

23

EMELLS

21/22

22

SART-LEZ-
ST VITH
(RODT)

3/112 23

23

23

A7
R7

D

HINDERHAUSEN

A7
B7

22

VIELSALM

24

SART

23

SALMCHATEAU

C R7
112

23

23

B7

CROMBACH

B9

23

22

PARKERS
CROSSROADS
8 MILES WEST
OF SALMCHATEAU

B

EIENBERG

BRAUNLAUF

21

OTTRE

22

A

HERE COLUMN
DISINTEGRATED
231630

ROGERY

23

112 22-23

MALDANGE

23

23

GRUFFLINGEN

B9
424

A- PROTECTIVE FIRE
OF 229 FA 23 DEC
B- ESCAPE ROUTE
C- ESCAPE ROUTE
D- ESCAPE ROUTE

BOVIGNY

FORTIFIED GOOSE EGG
22-23 DEC EVAC 23

424
112

23

AUDRANGE

BEHO

23

22

CHERAIN

SCREEN

GOUVY
TF JONES 20-23 DEC

22

22

22

22

22

112 INF

19 DEC

ADVANCE 20

17/18

19

N

WHAT HAPPENED AT
ST. VITH
16-23 DECEMBER 1944